THE SHAAR PRESS

THE JUDAICA IMPRINT
FOR THOUGHTFUL PEOPLE

A
SHAAR
PRESS
PUBLICATION

Tales out of Shul

The unorthodox journal of an Orthodox rabbi

EMANUEL FELDMAN

Published by **SHAAR PRESS**
Distributed by MESORAH PUBLICATIONS, LTD.
4401 Second Avenue / Brooklyn, N.Y 11232 / (718) 921-9000

Distributed in Israel by SIFRIATI / A. GITLER
6 Hayarkon Street / Bnei Brak 51127

Distributed in Europe by LEHMANNS
Unit E, Viking Business Park, Rolling Mill Road / Jarrow, Tyne and Wear, NE32 3DP/ England

Distributed in Australia and New Zealand by GOLDS WORLD OF JUDAICA
3-13 William Street / Balaclava, Melbourne 3183 / Victoria Australia

Distributed in South Africa by KOLLEL BOOKSHOP
Ivy Common / 105 William Road / Norwood 2192, Johannesburg, South Africa

ISBN: 0-89906-517-1 Hard Cover
ISBN: 0-89906-518-X Paperback

Printed in the United States of America by Noble Book Press
Custom bound by Sefercraft, Inc. / 4401 Second Avenue / Brooklyn N.Y. 11232

Dedicated to
the members of

Congregation Beth Jacob

Atlanta, Georgia

A wondrous blend of
individuals who have created
one of the unique congregations
in North America.

זכרתי לך חסד נעוריך אהבת כלולתיך
לכתך אחרי במדבר בארץ לא זרועה

"I remember the devotion of thy youth . . .
when thou didst follow me in the wilderness,
in a land that was not sown . . ." *(Jeremiah 2:2)*

Other books
by Emanuel Feldman:

The 28th of Iyar
Law as Theology
The Biblical Echo
On Judaism

Table of Contents

By Way of Prologue: Beginnings

A twenty-four year old man stepped off the train at Atlanta's old Union Station on a Friday morning in August, 1952. A fledgling Atlanta synagogue was searching for a rabbi, and the young man, newly ordained and soon to be married, was searching for a pulpit. Fledgling synagogues do not with ease find experienced rabbis, and inexperienced rabbis do not with ease find established synagogues.

The rabbi waited for the committee that was to meet him at the station. The platform cleared, but there was no sign of anyone. From the end of the terminal two gentlemen approached him. "You're not the rabbi, are you?"

"Yes, I am. Are you from the synagogue?"

"We sure are. Pardon us for making you wait so long. We saw you earlier, but we didn't know it was you. We were sort of looking for someone who looked like, you know, a rabbi." The three men chuckled, but only two of them thought it was funny. The third was already sensitive enough about the difficulties of finding a pulpit at such a tender age.

As it turned out, the congregation took to him, and he to them, and so, on that sultry Shabbos of *Sedra Shoftim* in the year 5712/1952, the young man agreed to become the rabbi of the young congregation of forty families.

Both the congregation and the rabbi expected the arrangement to last, at most, for a few years, after which the rabbi would look for greener pastures and the congregation would begin searching again for a new rabbi. But somehow the arrangement lasted for almost forty years. There were no pastures greener nor pulpits more challenging. It was a marriage made in heaven.

The marriage analogy is apt, for accepting a pulpit is very much like taking a bride. In addition to the surface facets — seeing eye to eye on issues — there must be a chemistry between rabbi and congregation. One can never know beforehand if that chemistry will exist afterward. In this case, it developed that it did exist, which in no small measure helped them remain together for a full generation.

Today, when Orthodoxy is so self-confident and knowledgeable, it is difficult to conjure up the face of American Orthodoxy in the fifties, particularly in Jewish communities outside the major metropolitan areas. Orthodox Judaism was evidently gasping its final breath, and it was only a matter of time before it disappeared. Torah observance around the country was minimal, and serious Torah learning was almost non-existent.

It was thus not surprising that the fine men and women of Atlanta's putative Orthodox synagogue had never been exposed to the rigors, or to the pleasures, of a Torah life. The most pious among them observed kashrut and lit Shabbat candles. This, plus attendance at a Friday night Oneg Shabbat, marked one as being very devout. It was an axiom that in the twentieth century it was simply not possible to observe anything else. Shabbat, or daily *tefillin,* or the laws of *mikveh,* were not even on the agenda. Jewish observance extended only as far as the kitchen, and a scant ten families of the forty in the congregation kept even that. And this was the most Orthodox of the community's congregations.

One could live with this for a few years, while learning to be a rabbi and before children were born. Unaccountably, however, the synagogue began a slow but steady climb, both spiritually and physically. This was not without pain, as these pages will show, but it was remarkable nonetheless. And it was that climb that cemented the relationship between rabbi and congregation and kept them together through bad times and good.

Although this book is focused on one synagogue, it is not a history of that synagogue. It is, rather, an impressionistic look at events and individuals within that congregation and the larger Jewish community around it. As in an impressionistic painting, there is a sudden dab of color here, an outline of a figure there; there are suggestions of a likeness or a silhouette, a hint of a background, a tracing of a scene, an occasional still-life. Detailed structure is eschewed in favor of vignettes and quick brushstrokes, all drawn on the larger canvas of American Jewish life in mid-twentieth-century America.

During the years of my rabbinate I would sporadically record incidents or ideas as they occurred. It is from that notebook that this volume emerged. I have endeavored to retain the breezy, discursive style of the original journal entries, which were often recorded on the run, or while sitting at the dais of interminable dinners, or late at night just before exhaustion took over.

By and large, these entries bypass the cosmic for the commonplace. It is through the commonplace that the cosmic is apprehended, and it is within the daily activities of flesh and blood people that the authentic stuff of life is found.

This is a light book that is serious, and a serious book that is light. On one level it will entertain and will engender an occasional tear or chuckle. But on another level it is more than a series of incidents and stories. Just as a flash of lightning on a dark prairie can illuminate for miles, so also can an isolated incident expose profound aspects of life, revealing both the foibles and the greatness of human beings.

Of course, unless one covers all blemishes and presents a cosmeticized look at people, not every image can be flattering. A good portrait, after all, is a chiaroscuro of light and shade. A journal such as this depicts not only the shining faces of the pure and the virtuous, but also the faces of the confused and the unlettered. Since a community consists of a variety of individuals, each of whom contributes to it in his or her own way, all types are recorded here as they appeared, unadorned and without make-up.

Because the sketches are not airbrushed or retouched, all the names used here are fictitious. In some cases, to preserve anonymity, certain venues have been changed and disguised — although each and every episode remains true. As a further safeguard, most of these incidents happened so long ago that neither the people involved, nor their families and friends, are presently part of our community. In addition, I have not recorded matters that would be easily identifiable and might cause pain. (Nor have I included material that would assuredly have catapulted this book into an instant best seller.)

It is presented to the public in the hope that, beyond the narratives that may be engrossing or provocative, the reader will be enlightened, entertained, and perhaps even inspired. It is also quite possible that sensitive readers will discover in these pages a deeper knowledge of themselves as human beings and as Jews.

Acknowledgments

Several people had a major hand in shaping this book. My brother, Rabbi Aharon Feldman of Jerusalem, has taken time from his own studying, writing and teaching to give me the constant and unstinting benefit of his wisdom, judgment, and erudition. For his unflagging help I am very thankful.

My sincerest appreciation to Rabbi Hillel Goldberg, editor and writer, for the benefit of his vast experience and insight; to Rabbi Yonason Rosenblum, author and biographer, for judicious editing and important suggestions; and to Yosef HaKohen, author of "The Universal Jew," for sensitive and careful reading. Each of these talented individuals read the manuscript at various stages, and each of them made perceptive and valuable critiques.

My wife of four-and-a-half decades has of course experienced firsthand much of what is recorded here. This made her finely honed sense of language, her astute editorial skills, and her keen discernment even more beneficial. For this and for many other things I am grateful to her.

I also express my appreciation to the professional staff of Shaar Press, for their unstinting and unwavering assistance in many different ways.

These acknowledgments in no way implicate the acknowledgees in the shortcomings of this book. For these, the author retains exclusive rights and responsibilities.

As this volume sees the dawn of day, I express my gratitude to the One Above Who has afforded me the privilege of toiling in His vineyard ללמוד וללמד, לשמר ולעשות ולקים "to learn, teach, safeguard, perform and sustain" the holy Torah which He has granted His people.

Emanuel Feldman

Jerusalem
Chanukah, 5757/December, 1996

Chapter 1:
The Hebrew Name
for Nicholas

When your sisterhood president asks you about this, what will you say? If the answer is not clear and unequivocal, you will not only embarrass yourselves, you will also embarrass the yeshivah which ordained you."

This was the voice of our teachers as we prepared for the rabbinate. They tried to prod us into ever more intensive study by imposing upon us the fear of both God and layman. We spent many stressful days and nights worrying about the questions our future congregants would throw at us. I suppose we had some fear of God, but our greatest fear was of the layman.

I was duly ordained, accepted my first pulpit, and anxiously awaited my first religious question. It was not one for which my yeshivah training had prepared me: "We just had a baby boy. What is the Hebrew name for Nicholas?"

Now that's a fine name for a Jewish boy: Nicholas Greenstein. Nick. It has a certain panache to it, a certain cadence - *goyish*, but not completely. Not yet. If Nicholas still has its Greenstein to maintain some vestigial ancestral memories, Nick's own first-born, in the shifting sands of time, will probably be Nicholas, Jr. Not Nicholas Greenstein, Jr., but some other name with a less Jewish residue which, in a guilt-assuaging maneuver, will undoubtedly begin with a "G": Guerin perhaps, which still has some subtle greenery growing within it. Perhaps Graham. No vestiges of anything there. Grimes? Green? It will probably be Guerin: Nicholas Guerin, Jr., followed in a generation by Nicholas Guerin III, devoted member of the First Episcopalian Church of Atlanta.

Here was an infant in whose fate I was now an accomplice. By giving him a Hebrew name, was I not contributing to the delinquency of a Jewish minor? Rabbi, I said to myself, just tell Mrs. Greenstein that Nicholas is not a suitable name for a Jewish boy. Certainly the child was not being named after his grandfather.

"Mazal Tov, Mrs. Greenstein. Now, let me see. Nicholas is a very interesting name. Is he being named after anyone?"

"His grandfather. He had some really Jewish name that began with an 'N.' No one is really sure what it was, 'Nemmy' or 'Neemy,' something like that. We thought Nicholas would be a fitting remembrance because it retains the N."

Having grown up in a rabbi's home, I was not unfamiliar with such insipidities, but I could not help thinking to myself: Am I going to spend the balance of my life providing people with the Hebrew equivalents for Butch and JoAnn, Clete and BettyLou? (Baruch, Chana, Kalman, and Beracha Lea were my contributions to Jewish posterity.)

To Mrs. Greenstein I suggested Nehemiah. She liked it but could not quite pronounce it. It didn't matter, because I knew that Nicholas would not be called Nehemiah more than a total of four times in his life: at his Bris Milah, Bar Mitzvah, wedding, and, if he was still listening, his funeral.

I was young, sure of myself, and angry at the creeping assimilation that the Nicholases of the Jewish world represented — and I was wrong about little Nick. Over the years, strange things occurred in the Greenstein household. Against all odds, Nick's parents gradually changed their way of living: they added kashrut to their home, later they began observing Shabbat, and lo and behold, Nicholas Greenstein entered the local Jewish day school, went on to a Jewish high school in another city, and today is a professional who is an observant Jew. His shingle reads: Nehemiah Greenstein, Ph.D.

I was wrong about his children as well. Not only are they not "Juniors"; they don't bear secular names at all. They are Chaim and Devora and Yaakov and Meir and Lea, and this is what everyone, Jew and non-Jew, calls them. They are not headed for the First Episcopalian Church.

a slow learner

That was not the only erroneous prophecy I made about this congregation. Though I hoped they might grow Jewishly, I assumed any such growth would be unremarkable. I thought I would stay a few years with them, do what I could, learn how to be a rabbi along the way, and then move on. I stayed with them for almost forty years; I must be a very slow learner.

"Forty years": the phrase trips off the tongue, but the thens and the nows whir through my head. The congregation has changed, and so have I. They have surely changed for the better. In 1952, we were fortunate that ten old men showed up every Shabbat morning in the old house we had converted into a synagogue; sometimes we had to wait over an hour for the tenth man. Synagogue officers never came to shul on Shabbat morning in those days. That was only for old-timers. Now we have over four hundred every Shabbat in a large and graceful structure, plus an early Shabbat morning *minyan,* plus an adult beginners' learning service, plus people learning Torah every night, plus other Orthodox enclaves which have been spawned in the city.

In 1952, there was as yet no Jewish day school in the community. Most of the establishment communal leaders were against the very idea. It was, they argued, anti-public school and unAmerican. They discounted it as yet another aberration of the benighted Orthodox who wished to segregate Jewish children. Only one professional in the establishment community, the head of the Bureau of Jewish Education, lent his unofficial support and assisted in many ways in the founding of Atlanta's first day school. It was a major struggle to gain financial support and to find pioneering parents courageous enough to expose their youngsters to what was for them an untested concept in Jewish education.

Now there are a number of such schools in Atlanta, plus a high school and a *kollel.* Even the Conservative and Reform communities have their own day schools. And the Federation now supports day schools generously.

In those days there was no communal adult education to speak of. Now, our synagogue alone has nightly classes in Talmud, Mishnah, Bible, Jewish thought. Other synagogues and the Community Center also run study programs.

In those days there were no *shomrei Shabbat* under age seventy in the entire city. Perhaps two or three courageous women used the *mikveh,* which was located in a dangerous, run-down neighborhood. Now, there are several hundred *shomrei Shabbat,* and hundreds of women observe *taharat hamishpachah* in several well-kept *mikvaot* in the city.

One can measure the spiritual development of a community by the kinds of questions they ask their rabbi. From the simple questions I used to be asked to the ones that greet me now, a thousand spiritual miles have been traversed. Now I get calls on car phones from people who are puzzled over the Talmud text we studied together the night before. They call with questions about business ethics, *mikveh* practices, the subtleties of

Shabbat laws, *tefillin* and *tzitzis,* or about the prohibition of lending or borrowing money on interest. Now they keep me on my toes. Yes, there is still the occasional what-is-the-Hebrew-name-for-Claude inquiry, but I no longer find myself wondering why they wasted my time in yeshivah teaching me the intricacies of Talmud, *Shulchan Aruch,* Jewish thought, and other matters I would never need to know. Now I wonder why they didn't teach me more. We've come a long way from "Rabbi, what's the Hebrew name for Nicholas?"

Chapter 2:
The Fallow Field

How all the changes took place in the religious lives of this congregation of Jews is a mystery. People look for simplistic answers, and so they give me the credit. Yes, there was teaching and there were discussion groups and counseling and persuasion — there was sowing of the fallow field — but in my heart of hearts I know that it happened with overwhelming kindness and direction from Above, and that I had precious little to do with it except to preside over the changes.

Kindness from Above: six years into my rabbinate, we

were making herculean efforts to move out of our old neighborhood, which was rapidly changing and which Jews were rapidly abandoning. After much searching, we purchased several acres in a fairly nice section of town and paid a down payment of ten thousand (borrowed) dollars. We were delighted and excited by the prospect of constructing a new building.

Then the unthinkable happened. We engaged an architectural firm to draw up preliminary building plans. After several weeks they came back with a report. The site was unbuildable. It was slowly giving way because of a nearby creek which had affected the nature of the bedrock soil. We would have to invest another ten thousand dollars for special supports — literally sink it into the ground — before we could build. That was out of the question.

The company which had studied the site before we purchased it denied responsibility. The seller of the land denied responsibility as well, insisting that he had made no false claims about the property. Unless we chose to go to court, we had lost ten thousand dollars. We could not afford to go to court, and so we elected to take the loss and to look elsewhere.

Gloom enveloped the congregation. We were angry at ourselves for being taken in. Members dropped out, the neighborhood continued its deterioration, and we were certain that our congregational demise was close at hand.

But the hand of God was at work for us. Six months later we found our present property, surveyed it carefully, purchased it, and after a remarkable fund-raising campaign that was itself beyond the natural, we built on it. It turned out to be a far better location for us, one which enabled us to grow and develop in exciting ways over the next thirty years. As for the property that we lost, to have located in that area would have been a miscalculation of major proportions — for in just five years, that neighborhood became a commercialized honky-tonk.

religious or observant?

The religious growth within the congregation has been dramatic, but there are constant reminders that much remains to be done. One of the men who attends our daily *minyan* told me one morning how much he sacrificed in order to be in shul that day. "Last night I was up until two A.M. playing pinochle, and still I'm here at six-thirty in the morning. If you're really religious, no sacrifice is too great." I looked for a sign of irony in his comment, but he was completely serious.

I worry about this: I have taught my people to be more observant — which is the *sine qua non* of a Jew, and the essential first step. But to become more religious, more aware of God, more conscious of His Presence and less addicted to the pinochle of daily life — that is the next plateau and much more difficult to reach, for rabbis as well as laymen.

There is a yawning gap between being observant and being religious. Observance can be objectively measured: maintaining Shabbat and kashrut, *davening* regularly, wearing *tzitzis,* practicing *taharat hamishpachah* — these are all tangible aspects of observance. But what goes on within the heart while all this is being performed — that only God knows.

For example, I fret about what takes place every Yom Kippur eve as the shul begins to fill up: the incessant chattering in the minutes before *Kol Nidre* begins. Many people come to shul early to be assured of a seat (we have no assigned seats) and then just sit there and chat, as if waiting for the curtain to go up in a theater and the performance to begin. As more and more people enter, the volume of noise increases. At ten minutes before Kol Nidre, a time that calls for silent contemplation, nine hundred people seem to be talking at once. There are those who look through the Yom Kippur *machzor,* or study a Jewish text, or sit and think — but they are vastly outnumbered.

On the surface it seems like a minor issue, and perhaps I am being naive, but even after all these years I find it discouraging that, at the single most sacred moment of the year, when the heavenly books of life and of death are open before God, idle talk reigns supreme. It makes me wonder, despite the tremendous growth in Jewish practice that this congregation has experienced, if we have been at all successful in stirring any deeper levels of religious feeling.

And yet, perhaps I am not being fair. Remarkable religious growth has taken place within the community, not only in terms of formal observance but also in terms of depth of feeling and commitment. One sees a great amount of genuine *chesed*, giving and sharing, and much openness and acceptance of others. And there are manifestations of genuine God-consciousness and piety. How can I assume to know what lies within the hearts of people?

I must not forget that most of our members — even those who are fully observant — do not come from religious backgrounds. Most of them, to their credit, became observant in their adult years within this congregation. We probably have the largest percentage of returnees to Judaism of any synagogue in North America. And we have a large number of fully nonobservant members as well, who stick with us for a variety of reasons which I do not always comprehend, but which I don't attempt to analyze because I am delighted they are here. All of them — observant and nonobservant — have willingly followed even though I was leading them into what must have seemed like a religious no-man's land.

the love of thy betrothals

A little more tolerance from their rabbi would not be out of order. Instead of carping at their not being perfect models of piety, I should be singing to them the song from the second chapter of Jeremiah: "I remember the kindness of thy youth, the love of thy betrothals: thou following Me in the wilderness, through a land that was not sown."

The kindness of thy youth: I remember the patience and forbearance with which the vast majority of them accepted the many mistakes in judgment of this young rabbi. I remember their small and large kindnesses, their *esprit de corps,* their fierce love for our little shul, their volunteering to do anything from painting the building, to planting the grass, to fixing broken windows, to repairing leaks, to washing the floors, to cooking synagogue dinners.

The love of thy betrothals: Paul Abrahams, though not personally observant, single-handedly kept our morning *minyan* going for years. Fortunately, he owned a large Cadillac, and when he saw our *minyan* foundering because of the deteriorating neighborhood, he literally took the wheel into his own hands. Every single weekday morning he would drive all over town, pick up six men and take them to our *minyan, daven* with them, drive them home, and then go off to work. Without this Jew, who was not observant but who cared about Yiddishkeit, our daily *minyan* would have disappeared.

Following me in the wilderness: I remember with a mixture of amusement and pride their spirited defense of Orthodox Judaism among their non-Orthodox friends, even though many of my defenders did not personally observe Shabbat, kashrut, or anything else.

Yes, many of them did not seem to budge one iota religiously, but we felt betrothed to one another. I deeply cared for them, and I knew they cared for their rookie rabbi and his wife.

the drive for success

At the same time, I recognized that the few members who supported our little shul in those days were, with some happy exceptions, Jewishly insecure. Minimally observant themselves, they did not know the religious direction they or the shul should be taking. Many of them would not have objected if I had developed the synagogue into a non-demanding Conservative congregation with all the trappings of synagogue modernity: mixed seating, responsive English readings, movie and book reviews from the pulpit, and, inevitably, a rabbi adorned in a black clerical robe. In brief, they would have been delighted if I had faithfully mimicked the non-Orthodox rabbis who seemed so successful. They were convinced that if I would only follow their lead, our synagogue would also become large, wealthy, and stylish.

To make things more difficult, the largest and most affluent synagogue in the city, until then nominally Orthodox, had officially joined the Conservative movement a few years earlier. Another large Orthodox synagogue was experiencing internal dissension over the same issue, and was beginning to make compromises with the Orthodox character of its services. All this increased the sense of isolation and insecurity within our synagogue, and intensified the fears of being left behind.

I was still very young and inexperienced, but it was not difficult to recognize the root cause of my congregation's demands of me. Beyond the depressing effect created by the swing to the Conservative movement, my people had never really seen or experienced classical Judaism. They had no models to follow. The only Judaism they knew was what they witnessed in the large and influential non-Orthodox congregations in town.

During my first year, some synagogue board members asked me to recite *Birkat Kohanim* at the end of the Shabbat services. "But I'm not a *kohen*," I said. "Only a *kohen* may pronounce this blessing."

"But you're a rabbi. That's just like a *kohen*, isn't it?"

"No, a rabbi is a teacher of Torah, but he has no special privileges like a *kohen*. That's why the first *aliyah* to the Torah goes to a *kohen*, not to a rabbi — unless the rabbi happens also to be a *kohen*. A *kohen* is a descendant of Aaron, the first *kohen*; a *kohen's* ancestors were in charge of the services in the Holy Temple."

"Well, Rabbi_____ is not a *kohen* and yet he blesses the congregation in Hebrew after services each Shabbat. It's so beautiful: 'May the Lord bless you and keep you' and all that.

It's really meaningful. Maybe you ought to consider it."

"I grant you that it's beautiful. But Jewish law clearly says that in public it can only be pronounced by a *kohen*. I don't know about Rabbi _____. He's not Orthodox, so that might explain it."

"Well, maybe they're on to something. It sure is a beautiful thing to see."

down for the count

These were the fifties, and, as everyone knew, Orthodox Judaism in America was down for the count. Throughout the country, including Atlanta, once-proud Orthodox synagogues were tossing overboard their traditional practices — separate seating for men and women, prayer in Hebrew, serious Torah study, emphasis on the sanctity of *mitzvot* — and enthusiastically clambering aboard the ship of the future.

Many Orthodox rabbis rationalized their abandonment of the tradition by convincing themselves and their congregants that unless they took half a loaf and joined the burgeoning Conservative movement, traditional Judaism would crumble completely. What seemed like the golden mean of that movement was very appealing: it offered a Judaism not as flexible as the Reform, and yet not as demanding as the Orthodox. It was Orthodoxy without the restrictions; it was Reform with a yarmulke.

The Orthodox rabbis who led the flight into the Conservative camp encountered very little resistance among their congregants; on the contrary, they were applauded for their foresight. The ship was leaving the harbor, and it was time to jump aboard or forever be left behind. For a brief moment in history, it seemed irresistible.

No one in the fifties could possibly have limned the face of non-Orthodox American Jewry a generation later: a community ravaged by Jewish illiteracy and rampant assimilation; an intermarriage rate of over sixty percent — and, in a miraculous reversal, an Orthodoxy risen from the dead to become a learned and self-confident movement that has restored awareness of Torah learning and Torah living onto the agenda of Jewish life.

am I crazy?

No one could have foreseen it, certainly not a twenty-four-year-old rabbi about to enter his first pulpit. "Am I crazy?" I remember asking my father, who had been a rabbi in Baltimore for many years. "The town is owned by the Conservative and the Reform movements. They are personally decent people, but for them Orthodoxy is a back number, finished, dead. And my people don't really disagree. What chance do I have to bring anything genuine into my tiny congregation of forty families? Most of them are so unsure of this little Orthodox shul's future that they also belong to a non-Orthodox congregation as a kind of religious insurance policy."

"Don't worry about tomorrow," he said. "That's God's job. Just worry about today. Your job is to get up each morning and do your best to teach authentic Torah in the most effective way you know how. Remember that as a rabbi you teach in a hundred different ways, not just by using a text or by teaching a class, but by the way you and your wife talk to your people, by the way you relate to them, by your general demeanor. You even teach them by the way you go shopping for groceries. You do your job, and God will do His."

Because I sensed my people's envy of the larger congregations, I spent the early years trying to instill Jewish self-confidence into them. I began from scratch, teaching many of them how to read simple Hebrew, running small discussion groups, and ceaselessly preaching that those who study Torah and practice *mitzvot* are the true aristocrats of the Jewish people. It was important to inspire them with the adventure of swimming against the stream, of being different from the masses. I pointed out the excitement of living authentically and genuinely, and ridiculed the easy value system and gimmickry of the society around us. The constant, relentless theme was the contrast between phoniness and authenticity, between gimmickry and genuineness. I pointed to the silliness and futility of sisterhood Sabbaths and Boy Scout Sabbaths and birthday Sabbaths, and stressed that what we needed more than anything else was a Sabbath Sabbath.

A young man once said to me, "Rabbi, you like to knock all these gimmicks, but you have your own gimmick."

"Really? What's my gimmick?"

"Authenticity."

To their great credit, they listened respectfully, and in some cases they actually took me seriously. I think that despite their lack of Jewish learning they sensed in their soul of souls that what I was teaching was true.

the case of the missing mechitzah

Well, most of the time they did. Like any marriage, however, our relationship was not always without its tensions. During the third year of my tenure the congregation sold its tiny quarters and purchased a church building which we renovated into a synagogue. This was the natural time for me to install a physical *mechitzah* in the synagogue. Up until then we had had separate seating for men and women, but no actual partition. This was far from the ideal situation, but I accepted the pulpit after consulting with a number of rabbinic authorities who approved the arrangement with the understanding that it was temporary, and that within a reasonable time an halachically acceptable partition would be installed.

Today the concept of a *mechitzah*, though still misunderstood by many Jews, is an accepted fact of life for an Orthodox synagogue. But in the fifties the idea of a physical barrier between men and women in a shul was anathema. The loud noises one heard emanating from American

Orthodox synagogues were the sound of *mechitzos* everywhere crashing to the ground, one after the other. Without doubt, the availability of mixed seating was one of the great attractions of the Conservative movement, which liked to point to its fusion of tradition and modernity (a fusion which soon enough was to become confusion).

If timing is all, the timing of my effort to introduce a *mechitzah* into the shul could not have been worse. Furthermore, it threatened to abort the very dream of some of our members: to become popular and accepted, just like the large non-Orthodox synagogues in the community.

It was absolutely clear that if I brought the matter up for a vote, the *mechitzah* idea would lose by a landslide. So I simply informed our president that this was something we would be doing as part of the renovation of the new building. He did not at first realize the full ramifications of what I was saying and posed no objections.

I had the *mechitzah* built and installed — a series of wrought-iron stands holding a velvet curtain running down the center aisle — and proudly and anxiously awaited its public debut on the Shabbat preceding Rosh Hashanah. But since no more than a *minyan* of ten old men and two elderly women ever attended on Shabbat mornings, it was hardly noticed.

That night, however, was the night of Selichot, which was normally attended by many more people. I anticipated that there would be no great enthusiasm for the *mechitzah* but was not prepared for what actually took place.

When the wives of the leading members of the board walked into the shul at midnight and saw the *mechitzah*, they were aghast. They knew that in our shul they could not sit with their husbands, but this they had not expected. They immediately turned on their heels, stalked out of shul, and waited outside in their cars until Selichot was over. One can only surmise what they told their husbands on the way home.

The next afternoon I walked into the shul to check a few things and noticed that the *mechitzah* had disappeared. I was puzzled and called the chairman of the renovations committee to ask him what had happened. "Oh, yes," he said, "I should have called you. The fire marshal inspected the building and told us that it was a fire hazard because it was in the middle of the aisle. He said it would block a quick exit in an emergency, so he took it away."

"Please give me the name of the fire marshal. I'd like to talk to him."

"No use, Rabbi. His mind is made up. He was very firm about it. By the way, your sermon at Selichot was very nice."

I called the shul president and asked to meet with him that night. During the meeting, I had a ludicrous but entirely accurate insight: some individuals had absconded with the *mechitzah*, in full knowledge that in the few days remaining until Rosh Hashanah I would not be able to replace it. I told him that it was his task to talk to the fire marshal and to get the *mechitzah* back in place by Rosh Hashanah. And then I very quietly used my trump card: I wanted him to know in advance that if it was not in place when I walked into shul Rosh Hashanah evening, I would very regretfully but very definitely turn right around and leave — and they would have to find themselves another rabbi. I knew, too, that in the few days remaining before the holiday they would not be able to find a rabbi. I also knew that they liked me enough not to want to lose me.

I went home and asked my wife Estelle if she would be willing to pull up stakes if necessary. Without any hesitation she gave me her full backing. We had an eighteen-month-old baby; another was due in several months, I was facing the end of my rabbinate in Atlanta — but there was no alternative. They had challenged not only Jewish tradition, they had also challenged what little authority I had as a rabbi.

During the two days remaining before Rosh Hashanah I sent, through various channels, unmistakably clear signals to the congregational leadership that I was not bluffing.

One of the most effective channels was Oscar Brodsky. Oscar was the kind of person who was curious about everything and everyone. This in itself is not a character flaw, but he was constitutionally unable to keep any information to himself. Whatever he knew, the whole town knew within one day. I ran into Oscar in the drug store during the *mechitzah* crisis. "How you doing, Rabbi? Ready for the holidays?"

There and then I decided that Oscar's loose tongue would now be commandeered for holy purposes. "Unfortunately," I said, "I'm not really ready."

"What's the problem?"

"Well, you may not have heard about it, but I was told the fire marshal absconded with our new *mechitzah*. The fellows don't think it's a big deal, but I told them that unless it gets put back I won't be able to *daven* with them on the holidays."

"Wow, that is serious."

I wished Oscar a good year and silently prayed that God would permit him to continue to be loose-tongued at least until Rosh Hashanah.

The officers met with me several more times. They tried to convince me that a *mechitzah* was not very important. Furthermore, it would prevent people from joining our synagogue and would tear the shul apart. I should not act impulsively, they said; perhaps in a few years the congregation would be more amenable. I was courteous and sympathetic, but I told him that this was something I had to have if I were to remain with them, and that I was particularly unhappy with the fact that the *mechitzah* had been removed without any consultation with me.

On the morning before Rosh Hashanah I walked into the main shul, and there was the *mechitzah* back in its place. It was wrought-iron, it was black, the curtain was hardly luxurious, but it was one of the loveliest sights I had ever seen in my life. I was overjoyed but said nothing to anyone except Estelle.

When I entered the shul that night I behaved as if nothing unusual had occurred. I said nothing about it to the officers, and they said nothing to me. I did, however, devote the first Rosh Hashanah sermon to the idea of sanctity and *kedushah*, and used as one of many examples the concept of the separation of men and women during prayer. I stressed that the purpose of a *mechitzah* was not to suggest that women were in any way inferior or unworthy, but that it was designed to increase intensity and concentration in prayer. I noted that a synagogue is a replica of the ancient Jerusalem Temple and that separate seating was a feature of that Temple. A *mechitzah* is a statement that prayer is not a social event but a serious encounter between man and God.

public and private

I also stressed that classical Jewish prayer strives to maintain the atmosphere of a private relationship between God and us during prayer — and to do this in a public setting. It tries to maintain the relationship of the single, lonely Jew to the single, lonely God (for God represents the ultimate loneliness: there is no one like Him) and to do this within the setting of the *minyan,* which represents the community of Israel.

Thus we have the *amidah,* which is first whispered silently and then repeated aloud by the chazzan. Thus, too, we have the concept of the *mechitzah.* In one sense, a total community prays. In another, a group of individual Jews is praying at the same time and in the same place, but each at his or her own level of understanding, each at his own pace, with his own rhythm. Each individual brings to prayer his or her own fears, yearning, sadness, gratitude, triumph, disappointment, ecstasy. The separation of men and women during public prayer symbolizes the separate and distinctive paths which men and women follow in their approach to God.

And then, striking the theme that I had struck so many times before, I told them that I realized that a *mechitzah* was not a universal favorite, but that this was due to the fact that people viewed it from tired and stale perspectives. It is a major symbol that distinguishes an authentic Jewish community that adheres to tradition unflinchingly, whether or not it wins popularity contests.

To their eternal credit, these people — who did not observe many *mitzvot* — listened attentively, absorbed what I had to say, and never troubled me about it again. Those who remained unhappy with the *mechitzah* simply left the shul. Blessedly, there were very few of them. The synagogue's religious identity was established, people knew who we were and what we stood for, and we began a steady growth. In retrospect, it was not only a good move ideologically, but also practically.

That episode reinforced for me a basic truth about success in the rabbinate: a rabbi must always be prepared to resign from his position if necessary. If he feels beholden to, or dependent upon, his people; if he is fearful of not finding another position; if he is not ready to leave when his bottom-line principles are trampled upon, then these principles begin to totter and he begins to rationalize and justify his every retreat. Soon enough, he will find his authority as a rabbi depleted and he will become a glorified rabbinic rubber-stamp, indispensable for the delivery of invocations and benedictions, essential for filling up a dais — and quite inconsequential.

I am not suggesting that a rabbi change pulpits constantly — to do so is debilitating in physical and spiritual ways and does not permit him to tend the seeds he is sowing — but he must be prepared intellectually and emotionally to do so if necessary. In a word, he must feel a sense not of dependence on his congregation, but of independence. This kind of attitude, cultivated over the years, will transmit itself to his followers and will enable him to be a true leader — and, paradoxically, it will ensure greater longevity in his pulpit.

On the Shabbat following the great *mechitzah* showdown, our *minyan* consisted of the usual ten men and, now sitting on the other side of the new *mechitzah*, our two regular Shabbat women: Mrs. Kaminsky, eighty-eight, and her friend Mrs. Weinstock, eighty-five. Younger women in those days had better things to do on Shabbat mornings than go to shul.

These two were genuinely pious and God-fearing ladies; they came early to shul and stayed late, and they were delighted with the *mechitzah*. "I feel much better *davening* here now," Mrs. Kaminsky said to me as we left shul.

Fortunately, neither of them was aware of what old man Fischer had whispered in my ear just before Torah reading: "Now I understand why you fought so hard for a *mechitzah*. Look who's sitting over there: Miss America and Miss Universe." Not a very charitable observation, nor an informed one, but nevertheless very amusing — for Fischer himself was almost ninety.

Chapter 3:
Honor Your
Clergyman Week

Rabbis: I admire them, sympathize with the responsibility they bear and their grueling work load, but they do from time to time frustrate me. For example:

Congregational rabbis exchange synagogue bulletins as a matter of course. It is worthwhile to know what is happening in other congregations, and occasionally one can discover a good idea for a program or a lecture series.

I was reading Rabbi _____'s High Holiday bulletin article. It was, I thought, rather well done. But something about it nagged at me: I had known this rabbi for many years, and while he was a very good scholar, I knew that he did not write well. In addition, the article had a vaguely familiar ring to it, and I was convinced I had read it somewhere before.

I read and reread it in an effort to remember where I had first seen it, but to no avail. I put it aside. A day later it struck me: the article had originally been written by none other than me, some five years earlier. I remembered how hard I had worked on it, that it had gone through a number of drafts before it was printed.

I checked the synagogue files and found my article. Rabbi _____ had changed only one word: I had written in my closing sentence that "Estelle and I and the children wish you a good year," but he, in a burst of originality, had removed "Estelle" and inserted his wife's first name.

He made one additional change — instead of signing my name to it, he signed his own name.

If imitation is the sincerest form of flattery, what is plagiarism the sincerest form of? The Talmud says that he who honestly cites the sources of his ideas brings redemption to the world, while he who uses the words of others without attribution is guilty of theft and brings destruction to the world.

I wrote him a note. "It was nice to see one of my articles in your bulletin. I am flattered that you used my piece, but I was rather surprised to see that you signed your own name to it."

He wrote back that since we exchange bulletins, he assumed that everything in each bulletin automatically enters the public domain and is available to anyone who wants to use its contents. Besides, he was under desperate pressure just before the holidays and he had simply instructed his secretary to copy my article and send it off to the printer. It was she who had signed his name, and it was she who had inserted his wife's name. He apologized and hoped that in the spirit of the season I would forgive him this oversight.

It was a reasonable explanation. No one better than I knows the overwhelming rabbinic pressures of meeting deadlines for speeches, lectures, sermons, and articles. It was sloppy of him, and even reckless, but I tried to understand.

being a shepherd

Writing and speaking are very important tools for a rabbi, but the key ingredient in a good rabbi is the ability to be a shepherd to his flock. Impressive speaking may help the rabbi land the pulpit, but good shepherding helps him stay there and be effective. Shepherd, do not neglect your flock: that is the message. A rabbi may be the most gifted speaker in the world, an outstanding teacher, the finest counselor, an efficient administrator, a charismatic leader blessed with great personal charm and vision, but if his community has the sense that he neglects them personally, he is in their eyes a mere executive, a person who cares nothing about them, and he might as well get out of town on the next plane.

Conversely, he may be a poor speaker who knows nothing about running a shul, is hopelessly disorganized, is notoriously late for everything and regularly forgets appointments, but if he is affable and caring, a loving shepherd, especially when they are ill or in crisis, then all is forgiven. If the congregation feels he loves them, they will reciprocate that love.

How does he show the flock he cares? It is important, first, that he genuinely care. This cannot be faked. If he does not like people, if he looks down on them for whatever reason — because they are unlearned, or not sufficiently pious — it will become evident soon enough. One need not fawn over people or flatter them, but one must respect them and see the good in them. Some congregants may be Jewishly unlearned, but they are not fools. They can sense if the rabbi is a genuine shepherd or not.

(The shepherd analogy is apt. Moses was chosen for the leadership of Israel because God saw how he treated his sheep. The famous Midrash says that when one little sheep ran off into the desert, Moses followed it, picked it up, gave it water to drink, and carried it back to the flock. This demon-strated not only compassion, but also wisdom: Moses knew that the sheep was not straying, but merely thirsty. Similarly, our people occasionally stray only because they are thirsty and have not been receiving effective thirst quenchers from their leaders.)

A good shepherd will not only visit his people when they are hospitalized; he will remember to give them a call a week or two after they are out of the hospital. He will not only make a *shivah* visit; he will also call the bereaved family after *shivah* is over, after everyone has stopped visiting and stopped offering their sympathy. When the family returns to its normal routine, and the routine is not normal because someone will never return, an expression of concern from the rabbi is very helpful and forever remembered.

Every once in a while, before the High Holidays, I would send a personal note to those people in the congregation who had been bereaved during the past year. I would simply write that I realized that the forthcoming holidays, with someone missing, would not be easy, that I wanted them to know they were in our thoughts, and that they should take comfort in the knowledge that their loved one was enjoying eternal life and peace in the World-to-Come.

It was a simple gesture, but it was profoundly appreciated. Once, at a Bar Mitzvah reception, I greeted an elderly widow who had left Atlanta ten years earlier. She pulled out a crum-pled piece of paper from her purse and, tears welling up in her eyes, showed it to me. It was the note I had written her when her husband died a decade ago. She told me that she had kept it with her all these years and reread it whenever she felt sad and depressed, because it made her feel so warm to know that someone cared about her.

One must not forget the obvious: people need to be loved.

A rabbi is not expected to call his members on their birth-days and anniversaries, or to attend every social event with-in the congregation, but there are many ways he can show that he cares. An occasional call to someone he has not seen for a while; giving undivided attention to every person who comes to see him; being patient with people who are "noodges" even when they get under his skin; trying to see something good in people even when they seem far from good. And, yes, rabbi, keep smiling.

the shepherd as leader: Moses and Aaron

The rabbinic dilemma is that the rabbi must be more than just a sensitive and caring person. The shepherd has to transcend himself and offer vision and inspiration. He must love his flock, but he must be a leader, and in order to lead he must be able to demand discipline and sacrifice.

A rabbi often wonders whom to take as a model of rabbinic leadership, Moses or Aaron. Each of these towering figures is an archetype of the ideal rabbi. Aaron was fully aware that his flock was only human and had human weaknesses. He was patient with their failings, for he realized that one does not with great ease attain spiritual heights. Aaron represents the understanding leader who brings peace between man and wife and between man and his fellow, and mostly, between man and God. He is the rabbi as shepherd.

Moses represents the rabbi as commander. He is possessed of a vision of a spiritual and temporal promised land, and knows precisely where he wants to lead his people. He has high expectations of his followers and makes great demands of them. Yes, he loves them as much as Aaron, and he is willing to lay down his life for them. Though Moses was in fact a shepherd himself, the rabbi who chooses him as a model must also have the capacity to be uncompromising and transcendent. His interests and his people's interests are not identical. His essence is not on earth among the people but in the rarefied atmosphere of the Sinai summit, in communion with God. He soars above his people and demands that they reach the stars.

While Moses communes with God on Sinai, it is Aaron who remains down among the people. It is Aaron of whom the Mishnah in *Avot* says that he was "a lover of peace, a pursuer of peace, loving God's creatures and bringing them close to Torah."

Whom should a contemporary rabbi attempt to emulate? If he is exclusively a commanding and visionary Moses, he could soon enough become a general without an army. If he is exclusively a loving, understanding Aaron, he will be unable to budge his people from their fixed positions, and soon enough his army will be leading him.

A rabbi must strive to become a fusion of the two. He must be a shepherd, but also maintain within himself the long view. He must be considerate and patient, but at the same time must make it clear that he has great expectations of his flock. He has to be understanding but also stubborn, and he must not flinch from demanding that they move to higher ground.

No one said it would be easy.

rabbinic authority:
Yankees 5, Dodgers 3

They taught me many things in the yeshivah and prepared me for many rabbinic eventualities. But one subject they never discussed with me was the concept of rabbinic authority. No one ever sat me down and said, "Remember, as a rabbi you are the living embodiment of the Torah; you represent the holy traditions of Judaism. Your opinion on any religious subject is in effect the word of God filtered down through our sages and wise men through your own piety and learning, refined by years of exposure to the purifying atmosphere of the Divine wisdom of the Torah. What you as a rabbi say on the subject of Judaism is in a way a distillation of the Divine will."

It is just as well that I was not informed of such things. My people would have had difficulty accepting the very idea of a twenty-five-year-old who was the bearer of the wisdom of the ages. Not only would they not have invested in me any real authority that might affect their lives; they were at first not even willing to bring their personal problems to this raw young man. Being Southern, friendly, and informal, many of them, without any self-consciousness at all, even called their rabbi by his first name during those early years.

I did have rabbinic authority when I answered questions about the time for Yizkor, or the date for next year's Seder, which answers they accepted fully and unreservedly, no doubt sensing that I represented four thousand years of Jewish tradition. And when I unhesitatingly suggested the Jewish equivalents for the Butches and Rosemaries (Baruch and Rivkah Malka) that they brought into the world, they took this not only as evidence of a superb rabbinic education, but were convinced that I was reflecting the Divine will. When, thus encouraged, I tentatively suggested to a father that he buy *tefillin* for his Bar Mitzvah boy, I was informed: "I got a set for my own Bar Mitzvah and they're still brand new, so why do I need to buy new ones?" And when a fine lady told me that she "didn't do any rituals but only lived by the Ten Commandments" and I made bold to inform her that Shabbat was the fourth of the ten, she was mildly surprised but recovered quickly enough to ask, "Are you absolutely sure?"

Only Ike the incurable gambler was convinced that I had a direct line to heaven. One Erev Yom Kippur he called me with his own awesome concern: the World Series was about to begin and would I please pick the winner for him? "But Ike," I protested, "you'd be risking hundreds of dollars on the word of someone who is not an expert in these things." Ike, overcome by genuine faith in my millenium-long authority, insisted: "Whatever you pick, Rabbi, I'm ready to lay money on it."

For four years running, in an amazing display of rabbinic *mazal,* I picked winners, and Ike happily gave ten percent of his earnings to the shul, informing all who would listen that his rabbi truly possessed the Divine spirit. For him, I was the very model of a modern rabbinic authority.

One Yom Kippur day, having bid more than anyone else for the honor, he opened the Ark for *Unesane Tokef* and stood respectfully beside me during the prayer — "Who shall live and who shall die, who by fire and who by water, who before his allotted time and who at his allotted time . . ." When the prayer ended he closed the curtain, shook my hand, wished me a good year, and whispered, "Good news, Rabbi. Yankees 5, Dodgers 3, top of the eighth."

God punished us both that year, him for thinking strange thoughts before the Ark, and me for accepting his good news with equanimity. Because of a big rally by the wrong team in the bottom of the ninth of the seventh game, my shul lost its ten percent and I lost my Divine pipeline.

Of course, at births, weddings, Bar Mitzvahs, and funerals, mine remained the unquestioned voice of our hallowed tradition. In sickness and in domestic crisis I was their entree to the Holy One. But when it came to life's major decisions — how much *tzedakah* to give and where to give it, where to send a child to school, how to live life as a Jew — it was "Rabbi, you are great and we love you, but the Torah was for then and this is now."

When I spoke about anti-Semitism, I was their halachic decisor, but when I asked why black athletes are called Isaiah and Jewish children are called Lucas, I was their very young rabbi who would some day mature.

When I taught about our glorious past, they had faith in my every word; but when I suggested that without Torah living we may not have a future, I was out of touch with the present.

When I supported the State of Israel in its crises, mine was the voice of Jewish authority; but when I asked why we could only manage a bare *minyan* on Shabbos mornings while the churches down the street overflowed on their Sabbaths, I was being impractical and utopian.

The rabbi as religious authority and as shepherd; the rabbi as the embodiment of Moses and Aaron; the need to be loving and patient with the flock — this is all good theory. But when it confronts the mundane reality of synagogue life, theory is not always lived up to.

true confessions

Being patient with "noodges" — glib, easy, theoretical advice, but not always lived up to. True confessions:

At four o'clock one afternoon, after a full day of difficult meetings and counseling and teaching and hospital visits, I get back into my office bereft of energy, time, or patience. On my desk is a note from the secretary: Mr. Blackstone called and is coming in to see me at four-thirty.

I groan out loud. Please, dear Lord, not Blackstone and his insufferable pontificating. For ten years he's been solemnly telling me how to cure the ills of mankind. The panaceas all occur to him while he is on the road selling his fabrics. Please, not Blackstone, not today.

A knock on the door. Enter Blackstone with a big smile. He pulls off his coat, clears his throat, sits down, begins. I tell myself: Remember, you're tired, irritated, under pressure; this fellow means well; you've always listened patiently to him; don't let him get under your skin.

He begins slowly, ponderously, as if he were about to reveal the secrets of the universe. "Rabbi, I've been thinking. (*Control, control.*) I been doing lots of thinking, yes sir."

(*It will only take a few minutes. Let him say his piece.*) "I have finally come to a conclusion, after a great deal of soul-searching, mind you. Rabbi — and I ask you to please listen to me carefully — the youth of today are the leaders of tomorrow!"

I have work to do, the clock is moving, and this fellow is

rediscovering America on my behalf. I say nothing.

"What do you think of that idea?" he asks.

"What idea?"

"That the youth of today are the leaders of tomorrow."

"Oh, I can't argue with that."

"I once knew a brilliant rabbi back in Jersey. This man was dynamic, mind you, a tremendous man, an orator, a scholar, a real brilliant rabbi. He once said from the pulpit — from the pulpit, mind you — that all the youth should come to the synagogue on Shabbos morning, and that on Shabbos afternoon they should play football and he would play with them! That way they would be attracted to Judaism, he said. Rabbi, have you ever thought of doing that?"

"No, I can't say I have." My resolve is beginning to melt. I notice that my fists are clenched.

Blackstone leans forward for the *coup de grace.* "Rabbi, these kids are our future. Why don't you try this idea out?"

Something begins to give within me. "It won't work," I snap. "It won't help and it won't work. The problem goes much deeper than that."

"Rabbi, if you don't try it, how do you know it won't work?" He was peddling drapery fabrics with his best soft-sell smile. "If it was good enough for Dr. Braun back in Jersey, it should be good enough for you," he purrs.

Control, control. Don't let him get to you. But it was too late. That which earlier had begun to give way had now become a full collapse. "Sam, I don't know Dr. Braun, but if that's his solution for today's Jewish problems, he's a total and complete fool. I want you to go back to Jersey and tell Dr. Braun that Rabbi Feldman of Atlanta said that if this is his prescription to save Jewish life, he's an unmitigated fool."

"You don't mean that."

"I mean that. Find me one Jewish child he has saved by playing football with him on Shabbos afternoon."

I feel sorry for Blackstone and don't want to hurt him in any way, but for ten years I have been humoring him as I listened to his bromides. I could not contain myself any longer.

It was only later that night that I realized that the true fool in the story was I for having allowed an innocent, unsophisticated person, who meant no harm, to irritate me to the point of explosion.

So much for the patience of an Aaron.

I did much better with Don Taubman. Don had a drinking problem, and late one evening he came over to discuss it with me. The problem was that when he came into the house he brought his problem with him; he had already had too much, and he had a bottle of Canadian Club in his hand. He did not — could not possibly — discuss drinking with me. Instead, he said he wanted to discuss philosophy with me: the purpose of life, why we are here, the nature of God, the concept of Messiah. "Rabbi," he kept repeating, "what's it all about, what's it all about?"

Despite all my efforts to give him black coffee or ginger ale or juice, he kept pouring himself drinks from his bottle. He became very agitated when I tried to move the bottle from his reach. Finally, I convinced him that it was time to go home, and offered to drive him. He refused, insisting that he would be fine, just fine. Despite my protestations he drove off.

I pictured the scene later that night: Don staggers into his house. His enraged wife asks him where he has been the entire evening. He answers innocently, "Honest, honey, I was at the rabbi's house."

the private rabbi

What was it I said earlier about a rabbi always having a smile on his face? That is not always possible. Not only because of frustrating discussions with laymen who are convinced they have simple solutions to complex issues, but because the rabbi does not have the answers to the perplexing issues of theodicy that arise at times of tragedy and that cut so deeply. Sometimes silence is the only response: the death of the young and the innocent; natural disasters; the eternal questions of why the righteous seem to suffer and the wicked seem to prosper. One wants to be of help, one is willing to be God's deputy on earth, to explain the ways of God to man, but the feeling of inadequacy is staggering.

Why is it given to me to be the defender of the faith when I myself am far from knowing the answers? Why is it my lot to immerse myself in endless meetings, in persuading people to do the right thing, in attempting to raise money for crucial causes, in public wranglings and communal disputes over religious issues, in fighting for higher standards of Jewish living?

It is not only that I grow weary of being the Divine deputy; I am also by nature not a public person. Sitting up front at the *mizrach* wall is an honor, and I am not beyond *kavod*, but in the final analysis I would much rather be on the sidelines than before the public. Given the choice, I would opt for the *beit midrash*, the library, the musty aroma of old books in the stacks, and not the pulpit and the lectern. Although I find people fascinating and enjoy being with them, I can without any pain forgo most social events. In general, I would rather listen to a sermon than give one, and rather be a student than a teacher. I am constantly torn between my deep desire for privacy and my equally deep desire to teach God's ways to His children.

Yes, it is a privilege. I know what Moses said to Joshua when he handed over to him the reigns of leadership of the Jewish people: *Ashrecha shenismanisa parnas al Yisroel,* "Fortunate are you who was appointed a leader over Israel." But I also know what Moses said to God in Numbers 11:11: "Why have I not found favor in Your eyes, that You have given me the entire burden of this people?" Although I certainly do not carry a fraction of the burden of this people, and although no sane person would compare himself to Moses, only a rabbi can fully appreciate this verse.

And yet, and yet . . . Would I rather be doing something else? No.

Is anything else more worthwhile or satisfying? No.

Is anything else more lasting? In what other field can one affect adult lives, and build souls, and teach the ways of God, and inspire and uplift and elevate Jews to their historic roles? None.

If the cliche fits, wear it: the pulpit rabbinate is a burden and a privilege. It is not unusual for great privileges to be great burdens.

If I were twenty-five and knew what I know now, would I choose the pulpit rabbinate again?

A very good question. The answer — with a deep sigh at the vivid memories of the frustrations, defeats, despairs, and discouragements which are endemic to the pulpit rabbinate — is a definite Yes.

what it's really like

Ah, the rabbinate, the rabbinate. Some day I'll write a book about it: what it looks like from the outside, what it's really like on the inside. Most parents don't want their children to become pulpit rabbis, usually for the wrong reasons. And those few who do encourage their youngsters to become pulpit rabbis often do so for the wrong reasons. They look at the rabbi in the pulpit, the object of so much attention, wielder of so much authority, admired by so many, at the center of so much activity. So they say to their son, "You know, you really ought to become a rabbi."

Such parents know nothing of the agony of the rabbinate, the loneliness of the life, the sheer physical and emotional travail that is involved in becoming — and remaining — a good rabbi. If they had to have one conversation with the mother of a stricken child, or make one agonizing *shivah* call, one tragic hospital visit, one counseling session about intractable problems; if they had to live through one weekend in which they officiated at a Bar Mitzvah, a wedding, a funeral, and tried to comfort a terminally ill patient; if they had to undergo the rigors of writing one speech, one lecture, one article — while trying to balance all this with the domestic roles of husband and father — they would think twice before encouraging their youngsters to enter this supposedly glamorous life.

Not to speak of the loneliness which comes from people treating the rabbi as an icon and not as a person. The rabbi is not seen as an individual with needs and hopes and aspirations and human flaws and problems, but as a mute symbol of the religion. He represents the ideal which everyone would want to be. He is not just a man who is trying to teach Torah; he is God's deputy, His representative on earth, and therefore different and special. This serves to intensify the rabbi's loneliness and his sense of isolation from others. Because he is different and special, the demands and expectations which his community places upon him — demands which would be overwhelming in any other field — are considered perfectly reasonable.

He is expected to be available twenty-four hours a day; to be an expert speaker, an expert teacher, an expert organizer, an expert counselor, an expert writer, an expert administrator; to be friendly and outgoing and accessible and understanding, but also thoughtful and original and scholarly; to be available at all times to everyone, but also to find time for personal study and learning; to be one of the boys, but also apart from the boys; to be a nice guy, but not just another nice guy; to be everyone's buddy, but everyone should also admire him and look up to him; to be dignified, but not overly so. And above all else, to be a shepherd. And, of course, to be the embodiment of Moses and Aaron.

(An outstanding rabbi in Baltimore once told me: "A rabbi must remember occasionally to drop his dignity, but to catch it before it hits the ground." He never revealed to me how one can recognize the thin line between dropping one's dignity and holding it aloft. My own version of this is that he must take his job seriously — but not himself.)

Yes, the pulpit rabbinate is an exciting and satisfying life, and good people should enter it — but only with the right expectations and with full awareness of its tough demands. To paraphrase the famous comment about old age, the pulpit rabbinate is not for sissies. One should enter it for the right reasons: to play a role in the future of the Jewish people; to help shape individual lives; to try to teach, preserve, and sustain God's Torah among His people. In this lies the real glamour of being a rabbi in Israel. Those who enter the rabbinate for the wrong reasons will find only frustration.

The wrong reasons: prestige, power, being looked up to. These stimulants quickly evaporate, leaving only emptiness in their wake, and unless the rabbi has other things in his baggage, he will be left only with bitterness.

Even those who enter the rabbinate for the right reasons must always be vigilant lest they allow themselves to forget their mission and begin to believe their own press notices about the "beloved rabbi." It is very easy to allow ersatz glory to distort one's vision. To love *kavod* is never to get enough of it; worse, cynicism is often the result.

But there are also profound rewards. Because of what the rabbi represents, he is allowed entree into the most intimate aspects of the lives of his people. With them he smiles at their births and weddings; with them he prays at their bedsides and weeps at their funerals; and with them he beams with pride as their lives gradually change.

the authentic
and the inauthentic

It is curious and refreshing to keep in mind that when the rabbi eschews gimmickry, does not cater to popularity, and simply teaches authentic Torah, Jews will respond to the message. The soul rejects that which is tawdry and a sham; it yearns for the genuine and the holy. The problem is that by and large the message that many Jews hear from their rabbis and communal leaders is inauthentic and artificial, and panders to the latest fads. Some rabbis actually tell their congregants that God does not really listen to prayer; *Bris Milah* is a group identity ritual which we moderns have outgrown; kashrut and *matzah* and *succah* are vestiges of an ancient past and not to be taken seriously today; *tefillin* are a tribal symbol; God is not a personal God; there is no afterlife, nor is there any accountability for our lives on this earth; Shabbat can be observed any way you like as long as it relaxes you; we don't believe in a Messiah. Etcetera, etcetera.

By the time the contemporary, relevant rabbi gets through with his Boy Scout prattle, there is little left of the classic and majestic Judaism of Torah and *halachah* and God-consciousness and discipline. Not surprisingly, the whole structure collapses of its own weight. Is it any wonder that few Jews take Judaism seriously? Based on the non-doctrines that they hear, which intelligent and sensitive person would not abandon a hollow shell stripped of all mystery and grandeur?

a lift for the spirits

A rabbi's spirits are sometimes lifted from the most unlikely sources. Mine are always lifted when I think of Mrs. SaraLee Hirsch. She lives in a little town in South Carolina, and of the two hundred Jewish families in town, she and her husband and children are the only observant Jews. I first met her when she attended a lecture I was giving in her area. Later we had a long talk in which she asked me many questions relating to Jewish practice. One of them dealt with her immersion in the *mikveh*. I knew that her town had no *mikveh*, and I asked her how she observed it. She replied that she used the Atlantic Ocean.

"Isn't that a several-hour drive?" I asked.

"It's less than two hours."

"What do you do in the winter?"

"I use the ocean in the winter as well," she replied with a smile.

"Isn't it rather cold?"

"It's cold, but I manage."

I am in awe of this woman's sheer spiritual strength and commitment. Here is a person not brought up in a traditional home who has taken upon herself all the *mitzvot*, and performs them with great self-sacrifice. When I grow discouraged, I think of her commitment.

the rabbi's wife

All of which leads me to ponder: in all of this palaver about the glories and non-glories of the rabbinate, what of the rabbi's wife? She sits out there, my dear wife, in the same seat she has occupied all these years, still listening intently to my sermons. She is an astute listener, has a keen intelligence, and her critiques are perceptive. She began her career as a *rebbetzin* at age twenty, and she has proven to be a natural. She has an innate ability to deal sensitively with people, bears herself with dignity and serenity, and has earned the respect and affection of the community.

It is not easy to be a *rebbetzin*; she shares center stage with her husband and is viewed as an extension of him. She is watched, admired, criticized, talked about, because she lives her life in the same glass house as her husband.

But there is a difference: the rabbi is trained for the rabbinate. As the son of a rabbi, I had been emotionally and intellectually preparing for the role all my life. But the rabbi's wife becomes a *rebbetzin* by virtue of her marriage to the rabbi. To be suddenly thrust out on the stage in a starring role is a frightening experience. That certain women do it so well is remarkable. In fact, many mediocre rabbis thrive in their positions because their wives are so talented. (They are not that mediocre; if they were, these women would not have married them.) On the other hand, I have seen occasional rabbinic lives wrecked by a wife who was completely unsuited for public life.

Trials of the rabbi's wife: It is the eve of our twentieth wedding anniversary. I have kept this evening clear for weeks, and am going to take her to a concert of Jewish music. I am in the shower. She knocks at the bathroom door. "Refrigerated Transport is on the phone." There is an edge to her voice. "Tell them to get someone else. It's our anniversary."

Refrigerated Transport. Before I pick up the phone I know what they want. It happens all the time with trucking companies. A truckload of freshly slaughtered kosher meat is loaded at, say, Dubuque, Iowa, and trucked to Miami. Fresh meat must be kosher-prepared or frozen within three days of slaughter in order to maintain its kosher status. If it is apparent that freshly slaughtered kosher meat will not be kosher-prepared within the three days, it must be thoroughly washed down before the three-day deadline is reached.

The trip from the Midwest packing houses to the major eastern or western cities takes less than three days. Every so often, however, trucks break down on the road or a shipment is delayed, and the entire truckload — hundreds of thousands of dollars worth of kosher meat — could theoretically be lost to the owners. The drivers have clear instructions about what to do in such circumstances. They have a list of Orthodox rabbis en route whom they can call to have the meat washed down. The truckers call it "blessing the meat," but there is no ritual at all. It is merely the physical act of thoroughly wetting the meat so that the blood within it does not congeal. Should the blood congeal, it presents kashrut problems.

the meat expires in two hours

I picked up the phone, although I knew the script before the rough-hewn but respectful voice uttered it: "Sir, I got this here truckload of meat that expires in two hours. Could you come on down and bless it for me?"

When I was the only Orthodox person in town, I would don raincoat and boots, meet the driver at one of the truck stops on the edge of town, and with a high-powered hose would wet down every slab of meat within the interior of the truck. It was messy work, far removed from a blessing, but there was no one else to do it and so I did it. As the community grew, I was able to send someone else to do the work (since it does not require a rabbi, but only a reliable and knowledgeable person) and have him reimbursed by the meat company. I may have lost an opportunity for *chesed* by getting a pinch hitter, but I did maintain some semblance of sanity.

Tonight there was no question that I would have to find someone else, and I did. The vision of stopping off at the truck stop, doing the hosing, and then appearing at the concert in a wet, bloody raincoat and dirty boots was a bit disconcerting. Literally.

We enjoyed the music, but it brought to the surface the realities of being a rabbi's wife. A rabbi willy-nilly finds himself married to two wives. One is the woman to whom he gave the wedding *ketubah*; the other is the community to whom he gave another kind of contract. Wife Number One should take precedence over Wife Number Two, but the painful reality is often the reverse. Which accounts for the edge in my wife's voice on this night of our anniversary. I don't blame her for not wanting to play second fiddle to a truckload of meat.

This matter of washing the meat down from inside a freezing truck was one of several occasions when I was given an unvarnished look at the flip side of supposed rabbinic prestige and authority. The other occasions were the times when I was crouching down in the mud to inspect leaks in the *mikveh*. Once, as the plumber and I wallowed in the mud beneath the communal *mikveh*, we doubled over in laughter as he said to me, "So this is what they meant when they talked about the glories of being a leader in Israel."

Yes, I know: this is the true honor — getting down in the mud for your people. And I remember the Gemara about King David examining bloody garments because of the laws of ritual purity. These are great concepts, noble and true. But deep in the bowels of a dripping truck filled with slabs of meat, or wallowing in the mud beneath a leaking *mikveh,* it did give us a chuckle.

rabbinic glory

The supposed authority and glory of being a rabbi: I was driving downtown, and there in front of me was a billboard, big as life:

"HONOR YOUR CLERGYMAN WEEK, JANUARY 30 — FEBRUARY 6. Sponsored by National Civitans, Pat Boone, Chairman."

Now, wasn't that a nice idea? I could visualize it: everyone coming up to his clergyman and telling him how much he is honored and loved. It was really quite thoughtful.

January 30 to February 6, I mused, should be a great week. Testimonials for all clergymen; people suddenly taking notice of the ministers, priests, and rabbis within their midst; lives changed; a new awareness of God.

Maybe this is a sign that religion in America is finally coming into its own. Once they begin to honor clergymen, can honor of God be far behind? Those Civitans, they really know how to do things: a big billboard right there in the middle of downtown Atlanta.

But as I thought about it, my enthusiasm waned. So what if once a year clergymen are honored. And the other fifty-one weeks? Now we have achieved the status of Be Kind To Animals Week. Isn't it rather undignified to use a billboard to remind people to honor us? Does anyone become a clergyman because he seeks honor? And just how will it be done? "Clergymen, we honor you deeply. We may not follow your teachings, but we want you to know that we honor you from January 30 to February 6."

Still, honor is not to be sneezed at. If they want to honor us, let them. So what if it is only one week out of fifty-two —

that's better than nothing. After all, it's not us personally; we represent something. Let them realize how difficult our work is, how many hours each day we devote to our holy duties.

Yes, Pat Boone, it is a great idea. It's about time someone thought of it. Poor clergymen, everyone takes us for granted. More power to the Civitans for HONOR YOUR CLERGYMAN WEEK. Hmm, I wonder if the people in my congregation have heard of it yet . . . they live so far from this billboard . . .

I drove back to shul and walked into my study with new bounce in my step. I was one of that multitude of grey, unknown men who are finally receiving their just recognition on the American scene. I sat smiling and satisfied at my desk as I shuffled through my pile of mail.

Then my eyes fell on the calendar. It was February 7.

Chapter 4:
The Rabbinic Calling

Some people refer to the rabbinate as a "calling." A more accurate description would be a telephone calling.

It is eight P.M. I am eating supper. The phone. A woman.

"Rabbi?"

"Yes."

"Am I disturbing you?"

"No problem."

"How are you?"

"Fine. How are you?"

"Fine, thanks. Rabbi?"

"Yes."

"Rabbi, I hope you're not eating."

"That's perfectly all right."

"Rabbi?"

"Yes."

"What day of the week does Rosh Hashanah fall a year from now?"

"I don't have my appointment calendar in front of me, but if you'll call me in the morning in the study I'll be glad to give it to you."

"Oh, I didn't want to disturb you at the study because I know you're busy there."

* * *

One night I came home very late after a long meeting and found a written message as I walked in the door: "Mrs. Fine has been trying to reach you all evening. URGENT. Call her until two A.M." Before I removed my coat and hat, I dialed her number. The urgency? It concerned the local kosher bakery. Their Shabbat *challah* is not as tasty as it used to be, and why don't I see to it that we get a new kosher bakery in town?

a visit to her husband

"How are you, Rabbi? This is Mrs. Solomon."

She was not a shul regular, and I didn't remember who she was, but I replied, "Fine. I hope you and the family are well."

"Well, I don't have a family, you know."

"Oh, I'm sorry. Of course." I still couldn't quite place her, so I played for time and asked how she had been. "Rabbi, I'd like to visit my husband."

"Oh? How is he?"

"Rabbi, you buried him two years ago! He's at Greenwood

Cemetery. Rabbi, don't you remember me at all? Mrs. Solomon. You know, from Canada."

Her voice is pained. And I am in pain for not having remembered sooner. "Of course I remember you. Please forgive me."

"I'd like to visit my husband — you know, his grave. But I have no car, no way to get there, there are no buses that go out to the cemetery. A taxi costs twenty dollars one way, and I can't afford that."

"Perhaps I can get someone to drive you. Please call me back tomorrow morning."

I called several people and got a few maybe's, but when Mrs. Solomon called me back I had nothing definite for her. I sensed the disappointment in her voice: "Rabbi, you mean no one in the whole synagogue can drive me?"

"Well, not quite. I'll continue trying." But it was no use. So I volunteered to drive her to the cemetery myself. She was delighted. I was not so delighted; my schedule for the day was already crowded.

The cemetery was deserted when we arrived. She made her way between the tombstones to her husband's grave. "Would you mind reading a psalm with me, Rabbi?" We read Psalm 23: ". . . Though I walk though the valley of the shadow of death, I will fear no evil for Thou art with me." She sobbed lightly. The sun was warm above us. "Would you mind reading just one more psalm?" We read Psalm 15: "Keep me, O Lord, for I have trusted in Thee . . ."

She placed her hand on the stone slab. "It's so pretty here, such a nice view, so peaceful. He was a very good man."

"He certainly was. Would you like me to read another psalm?"

"No, those two were just right. Thank you."

I drove her back home. The people who couldn't drive her that day all did me a favor. Somehow, she brightened up my entire week.

* * *

A few snippets from this week's phone calls:

- "You don't know me, I'm not a member, but my husband and I are having real problems. It's very serious and very personal. I don't want to talk to you face to face because I'm embarrassed. Could you help me on the phone?"
- "I have a lot of old clothes, but in very good shape, that my late husband wore. Also some shoes, very nice ones. I'd like to send them to the poor people in Israel. How do I go about this?"
- "I am a Christian lady. Forgive me for bothering you, but I wanted to know whether Jews believe in God."
- "I have a really important term paper due tonight on Judaism. Could I come over and talk with you about it?"
- "Your sermon last Shabbos made me think. Can I make an appointment to discuss it with you?"
- "Is it okay to have a bridesmaid who isn't Jewish?"
- "If God is good and He is loving, why is there so much suffering in the world?"
- "The article you promised for *Tradition Magazine* was due three weeks ago. Is it ready yet?"
- "Could you do a book review for Hadassah in November?"
- "Do Jews believe in a Messiah who is a person, or just in a Messianic Age?"
- "What word in what book marks the exact midpoint of the Bible?"
- "What is the date of the first Seder next year? We're having a lot of guests and we have to plan."
- "What time is the *minyan* tomorrow evening?"
- "What's the point of the Mishnah mentioning minority opinions when we follow the majority?"
- "We really need a new *mikveh*, Rabbi. Please do something about it."

and then what?

A call from a stockbroker, obviously making random calls in search of new business. He is touting a new stock offering. "It will probably triple in value within six months," he purrs.

I was in a playful mood. "And then what happens?"

"Well," he says, "that means if you invest $5,000 today, it could be worth $15,000 in ninety days."

"And then what?"

"And then you will have made a cool $10,000 profit in only three months. That's a lot of money."

"And then what?"

"Then you could either reinvest it, or you could do whatever you want with the money."

"Suppose I reinvest it and I keep making lots of money. What happens then?"

"What do you mean? You could become a millionaire."

"Fine, but then what?"

By now he was surely cursing his luck for having dialed my number, so I said to him, "Look, you happened to call a rabbi. I have no objections to being financially comfortable, don't misunderstand, but I think there's no point to making money in order to make more money. Money is not an end, it's a means towards an end."

"Well, sir, you could buy a new home or a new car."

"But what if I'm perfectly content in the house I now have? And what if my old car is okay and I don't want a new car?"

"Yes, sir." He had given up on me and couldn't wait to get off the phone.

"Before you go," I said, "let me say that you are a terrific salesman. You have a great phone personality, you're intelligent, you don't push too hard. Maybe you really should tell the people on your list that they ought to reevaluate their priorities, that they ought to think what good use they would like to make of their money, and that maybe making lots of money should not be the highest priority in life."

"Yes, sir. Real nice talking to you. Bye."

why am I being punished?

An Erev Yom Kippur call from a woman who would not give me her name: "You may remember that I called you three years ago. I had five kids at the time and was pregnant with number six. I was beginning to panic, I didn't think I could handle six children, and I wanted to have an abortion. I talked to you on the phone because I was too ashamed to discuss it personally. We had a long conversation and you talked me out of it. Well, I had the child. He is now three years old. He has just been diagnosed with a brain tumor. Malignant. There is no treatment for it."

I was staggered, having expected a happy ending to her story. I told her how terribly sorry I was and asked her if I could do anything for her.

"Yes, you can do something for me. You can tell me why God is punishing me since I went the extra mile and didn't have the abortion when I wanted to. I did the right thing, so why is God doing this to me now?"

Anger, resentment, pain. Clearly, she was reaching out for comfort and solace. I tried to provide it as best I could. I asked her to come in and talk with me face to face, but she said she was less ill at ease on the phone.

I suggested that not everything that goes wrong in a person's life is an indication that one is being punished. God has His own mysterious and hidden ways of running the universe. Sometimes the purpose of a life is fulfilled in seventy years of a life, and sometimes in just a few months. What one needs to do is to strengthen one's faith through prayer and through opening up one's soul to God. I tried to keep her hopes up and at the same time to prepare her for the worst.

She listened carefully, but I was not certain I was getting through to her. I asked her to give me her phone number so I could call her from time to time, but she refused. She did promise to call me on a regular basis, and she has done that for the past several months. Every first of the month she calls, and we talk, and I try to help. It is only a phone call, but because I do not know the person to whom I'm talking, it is much more difficult than an actual hospital visit. But apparently my anonymous interlocutor finds it helpful to talk, so we talk.

$$* * *$$

It is ten o'clock at night, and I am preparing my Shabbat sermon. On the radio one of my favorite pieces is about to begin, the Sibelius Violin Concerto. I am looking forward to hearing it. My stomach tightens. I know the phone will ring as soon as the concerto begins.

The phone rings on the first note, as if the conductor had pointed with one hand to the orchestra and with the other to my telephone. It is Bessie Druckman.

"I know it's late, but do you know where I can get a fake beard?"

I am taken aback by the question, and also annoyed at the interruption, but it is only one week before Purim, and people are evidently looking for costumes. "A what?"

"You know, a fake beard. Where can I get one?"

Bessie is a good soul, and it is hard to get annoyed with her. "How would I know? My beard is real."

With Bessie one does not make jokes. "I know yours is real, Rabbi. I need a fake one for me for Purim."

"I don't know where you can get one, Bessie." The truth is that I really want to hear the music and would like to get off the phone as quickly as possible without offending her.

Her disappointment is palpable. "I figured you would know all about beards. Who do you think would know?"

"Look in the Yellow Pages under Costumes. I'm sure you'll find something there, okay?"

"Hey, that's a great idea. Thanks, sorry to bother you."

"Oh, no bother at all. Any time."

Any time.

＊＊＊

A call from a man who identified himself as "a Baptist and a former drunk" who was still attending sessions of Alcoholics Anonymous. He claimed that he had been receiving direct messages from God. Since most of the messages emanated from the Hebrew Bible, he would like to check them with me.

"In what way do you receive these messages?" I asked.

"Very simple. I flip open my Bible, I don't look at the page, I put my finger on a verse, and the verse gives me a message."

I tried to be noncommittal. "Interesting," I said.

"This morning my finger landed on some verses in Ezekiel which describe the construction of the Altar. Later on I landed on the Book of Joel, who was describing the building of the Holy Temple. Rabbi, do you think that maybe I am being told that I ought to stop drinking and begin learning a trade, such as a draftsman or builder, and that I should specialize in religious buildings?"

I told him he had really hit the nail on the head. He thanked me profusely.

He was fortunate, for his own sake, that his finger had not fallen on the passages dealing with wine libations on the Altar.

may I know who's calling? no

A random thought: I have never successfully reached an attorney on the first phone call. Has anyone? He is invariably "away from his desk," or "at a meeting," or "tied up with a client," or "in court." No lawyer ever seems to be immediately available for the phone, as if it were somehow unmanly to be available.

The "May-I-know-who's-calling?" syndrome, not limited to lawyers but heard universally, is another phenomenon that intrigues me. I once replied simply, "No."

Dead silence on the other end, then a giggle. "Did you say no?"

"Yes, I did."

There was an awkward silence, after which she recovered sufficiently to tell me that her boss was away from his desk.

Why people must know in advance who is calling is beyond me. I am told that people like to be prepared mentally for the call. My own feeling is that people do this because everyone else is doing it; if you don't do it, it could be perceived as a lessening of status or power — almost as bad as if you were immediately available to a caller.

When I first came to Atlanta, I instructed our synagogue secretary never to ask who was calling before putting me on. "But all the other places I worked all insisted on it," she said.

"I know," I replied. "That's why we're not going to do it."

She shrugged her shoulders. It was the very first inkling that anyone had that the new Orthodox rabbi was a bit untraditional.

Chapter 5:
Also a Rabbi

t is instructive to see what constitutes, in the pragmatic American mind, a successful rabbi. A flyer comes in the mail promoting a book written by a certain rabbi:

> "When in 1994 Rabbi Salzman retired from the active leadership of his congregation, he completed one of the most successful careers in the history of the American rabbinate. During his dynamic fifty-year ministry, his once-small congregation with

modest facilities had grown to a membership of nearly fifteen hundred families housed in one of the most beautiful and best-equipped synagogues in the world."

On the face of it, a great success story. But on closer inspection, this demonstrates only that Rabbi Salzman knew how to run a congregation, how to raise funds, how to attract and retain members. What we do not know is whether or not he affected lives, or changed people, or transformed them into better Jews.

Success in the rabbinate: sometimes the unknown rabbi with a handful of members in a humble synagogue in a poor neighborhood is much more successful in affecting the souls of his flock than is the big-name rabbi with the huge membership and high-powered organization. The unknown rabbi may not be a polished orator or a skilled executive, but he studies, reads, teaches, contemplates, and inspires his congregation with his intellectual honesty and his spirituality.

studying in the study

All of which brings to mind the matter of personal study. A person is revealed by the way he spends his discretionary time. For a rabbi, time must be utilized, as much as humanly possible, in "learning" — in the study of the classical Torah texts. There is an unending stream of valid reasons to postpone daily study, to hold it off until a more propitious moment. The only way to fight this tendency is to set up a designated time each day which is sacrosanct and devoted exclusively to study. Even a few minutes on a regular basis is helpful — but it must be regular and inviolable, not sporadic or haphazard. If the rabbi can establish a *havruta*, another individual with whom he studies together regularly, that is even better. And blessed is that rabbi who has a community to whom he can teach Mishnah or Talmud, because this motivates him to prepare, sharpen, and hone his personal learning of Torah. Without study of Torah, the rabbi can degenerate into a glorified master of religious ceremonies; with learning, he can grow spiritually and intellectually, and he will find greater satisfaction in his daily tasks.

Torah study is more than just another "thou-shalt." It is the paramount *mitzvah* which supersedes all others. With prayer we approach God through the heart. With certain deeds — *tefillin,* Shabbat, kashrut, *tzedakah, mezuzah,* doing kindness — we approach Him through our actions. With Torah study we approach God through our intellect.

Torah study, however, is not an abstraction. It contains within itself the three pathways to God: heart, action, and mind. That's because when we study Torah, we are uncovering the way in which God wants us to live on this earth. Careful study of Torah enables us to enter, so to speak, the mind of God.

Torah study is unique in one other respect. It is the only *mitzvah* of action which has no beginning and no end. The obligation to study Torah is constant, ongoing, day and night, in sickness and in health. Torah is the blueprint of the world and the pillar which holds it up (*Zohar II,* p. 161a, *Terumah*). It is said that God Himself studies His own Torah (*Avodah Zarah* 3b; *Bava Metzia* 86a).

Beyond all this, there can be no joy in the world that quite equals the joy of unraveling a difficult and subtle Talmudic text. I recall vividly that my father, who was an active rabbi in a busy community, spent hours daily in Torah study. He would spread his large Talmud volume across the dining room table and pore over the text as he chanted and hummed in intense concentration. Every so often he would look up at me, all of eight years old, and say *"Ay, Mendele, es iz azoi geshmak, azoi geshmak!"* ("It's so delicious, so delicious.") He was echoing the words of King David in Psalm 19: "The laws of God are upright, gladdening the heart . . . sweeter than honey and drippings from the combs."

I thought you graduated

Laymen frequently do not appreciate the importance of Torah learning for a rabbi. After all, if the rabbi already has his ordination, why must he continue to study? The following has happened to so many rabbis that it has become an apocryphal story, but it really occurred to my father: The president of his first American congregation once discovered him late at night in his synagogue study, engaged in Torah learning. "Rabbi," said the president, "I thought you had already graduated."

In the early years, my congregation was convinced that the two most learned rabbis in America were Rabbi Moshe Feinstein and I. Reb Moshe, of course, was the preeminent halachic decisor in the world. I was the local Reb Moshe because I knew: a)when Pesach would fall three years hence; b)the Hebrew names for Kimberly and Clete (Kayla and Kalman); c)the *Amidah* by heart; and d)I taught classes in Bible and Talmud.

I must confess that I never said anything to disabuse them of this notion. But I was soon to get my inevitable and deserved comeuppance. One of my members made a business trip to Toronto, where he met someone who had studied in the Ner Yisrael yeshivah in Baltimore. "Then you must know our rabbi," said my loyal congregant excitedly. "He's also from Baltimore."

"Of course I remember him," said the man. "He was the best left fielder Ner Israel ever had."

My board of directors once sent a representative to talk with me about what they considered my undue attention to reading, study, and writing. They felt that this was affecting my work in the shul. They would prefer, I was told, that I spend more time attending parties and receptions. To the credit of the board's representative, he was very embarrassed to relay this message to me. "Mind you, I don't feel this way personally," he kept repeating.

I was annoyed but also amused. Annoyed that the board should view me as an employee whose entire time belonged to them, and amused that they had so little understanding of the role of Torah study in the life of a Jew, much less in the life of a rabbi who was supposed to know enough to teach them.

I told the gentleman that I understood the board's concerns, but that I wanted them to know that the more I read and study, the better a rabbi I would be for them. He kept repeating, "Yes, yes, I understand fully, but I'm only carrying out their mandate for me to speak with you."

I felt sorry for him. "Fine, I appreciate that. Go back and tell them you have spoken to me and that I take their message seriously. But tell them also that I consider studying to be part of my job description, part of my duties to them. Study doesn't make me a less effective rabbi; it makes me a more effective rabbi."

I never heard another word about this. I think that, to their credit, they were sorry they brought it up in the first place.

the rabbi and his board of directors

A rabbi's interpersonal skills are always being tested, but nowhere more severely than in his relationship with the synagogue's board of directors. This is one area of synagogue life where the layman feels that he is superior to the rabbi, for here business acumen rules supreme. The rabbi's religious views are treated respectfully enough, but when it comes to finances, the rabbi, on the face of it, is less equipped to make the tough decisions than are the successful businessmen and professionals who sit on the board.

By and large, I have been quite content to let the board run the business end of the synagogue, with the tacit *quid pro quo* that I run the religious components of the synagogue. Inevitably, the lines of distinction have become blurred from time to time, as what I saw as religious they saw as financial, and what they saw as financial I saw as religious. But on such occasions we managed to muddle through. To make it clear that I was not interfering in their domain, I did not routinely attend a synagogue board meeting for most of the years of my rabbinate — unless it was at the board's express invitation.

Not being present contains its risks, however. On the morning after one meeting the president called me and asked if it was true that I was opposed to building a new driveway behind the synagogue. "Leonard," I said, "I have no feelings about it one way or the other. Whatever you fellows decide is fine with me."

"I kind of thought so," he said, "but you were quoted at the meeting as being opposed to it."

"Quoted? I don't recall speaking to anyone about it. Who quoted me?"

"Al Bernstein. He said you were against it."

I picked up the phone and called Bernstein. "Al, I am told that you quoted me last night as being opposed to the new driveway. But I don't recall ever talking to you about it one way or the other."

"Oh, you didn't have to tell me. When I mentioned it to you last Shabbos at *kiddush*, you said that it's not in your domain and that you didn't want to discuss it. But I saw in your eyes that you were opposed to it."

I let it go at that, but I began to wonder if, in addition to being careful with his words, a rabbi should also be careful with his eyes.

I have been blessed with officers and boards of directors who have been sensitive, caring, and serious about their responsibilities. I have been spared the agonies of other Orthodox rabbis whose lay leaders were constantly second-guessing them religiously, pressuring them to be less Orthodox and more in tune with the times. We went through this stage very early on, and since then the lay leadership has been extremely cooperative in all things religious, allowing me to take the lead and to set the tone. In addition, they gladly deferred to my judgment in issues dealing with Jewish priorities, such as the engaging of teachers or religious functionaries. By and large they realized that though they might be successful in their own fields, they had no training that qualified them to make decisions affecting the religious direction of the synagogue. They sensed that the values and experience they brought with them from their own professions or businesses were not necessarily transferable to synagogue life.

While most lay leaders innately possess this good sense, there are always those for whom the bottom-line mentality is the dominating frame of reference. The refrain that a shul should be run like a business is true, but not entirely. A shul office should be efficient and service its membership well; it should be courteous and helpful to those who walk through its doors — like a good business.

But a shul is not in business to be a business and to earn a profit. Its purpose is to teach Torah values and to elevate lives. That which may not make good business sense may occasionally make good religious sense if it serves the shul's ultimate purpose. Sometimes, if the need is urgent, a program has to be instituted and the money found later. That is not good business policy, but it is good synagogue policy. "Rabbi, we'd love to do X, Y, and Z but we can't afford it" may occasionally be literally true, but sometimes even if it is true, it is false. Sometimes a synagogue cannot afford *not* to do that which it is certain it cannot afford.

A minor example, symptomatic of many more significant ones: years ago it became apparent that our shul needed to have its own preschool program. We were running a large deficit, however, and the board refused to go along with the initial investment of some ten thousand dollars. I knew that this bottom-line thinking was short-sighted, not only spiritually but practically. After many conversations with the relevant people, I made an offer they could not refuse: I would personally raise the money they needed from fresh sources. They accepted my challenge, the preschool got off the ground, it more than paid for itself, and today it is one of the finest and largest in the city.

how I live is not your business

Although our board occasionally reached too far into the religious realm, these were not meant as challenges to my religious authority. The challenges that occurred in the first few years never happened again. For example, in my third year with the congregation, Jake Rubinoff erupted at a board meeting: "With all due respect to our rabbi, he is very young and he should stop talking about our personal lives. Why is it his business what I do on Saturday or what I eat the rest of the week? Someone has to tell him that he's driving people away with that kind of talk. We're never going to get bigger that way. I make a motion that the rabbi clear every sermon with the president before he delivers it."

There followed an embarrassed silence. Although his motion was seconded, it became evident during the ensuing discussion that the board members themselves realized that they were sliding down a slippery slope. They voted overwhelmingly to defeat the motion. But it was a warning shot across my bow. I had deluded myself into thinking that I was winning the congregation over, when in fact I still had much persuading to do. On a deeper level, however, his irritation was a sign that my message was getting through to him.

Jake was right about one thing: I was very young at the time — only twenty-eight. But he was wrong about one other thing: Even if I had wanted to, I could not possibly submit my sermons in advance, for one simple reason: although I thought about it all week, I invariably did not complete the sermon until very late Friday afternoon, and occasionally was still frantically composing it in my mind on Shabbos morning during the Torah reading.

The worst time to deal with a board of directors is, obviously, when the organization is experiencing the inevitable dry periods — membership is stagnant or decreasing; voluntary contributions are down; and the deficit seems insurmountable. At such times it is best not to suggest any new programs that will cost money. Good business practice demands that costs be cut. The first costs to get cut are, of course, salaries.

salaries and broken pipes

One year the shul was experiencing particularly tough going. A delegate came to see me with a message from the board. He was very apologetic, but the board had reluctantly decided to ask me to forgo my promised salary increase for the coming year. Instead, they were asking me to take a voluntary cut of one thousand dollars.

With five growing children in various schools, with tuition and other related costs I too was experiencing tough financial times. Even the small cost-of-living increase I was scheduled to receive would hardly have made a difference, but a salary cut would make things very difficult. It did not seem right that I should bear the burden of what was essentially the failure of the board of directors to raise the requisite funds. I have always felt that they are not elected just to attend monthly meetings and to vote on proposals. Their task is to make certain that the finances of the shul are covered, and if they are not covered, they themselves should be ready to do it the old-fashioned way: dig into their own pockets if necessary. Coming from what was essentially a very considerate group of people, the proposal was uncharacteristically unfair; it could only have been caused by their sense of desperation.

"Mark," I said, "I want to make a counterproposal. My salary is twenty thousand. One thousand dollars is a five-percent cut. If the board wants me to help solve the deficit crisis with a contribution of five percent of my income, that's fine, and I am happy to do that. But I think the rabbi should not be the only one who's giving. It's only right that every member of the board should also give five percent of his or her income. I'm sure the board doesn't expect me to be the only contributor. Let's make it an across-the-board five percent."

Mark was a very bright and successful entrepreneur, but from the look on his face it was clear that such an idea had never occurred to him. "I don't know if they'll buy that, Rabbi."

"Mark, do me a favor and try. Tell them at the next meeting that I am happy to contribute five percent of my income, but that I am proposing that every single board member do the same. Figure it out: if we do that, we will make a huge dent in the deficit, especially since most of the board members earn much more than I do."

"I'll tell you what I'll do. I'll bounce it off informally on some of the guys and see what their reaction is."

I was certain that I had inadvertently hit upon a wonderful fund-raising idea and that the financial crunch of the shul would now be solved. But I never heard from Mark again on the subject. Apparently the guys didn't think it was a workable idea, and it didn't even make it to the next board meeting. Too bad. In one fell swoop we might have raised a large amount of money. But it was not a total loss: after thinking about it, they dropped the idea of my salary cut.

At a board meeting of one of the local day schools, the house committee brought up the problem of the rusting pipes and the leaks in the roof. They recommended an expenditure of ten thousand dollars to make full repairs. After a brief, perfunctory discussion, the motion was passed unanimously.

There was no question that the repairs were needed and, although there was no money in the treasury, somehow the money would be found. But I couldn't help thinking of the meeting of that same board six months earlier. The principal of the school had requested a raise of three thousand dollars. It was well known that he was barely making it on his current minimal salary. There was a prolonged discussion, it was sent back to committee for further negotiation, and several meetings later the board voted, by a nine-to-seven vote, to grant him a one-thousand-dollar raise.

Unhappy conclusion: it is self-evident that pipes and roofs must be in good working order. But that educational personnel must be in good working order through a decent standard of living — this is not always self-evident.

And yet, despite the frustrations that boards often engender, they are obviously essential to the well-being of a synagogue. Although I occasionally yearn for a benevolent despotism (with me as the despot, of course) I can think of no substitute for them. They are capable of doing outstanding things. They work selflessly, and they are dedicated and committed to the welfare of the institutions they serve. They are concerned about its progress and raise much of the funds. I have known officers and board members who have literally spent sleepless nights worrying about the shul. In addition, the board makes it possible for a broad range of people to have a sense of participation in the affairs of Jewish life. And, yes, they do help contain the enthusiasm of rabbis like me who would spend first and worry about paying later. It is not always easy to live with them — and I still flinch when I hear the phrase "With all due respect to you, Rabbi" — but it would be impossible to function without them.

also a rabbi

I close these rabbinic musings with my favorite rabbinic story. It concerns the first visit of my father, Rabbi Joseph Feldman, zt"l, to Atlanta, a few months after I arrived in town. When he walked into our shul on Shabbat morning, one of our gentlemen offered him a *siddur* and asked him his name.

"My name is Feldman."

"Feldman? Are you related to our rabbi?"

"Yes, I'm his father."

The gentleman, sensing something about my father, asked, "Are you also a rabbi?"

My father immediately responded, "You have it backwards. I am a rabbi. My son is also a rabbi."

Chapter 6:
Do You Always Fly
First Class?

One never knows what images congregants have of their rabbis. Sometimes, one suspects, they have a grossly inflated view of us. A woman, a relatively new member, called me to ask me a question. In passing, she said, "I would tell you how much your sermons mean to me, but I was told I was not supposed to do that."

"Why not?"

"Because I was told you don't like to hear praise about yourself."

"Not so. Any time you want to tell me I am doing a good

job you can call me collect. Don't hold back."

She chuckled: "You mean you're human like the rest of us mortals?"

"Yes, but let's keep it a secret between us."

Amazing, this picture that some people have of a rabbi: a spiritual superman, impervious to temptations, ascetic, totally other-wordly, transcending the mundane cares of daily life, without ego, without weaknesses, without needs.

Would that it were so.

More images of rabbis: during one of my visits to a bereaved family, Shirley Warner good-naturedly announced to the group sitting in the living room, "I've known Rabbi Feldman for twenty-five years and he has never changed his convictions."

The comment contained some pride, but only some. I would have expected her to say that she was proud of the fact that her rabbi had principles and stuck to them.

I responded: "You really wouldn't want me to change them, would you?" It was a powder-puff question which gave her a chance to say no.

But she surprised me. "Well," she smiled, "maybe just a few of them you might have changed over the years."

The voice of today's society: by all means, do have convictions and principles, but for goodness' sake, be flexible, don't let them stand in the way, and don't hold on to them "over the years."

I didn't bother to ask her which one of my convictions she did not approve of.

my rabbi is more fabulous than yours

The fact is that even if people do not always listen to their rabbis, they do take a certain pride in them. One of our local ladies, widowed for many years, recently remarried.

She is seventy, he is seventy-five. She has already begun spatting with her new husband and is seriously thinking of divorce. One of their fights was over me. According to her, it went like this:

She: My rabbi is the greatest.
He: He's okay, but nothing like the one we had down in Shreveport. That one was tops, really the greatest.
She (raising her voice): There is only one greatest, that's Rabbi Feldman. There's nobody like him.
He: Too Orthodox, much too Orthodox. Now, my rabbi, he's fabulous.
She: You're just a stubborn old man.
He: Look who's talking. You're as stubborn as anyone I've ever seen. I say my rabbi is fabulous, and that's that, and I don't want to hear another word about it.
She: What are you, some kind of god or something — telling me about rabbis? What do you know?

(Nice to know that I am a key element in their blissful marriage.)

doing the Lord's work

In the busyness of keeping up with his day-to-day obligations, a rabbi tends to forget that the obligations themselves are holy. A rabbi is a living embodiment of the famous Baraita in Tractate Shabbat which speaks of *mitzvot* such as daily worship, hospitality to strangers, visiting the sick, bringing a bride to the wedding canopy, bringing peace between man and his fellow, escorting the dead: all the things a rabbi does every single day. Certainly a sermon, if it teaches Torah and inspires, is among the holiest of tasks: "And the study of Torah is equivalent to them all." But if we are not careful, our duties can become just another job.

This was brought home to me by a church group to whom I had spoken about the main ideas of Judaism. (Among other questions, I was asked by a little, white-haired Christian lady, in the politest and sweetest of ways: "Are you as a religious Jew disappointed that Isrul (sic) is a godless country?") A week after the program I received a gracious note from the chairperson who thanked me and blessed me to be able to continue "doing the Lord's work."

Though the term is a cliche, it suddenly struck me that for a very long time I had not consciously viewed my work as the Lord's work, as *avodat haShem*. And yet, that is just what it is. Everything a rabbi does — teaching or visiting or counseling, even just schmoozing with someone — is an opportunity to bring people closer to Him. And even though rabbis have no special rules and no special privileges and are technically only teachers, the fact is that for the masses of Jews the rabbi represents Jewish tradition and Torah and, yes, God himself. What the rabbi does, how he behaves, how he interacts with people, reflects in some way upon Him. But the work is so time- and emotion-consuming that rabbis often forget the sacred nature of the work.

I am hard pressed, however, to justify every single thing I do as God's work. Attending receptions? Making small talk at parties? Sitting like a potted plant at the dais of a hopelessly dull banquet, or through endless meetings and interminable organizational functions? In a small sense, yes; in a larger sense, not really. But the lady's letter was a good reminder.

(By the way, what *do* rabbis do all day? Laymen often ask this question. When our daughter Geulah was six, she gave me a new insight into my role: "I know what a rabbi does. When a man dies, you tell him what to do.")

rabbis, doctors, and professors

A confluence of two incidents brought home to me that Jews need to be reminded of the sanctity of the rabbi's job. I had been invited to give a course on Jewish law in one of the local law schools. When time came to print their course catalogue, they were unsure how to list my name among the faculty: "Professor," "Dr.," or "Rabbi." I happened to be in Israel and could not be reached. I was later informed that the committee — all non-Jewish professors — decided that anyone could be a professor or obtain a doctorate, but not everyone could be a rabbi. So they decided to list me as "Rabbi."

What saddened me was that I had just received in the mail an announcement that a national Jewish organization — an Orthodox group — was honoring a number of rabbis for their work. All the names were listed. But those rabbis who also had doctorates were not called "Rabbi Dr." but simply "Dr." Those without the degree were called "Rabbi."

The message was clear. With such self-denigration taking place within the traditional community, it is good to be reminded about the Lord's work.

***

Instructive, the kind of reputation Orthodoxy and its rabbis have among non-Orthodox Jews. After visiting a gentleman from South Georgia in the hospital, I received the following letter from his wife:

> "Dear Rabbi: Thank you for visiting my husband when he was sick. I never met an Orthodox rabbi before, but you sure don't look like one of them. I never thought Orthodox rabbis visited the sick at all. I thought all they did was pray all day and study. I'm grateful to you that you don't pray and study."

A fascinating breed, pulpit rabbis. Certain rabbis are superb scholars, truly brilliant and learned in Torah, and no matter how busy they are, they manage to invest a good bit of time into their Torah studies.

It takes a perceptive layman to distinguish between rabbinic excellence and rabbinic mediocrity. I think any layman can sense a rabbinic phony, the rabbi who is merely an executive and does not believe what he says. But few can recognize the extent of a rabbi's learning or piety — or its absence. For too many people, the "bedside manner" of the rabbi is the key to his acceptance, just as it is with physicians. (I am all for sensitive and pleasant physicians, but I'd prefer a gruff and brusque physician who finished at the head of his class and is on the cutting edge of medical developments, to a sweet and gentle one who finished last in his class and is practicing the medicine of twenty years ago.)

Erev Yom Kippur lashes

Some Jews administer symbolic lashes to one another on Erev Yom Kippur as a form of penitence. The call from Lil Rothman one Erev Yom Kippur served as my personal lashes. I still wince when I think of it.

Lil is a bright, articulate, self-possessed divorcee, an attorney in her mid-fifties. She was leaving town for a new job in a law office in Los Angeles and called to say goodbye — and to tell me how disappointed she was in me. "You are always giving sermons about doing *mitzvot* and about being considerate, but not once in the five years since my divorce have you ever shown me any support or indicated any concern about how I was getting along."

I was stunned, although there was some element of truth in what she was saying. But she had always appeared so self-assured and self-confident that I never sensed the turmoil that lay underneath. "All the honor and respect that people give you, they mean nothing if you don't help people when they need you," she snapped. She was obviously expressing a deep hurt and pain that had been suppressed for a long time and that was finally erupting.

I told her that of all the people I knew, she seemed most secure and in control of her situation, and that therefore I did not sense her need for some attention. I admitted that I was mistaken and apologized profusely, but of course it meant nothing.

Her call was like a body blow. I tossed and turned all that night. In her case, an occasional call to let her know that I was aware of her existence would have been sufficient. I hadn't even done that. I had violated the first rabbinic commandment: to be a good shepherd.

* * *

I am fortunate that, because of my rabbinical upbringing, I am not disturbed by the glass-house syndrome. I know that a rabbi's children are held up to a different standard, and that a pulpit rabbi and his wife are constantly being observed — but am untroubled by it.

Once in a while it even has its amusing sidebars. On any given Shabbat in shul, someone will approach me and say, "Rabbi, you look tired today. Is everything okay?" A few moments later, someone else will say to me, "Thank God, you look great." A third person will say, "Are you all right? You look like you're losing weight." A fourth will say, " Are you putting on weight?" Rabbis try to create observant Jews among their flock, not realizing that the flock is already quite observant. It took me a while to realize that they all mean well and are merely trying to express their affection and concern.

There was one layman's view of a rabbi, however, that still puzzles me. It happened on a flight to Israel. When I approached the ticket counter, the agent happily informed me that the coach section was filled and that I was being bumped up to first class. I had never before flown anything but coach and was delighted.

It was one of those classic 747's with the first-class compartment on the upper deck. There seemed to be more stewards than passengers. The seats were wider and roomier, everything was more comfortable, and the staff seemed dedicated only to the one ideal of pleasing us. Throughout the flight I had a wondrous, and somewhat sinful, sense of physical well-being.

Among my fellow passengers in the cabin was Mr._____,

a world-class Jewish philanthropist. I had seen him as the honoree at numerous testimonials and had even solicited him on occasion for some important national Jewish causes. As we entered the compartment, I introduced myself and wished us a good trip.

When we arrived in Tel Aviv, we approached the passport counter together. He turned to me and said casually,"Tell me, Rabbi Feldman, do you always fly first-class?"

I couldn't resist. "Doesn't everyone?" I heard myself blurting out.

His remark puzzled me. Why should he have asked me that question? Would he have asked it of a fellow businessman? Was he expressing pleasure at a rabbi flying first-class, or did he think it was inappropriate? Was he wondering how I could afford it on a rabbi's salary? Was he thinking that now that rabbis are also flying first-class, what's left for important people like himself? Or was it just an innocent, innocuous question? And did he wonder what I meant by "Doesn't everyone?" I could have simply said yes. Or I could have told him the truth, that I was bumped upstairs. Or I could have said, "Not always, just once in a while when the mood strikes me." That last one has a certain casual panache to it and would have been much sharper than my flippant remark. I must try to remember it for the next time.

Chapter 7:
Man in God's Image,
God in Man's Image

Atelephone call from a national Jewish organization urging all rabbis to sponsor a day of prayer for Jews behind the Iron Curtain: "We want to mobilize all of America's synagogues for this day of prayer," said the official.

"Sounds like a good idea to me," I responded.

Then he added something not in the script: "I don't know how much good the prayers will do, but it will arouse public opinion if we publicize it and the media pick it up."

Only after he hung up did I realize just how sad this last

statement really was. For him, prayer has no value in its own right. It is strictly a PR gimmick, another kind of technique. He probably sends his prayers up to heaven with a notation in the upper right-hand margin: FOR IMMEDIATE RELEASE TO ALL MEDIA.

This was not very different from the request by an influential community leader: "Rabbi, we're planning a Bar Mitzvah for our son this summer in Israel. I thought of Masada, but it's stifling up there in August. We also considered the Wall, but I hate to say it, that's old hat already. I need a place that's dramatic, moving, you know, and not too hot in the summertime. Can you recommend a spot for me?"

creative services:
God in man's image

A notice in *The Jewish Times* invites everyone to join a local group in "creative prayer" on the following Friday night. Are they implying that classical *davening* is not creative, but static and lifeless?

Creative prayer: all one needs for this are a few records, some poems, and a guitar. Obviously, Judaism encourages spontaneous prayer: we can reach out to our Maker at any time and in any language. But Judaism also insists on a certain discipline in prayer. When and how we pray is not left completely up to us.

I try hard to understand the devotees of non-traditional *davening*. They are innocent; their hearts are in the right place; they are striving mightily to reach out to God and don't quite know how; we have not succeeded in touching their souls. But in less understanding moments I sense that one of the key motivations of these creative services is to discard the classic *siddur* entirely. "Why bother with stuff that was written by someone else? Roll your own," said one of the creativists to me.

Some of this stems from naivete and from a complete unawareness of the nature of real prayer; but there is also a healthy dose of arrogance mixed with insensitivity. Is it not an effrontery to refuse to "mouth prayers written by someone else," and to convince ourselves that our own home-grown variety can equal the power and majesty of the classical Jewish liturgy? Especially without having troubled to familiarize oneself with the classic prayers offered up by Jews for millennia.

If we were religiously sensitive, we would tremble when we approach God, for we really do not know how to address Him. We — lonely and mortal, filled with doubts and fears, hate and suspicion, made from dust and returning to dust — are given the privilege of standing before the Creator of all and speaking to Him.

We know not what to say nor how to say it. Because of this, we draw our prayers from the classical vehicles of expression created for us by our heritage: the Psalms of King David, the songs of Moses, the praises of Joshua, the hymns of Yehudah HaLevi and other religious geniuses. Are these beneath us?

All of these create a mood of prayer, identify us with our people — past and present and future — make us as one with them, channel our hearts and minds towards the Creator, and express — beyond the written words — our innermost, inchoate feelings.

Does a musician consider it beneath him to play Beethoven? And doesn't Beethoven say something new to us every time he is played?

In our narcissistic age, we have seen our reflection in the water and can see nothing else. With us, man is created in man's own image. We even create God in man's image.

✳ ✳ ✳

Prayer, however, is resilient, because the soul needs to pray just as the body needs to drink. Frequently, when I walk into the empty main shul during the week, I find a man or a woman sitting all alone, engrossed in personal prayer. I often find a few people alone in shul on Shabbat, long after *daven-*

ing is over and everyone has left. They are praying on their own or catching up with parts of the service they may have missed, or just meditating. The experience clearly uplifts them; what these folks don't know is that seeing them also revives me. There is a certain magnetic power within prayer, and there is a similarly powerful need within each of us to reach out to something beyond the self.

red slacks and the house of God

The reverential attitude that prayer requires, however, does not come automatically. It needs to be imparted.

The guests in shul for a certain Shabbat Bar Mitzvah, all from out of state, were particularly ill-mannered. It was evident that few of them had ever attended a Shabbat morning *davening*. One young woman even arrived in what looked like a tennis outfit. For these guests, this was strictly a Bar Mitzvah party, the unavoidable prelude to which were the religious services.

But it was not only that they were ignorant of synagogue practice. That in itself is excusable. What was inexcusable was their insensitivity to the occasion and to the place. Many of them talked to one another incessantly, waved to friends and relatives across the synagogue, and made not the slightest effort to participate, to learn, to listen. It is a tribute to our regular worshipers that they were disturbed by this as well.

One man, wearing a loud yellow shirt with flaming red slacks, was particularly oblivious to the fact that he was in a house of God. He laughed boisterously, walked up and down the aisle, and stopped to chat with everyone in sight. He could have been at a baseball game.

I sent someone over to him to quiet him down, but to no avail. Several times I resisted the temptation to interrupt the services to remind everyone that this was a shul. But such pulpit interruptions are themselves not conducive to good prayer, and there was no point in publicly embarrassing the out-of-state guests, so I held back. My annoyance, however, welled up within me.

Toward the end of the *davening,* he of the red slacks — an uncle of the Bar Mitzvah boy, as it turned out — was asked to mount the pulpit to open the Ark. As he stood next to me, I whispered, "The only way we can keep you quiet is to have you stand up here next to me." He was taken aback but said nothing.

A moment later, while the Ark was opened, he turned around and waved to someone down in the congregation. "Please face the Ark and be still," I snapped.

"You certainly do observe things, don't you?" he said.

"Please show a little respect for the open Ark," I said, trying at the same time to concentrate on the lovely words of the *An'im Zemirot:* "*Homeh libi el dodekha* / My heart yearns for Your love . . ."

I met him again at the Saturday night reception. He was dressed in a formal black tuxedo. Obviously, the red and yellow outfit was reserved only for religious services. He approached me, drink in hand, and with a gracious smile shook my hand. "Rabbi," he said, "it was a lovely service this morning. I enjoyed every minute of it. And, by the way, I want you to know that I'm not angry with you."

* * *

Sometimes I feel sorry for our magnificent prayers. A woman calls from her hospital bed. She apologizes for bothering me, she is not a member of any synagogue, but since she is going to undergo surgery in the morning, she wants my help. "Rabbi, do you mind saying a prayer for me? I'm superstitious."

Did she mean "religious"? Was she referring to the "supernatural"? Did she mean to say that she believed in the efficacy of prayer? Whatever she meant, I hope she didn't mean "superstitious."

suddenly in shul

Even more amusing was Ted Sabin. One Shabbat morning Ted suddenly appeared in shul. "Suddenly," because for twenty years Ted has come religiously once a year — on Yom Kippur immediately prior to *Yizkor* — and just as religiously has left the moment *Yizkor* was over. He is a twenty-minutes-a-year Jew. He is a fine person and I am fond of him, but he is not one of my major success stories.

On this Shabbat, Ted took a seat as far in the back as he could and sat rather restlessly throughout the *davening*. It crossed my mind that perhaps he thought today was Yom Kippur, but since it was mid-February I dismissed the idea.

As soon as *davening* ended Ted came over to me. After a few pleasantries, he asked, "Rabbi, isn't today the Bar Mitzvah of Al Greenberg's son?"

"No, Ted, that's next Shabbat."

"Next Shabbat! I thought it was today. Darn," he muttered to himself, "I killed the whole morning."

Let me not be too critical of laymen and prayer. A woman once asked me to pray for her husband who was critically ill. I promised to do so but added, as I always do, that she should not depend on me alone but should pray herself as well. That same day I was suddenly called out of town and was gone three days. When I returned she called me. "Thank you, thank you, for praying for him. He had a miraculous recovery. Even the doctors are surprised. I am forever grateful."

I realized then that during my trip I had completely forgotten to pray for his welfare. In a kind of shock, I mumbled something about not needing to thank me, that her own prayers were the ones that were answered.

She insisted: "No, Rabbi, it was you. I know it was you."

I tried to convince her of the truth: that I had done nothing, that it was her prayers alone that had been effective, but the more I tried, the more she was convinced not only of my influence with God, but also of my modesty.

It was not my finest hour. I really needed to pray to offset that forgotten duty to pray.

If rabbis occasionally forget to pray for their congregants, what can we expect from laymen? Sometimes this has ludicrous overtones. One year I took a six-month sabbatical in Israel. That meant that I was away from shul for twenty-four consecutive Shabbat mornings. On the first Shabbat of my return Harry Glickman, not one of our regulars, was in shul for a Bar Mitzvah. In jest, I said to him, "Harry, I haven't seen you in six months. Where have you been?"

Harry proceeded to explain to me why he had not been in shul all this time. It became evident to me that he was not even aware that I had been gone for half a year. How nice, as they say, to be missed.

This says something about Harry. It also says something about Harry's rabbi.

please, dear God, not on Tish'ah B'Av

That was not a good week for prayer in general. The next Saturday night was Tish'ah B'Av, the saddest day in the Jewish calendar, the national day of fasting and mourning for the destruction of the two Holy Temples, as well as for countless other national tragedies that occurred on this date. It is the tearful anniversary of the incursion of tragedy into the Jewish world. It is a time for introspection, the recitation of dirges and laments, as well as prayers to God to reverse the fortunes of our beleaguered Jewish people.

Tish'ah B'Av is not everyone's favorite time, and most American Jews are not even aware of its existence, but it is a singularly important day in the Jewish calendar — because of what it says about Jews: that we are a people that remembers. A people that remembers its past will have a future.

There are many more Italians in the world than Jews, but no one laments for ancient Rome. There are many more Greeks than Jews, but the Acropolis and the Parthenon are tourist attractions; no one mourns their destruction. Tish'ah B'Av is crucial to us, because only a people that is capable of weeping will some day be able to laugh.

Particularly in the Western world do we need this day. In the midst of all the affluence and the creature comforts, we need to remove our leather shoes and dim the lights. We need to fast and not indulge ourselves. We need to read Lamentations and weep for our people's martyrdom and for its bloody history. We need to be reminded of what it means to be a Jew, that Esau hates Jacob, that Pharaohs wish to enslave us and Hamans and Hitlers to destroy us, and that the empires of the world abhor the Jewish people because we belong to a "nation that dwelleth alone." We need to be reminded of the Holocausts of our history.

A man once asked me: "Why bother with an event like the destruction of the Temple that took place two thousand years ago? Why mourn? We have modern Israel, we should rejoice."

I replied that while modern Israel is a source of joy, it is not unalloyed. Is there a country more worried about its daily security than Israel, or one that has more bitter experience of friendly countries suddenly growing cold and distant at the slightest provocation? No other countries have to struggle over the sovereignty of their ancient capitals. No others are restricted in their rights to visit and worship at their ancient holy sites in their own land.

Tish'ah B'Av is important because it contains a message of profound hope and faith. On this day, our tradition tells us, the Messiah was born. On the day of destruction, redemption. The end was also to be the beginning. On the Shabbat preceding Tish'ah B'Av we read the first chapter of Isaiah, in which God severely rebukes us. On the following Shabbat we read the fortieth chapter of Isaiah: "Comfort ye, My people."

As the tears are real, so will the comfort be real.

Immersed in these sobering thoughts, I am walking to shul on late Saturday afternoon. The fast would begin in a few moments, just at sunset.

An unmistakable, heavy aroma wafts across our lovely little street and into my nostrils. Someone is barbecuing meat. Shabbat and Tish'ah B'Av and barbecue: it is too much to bear. I groan aloud, and within me there wells up a profound dread. Involuntarily, the following questions race through my mind:

a) Is someone violating Shabbat by barbecuing, or is some-one about to violate Tish'ah B'Av by eating?
b) Is it theoretically possible to violate both Shabbat and Tish'ah B'Av simultaneously?
c) This meat they are cooking — is it kosher?
d) What difference does it make if they commit the violations with kosher or non-kosher meat?
e) How low have we as a people sunk, to do this on Shabbat as Tish'ah B'Av approaches!
f) Why am I so hysterical? Perhaps one of the non-Jewish neighbors is barbecuing?
g) But if it is in fact a Jewish neighbor, is there a man-hole nearby into which I can crawl and not reappear for a very long time?

Dear God above, please, I beg of Thee, let the barbecuer be one of the non-Jews in the neighborhood. Please, not a Jew, not on Shabbat, not on the eve of Tish'ah B'Av.

It is one of the most heartfelt prayers I have ever uttered. But it is too late. I pass the house from whose backyard the smoke is rising in a thick, black, miasmic cloud. They are not members of ours — at least that — but that is small consolation; they are Jews.

My heart sinks every time I think back to that Tish'ah B'Av. Here in microcosm was contained all the innocence and igno-rance of American Jewry. The barbecuing Jewish family had no idea that Shabbat was a holy day. Their own parents in all likelihood had never observed it, and probably no one had ever informed them or taught them or exposed them to the beauty and sanctity of this day. They knew that many of their Jewish neighbors walked to shul on Shabbat, but so what? Those people were Orthodox.

Like most American Jews, Saturday for them was just part of the weekend, nothing more. They believed in God and probably even prayed to Him occasionally. They did not mean to deny that which Shabbat represents: that there is a Creator Who created the world in six days and rested on the seventh.

As for Tish'ah B'Av, they probably had never even heard of that either. They are good, upstanding people — friendly, helpful, charitable, honest. They would be very upset if they ever learned about the kind of spiritual indigestion their barbecue had created in me.

If Jews are not exposed to Judaism in any form, the results are inevitable. When Jews are taught properly, their souls respond, because the Jewish soul yearns for truth and authenticity. The great frustration lies in our inability to reach them in any meaningful way. Yet, we cannot give up on them, because the situation in Jewish life is beyond desperate. Unless their hearts are somehow touched, in one more generation they and millions like them will be lost completely to the Jewish people.

casino night at the synagogue

Recent studies show that almost eighty percent of Atlanta's Jews are not formally affiliated with any type of synagogue or temple. These figures are not unusual for North American cities. The issue is complex, and one should not simplify, but it is not difficult to isolate one of the causes of the low esteem in which prayer and synagogues are held by ordinary laymen: the lack of dignity and self-respect with which synagogue leaders and rabbis often present the synagogue to the community at large.

This is a notice — not atypical — from a local synagogue:

> "Casino night at the synagogue. Gambling, food, drinks, prizes. Learn to shoot craps, play roulette, blackjack. Real Las Vegas tables and professional croupiers. Bring your friends to the congregational event of the year.
>
> Saturday night, 7:00-12:00 midnight."

How would one expect a sensitive young person, looking for religious meaning in her life, to react to this "congregational event of the year" within her family's house of worship? That such young people often find spiritual solace in non-Jewish religious groups and cults that are not bashful about the presence of God should not shock anyone.

Another manifestation of this tendency to Jewish self-denigration is the annual rash of synagogue-sponsored New Year's Eve parties, complete with dances, smorgasbords, noise makers, and funny hats. Synagogues across the spectrum sponsor them — Orthodox, Conservative, Reform, Ashkenazi, Sephardi — without shame or self-consciousness.

In the early years, when my own synagogue leadership, following the lead of the larger congregations, suggested to me that we do the same thing "in order to attract the youth," I was able only with great difficulty to persuade them that this was undignified and not in keeping with the mission of a shul. They accepted this, albeit reluctantly and unenthusiastically. But they never brought it up again, and as they matured they recognized, to their everlasting credit, that this was unseemly for a house of God.

The popularity of these events calls to mind the statement in the *Aleinu* prayer which is recited three times a day and which is central to Rosh Hashanah and Yom Kippur: "*Shelo asanu k'goyei ha-aratzot*, Who has not made us like the nations of the earth . . . nor our destiny like that of their multitudes." It is ironic that, unwittingly, American synagogues often mock this majestic declaration of Jewish distinctiveness.

Jews know the secret of how to express the combined hope and trepidation which marks the beginning of a new year: with prayer, atonement, introspection, a turning towards a new relationship with God. But the nations of the world historically ushered in a new season with pagan revels and orgies, of which the contemporary New Year's eve parties — with their boozing and carousing — are a tribal vestige.

What an individual does on his own is, of course, his own business. But synagogues that officially sponsor such parties, with all their paraphernalia and accouterments, are remiss in their obligation to march to the beat of a different drummer. This falls considerably short of the sacred mission of a Jewish House of God, and is another dim chapter in the annals of Vulgariana Judaicana Americana.

It is a long, dark, and winding road from the awesome shofar of Rosh Hashanah ("*Ha-yitaka shofar ba-ir* . . . Can a shofar sound in the city and the people not tremble?") to the tin horns of New Year's Eve. Some institutions make the trip in the short time between Rosh Hashanah and January 1.

the genuine vs. the phony

All this is rationalized by the spurious notion that it is important simply to get people inside the synagogue structure — for any reason. Get them there for a dance, goes the litany; get them there for bingo, for Casino Night; just get them inside the building. As if the inside of the building will of itself transform the lives of those who enter. This is a rather mystical notion that has no empirical basis. What the gimmickers do not understand is that the people will enter the building for the bingo and for the games and for the fun — but when you attempt to get them to enter that part of the building in which study or prayer takes place, they stay away. They are not to blame. In order to get them to come inside for serious things, the heart has to be touched and the mind stimulated. This begins not with gimmicks but with instilling

into our people a sense of the dignity and awe of a synagogue, a sense that this is in fact a house where God dwells.
People will respond to such signals; they will not respond to
signals that debase and degrade. The fault, dear rabbis, lies
in our brutishness.

To gain entry in the hearts of people — how excruciatingly
difficult and frustrating this is. But Jews will respond to intellectual and religious honesty. Deep within them they have
contempt for tricks and contrivances.

Phil Lederman, a well-known neurologist, is a regular at
our daily early morning *minyan*. He and his family are fully
observant Jews. Only five years ago he kept nothing and
knew nothing about Judaism.

Then his father died. Out of a sense of loyalty to his father,
Phil determined to say *Kaddish* for the week of *shivah*. Then
he decided to come to *minyan* every day for thirty days. The
thirty days extended into another thirty days and then another. Before he knew it, Phil was attending Torah classes, studying classic Jewish texts in translation, learning to read
Hebrew fluently. When the year of mourning came to an end,
Phil decided to maintain his daily *minyan* commitment. No
one understands fully the dynamics of change within a
human being, but years later Phil confided in me that he had
been attracted by the simple discipline of coming to *daven*,
and by the basic truth that there was a Creator Whom he
needed to acknowledge on a regular basis. The daily regimen
of prayer, he said, provided him with an anchor and a
reminder of who he was.

✳ ✳ ✳

There is, of course, more to prayer than meets the eye —
even on a practical level. Irene Koppel, our member and an
influential leader in local women's circles, fancies herself a
great patriot of Israel. She has been nagging me for years
about the fact that our synagogue does not recite the special

weekly prayer for the State of Israel.

We do not recite this prayer because it is not part of the classic liturgy and adds nothing to the prayers for Zion and Jerusalem that already mark our normative prayers every morning, noon, and night of the year. In addition, I have an aversion to specially written contemporary prayers. One can pray to God for anything at any time, but to compose a prayer and to force it into the set liturgy smacks of a certain presumptuousness before the tradition. I never went along, for example, when some rabbinic groups — including some Orthodox ones — suggested a special Pesach Seder ritual in which a fourth matzah was added to the Seder plate and a special prayer recited on behalf of Soviet Jewry — although I certainly prayed privately for them. I never recited special public prayers for the welfare of the U.S.A., although it is printed in many *siddurim* — although I would pray privately for its welfare. I am as uneasy about adding to our set liturgy, which is a delicate jewel, as a musician would be about adding a fugue of his own to Beethoven's Ninth.

In the case of the prayer for Israel, I also find it presumptuous to inform God, as that prayer does, that the modern state is the "first flowering of the redemption of our Land." Who says so? The authors of the prayer — apparently the Israeli Chief Rabbi's office, assisted by S. Y. Agnon, the famous Hebrew writer — were certain that this was the case. But who knows? As great as they were, they were not divinely inspired psalmists; they could have been wrong. After all we have been through in this century, the thought is too terrible to contemplate — but the fact is that there are no guarantees, and perhaps the twentieth-century State of Israel is, God forbid, only a blip in Jewish history. (Every Shabbat morning, our synagogue does say a special prayer for the Israel Defense Forces and for their wounded and injured.) The only guarantee we have is that there will always be a Jewish people. But in what shape we will be, and how many of us there will be, and whether or not we will live uninterruptedly in our ancestral homeland before the advent of Messianic times —

all this is unclear. Granted, there are fine rabbis and fine synagogues that do recite this prayer, and I have no quarrel with
them. But these are my considerations, and the considerations of many authorities much greater than I.

Irene — who observes absolutely nothing Jewish, appears
only rarely in shul, and sends her children to private non-
Jewish schools — is more perturbed than ever about the
prayer for the State. She makes an appointment to talk with
me about it, and I explain all this to her.

She comes in angry, her mind is clearly made up, and of
course she is not persuaded by anything I say. Never overly
timid, she suggests that I am under the sway of the ultra right-
wingers who oppose the State, that I am in fact a closet
Neturei Karta-nik. I point out to her that even some of the
most militantly pro-Zionist synagogues in Judea and Samaria
have stopped saying the prayer because they were outraged
by governmental policies concerning the settlers and the so-
called peace process — but even this does not sway her.

I finally say to her, "Irene, if we were to institute this prayer
next Shabbat morning, you would never know the difference."

"Why not?"

"Because you are never in shul on Shabbat anyway." What
I did not say was that I found it most hypocritical that a person who clearly does not believe in the efficacy of prayer was
making such a to-do about this one prayer. For her, clearly,
praying to the Creator of the universe was not a religious
issue but a political issue.

Several weeks after our meeting, our president informed me
that Irene and her husband had resigned from the congregation, and that in their letter of resignation they stated that they
"cannot be members of a synagogue which does not support
the State of Israel and refuses even to pray for it." That they
resigned does not surprise me. Rather well-to-do and stubborn
by nature, Irene is accustomed to getting her way, particularly
with rabbis, and does not suffer gladly those who challenge her.

What did surprise me was the distortion of my words. I had
explained to her that my refusal to utter the contemporary

prayer was based not on politics but on purely religious considerations. To call our synagogue anti-Israel is a stunning accusation. We boast the single largest percentage of members of any synagogue in North America — about seventy families — who have made *aliyah* to Israel. In addition, each year we send dozens of young people to study in Israeli yeshivot, seminaries, and universities. Hell hath no fury like a wealthy person spurned.

A few days later I received a phone call from a non-member friend who said that he heard something that he found astonishing: that I adamantly refuse to permit a prayer for Israel in my synagogue because I am philosophically opposed to the State.

It had not taken long for the character assassination to begin, a whispering campaign in the community against the Orthodox rabbi. I told the caller that I cannot imagine who would spread such malicious gossip, that anyone who would seriously believe that I oppose the State of Israel is welcome to his madness. I asked the caller to have his informant speak to me directly. No one ever did.

Chapter 8:
The Sermon Heard
Round the World

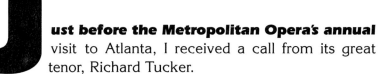

Just before the Metropolitan Opera's annual
visit to Atlanta, I received a call from its great
tenor, Richard Tucker.

"I'm going to be in town with the Met next week," he said.
"On Monday night I have *yahrzeit* for my mother and I wanted to know if you have a *minyan* daily, and if I could *daven*
Maariv from the *amud* that night." I told him that we do have
a daily *minyan,* and that we would be delighted to have him
lead us in *Maariv.*

Gradually, word leaked out that the great Richard Tucker was going to *daven Maariv* for us on Monday night. That soon escalated into Richard Tucker is going to give a *Maariv* concert for us on Monday night. On Monday night, instead of the usual ten men for *Maariv* in those early years, over one hundred people gathered in our little shul to hear the great tenor himself in a *Maariv* concert.

Tucker mounted the *bima* and began the *Maariv: Vehu rachum yechaper avon . . .* He recited it rapidly in the traditional low chant, without any particular effort to sing the words. And so it went through the *Maariv:* he *davened* the way an ordinary Jew *davens*. No arias, no solos, no performance. No one had promised a concert, and he gave none. At the end, he recited the *Kaddish* for his mother, graciously shook everyone's hands, even signed a few autographs, and I drove him back to the performance hall.

On the way, I jokingly asked him if he was nervous about tonight's opera performance. "Of course," he said, "I'm always nervous before I sing."

"But this is not New York. For you this is the sticks. What is there to be nervous about here?"

"I'll tell you something," he said. "It's always good to be a little nervous before you go on stage. It gives you a certain extra energy. When I'm not nervous I'm stale and flat."

Thus did I learn an elementary but important fact of pulpit life. The great nemesis of young rabbis delivering their first sermons is fear. Somehow, the very idea of standing up before a group of people to express one's views causes trembling in the hearts of the most talented of men — and in the knees and in the jaw. No matter how many public speaking classes one has attended prior to his first pulpit, there is nothing that quite equals the dread that one experiences when first speaking to his own congregation. But after the Tucker conversation things changed; instead of fearing the fear and being nervous about the nervousness, I learned to welcome it as a friend and to utilize it for my own needs. Now I'm nervous when I'm not nervous.

the ache within

I remember discussing the matter of stage fright with my father just before coming to Atlanta. "It's very simple," he said. "Just make believe that there is no one sitting in front of you. Make believe you are speaking to empty benches."

After my first month in the pulpit I called him. "About those empty benches," I said. "I don't have to make believe. That's exactly what I have in front of me when I speak: empty benches."

With my father I made light of the lack of worshipers. I did not share with him the aching feeling in my gut while I prepared my sermons week in and week out. As I researched and organized and rewrote, I wondered what the point of it all was when nine people at most would be listening. I kept telling myself that the handful of Shabbos regulars were worth my best efforts. If they cared, I cared. I reminded myself that my task was to teach Jews, whether a few or a multitude. And I consoled myself that if I felt bad when barely a *minyan* showed up, imagine how God Himself feels after all He has done for us. If He can continue to love His people and do His best for us, I could do no less. But Imitatio Dei was never easy, and although the pep talks helped a bit, the ache within me did not entirely disappear in those early years.

frothy and fluffy sermons

The matter of public speaking — in the case of a rabbi it is really public teaching — is endlessly fascinating. One never knows when, or if, that mysterious electricity will be kindled between speaker and listener. Without that electricity, even the most finely constructed sermon falls flat. Sometimes the sermons to which one devotes hours of research and shaping emerge bland and stale. And occasionally one lets fly an unprepared sermon — an idea that entered the mind that same morning during the Torah reading — and the impact is powerful.

A certain rabbi friend of mine never thinks about his sermons. In fact, he never works on them at all. He is a fine and good person, learned and intellectual, and undoubtedly a good shepherd to his flock. But he has one weakness: he simply is unable to prepare a sermon. He cannot collect his thoughts and organize them in an effective manner. In fact, he once confided to me that frequently, in sheer desperation, he lifts his sermons verbatim out of books of sermons that are readily available (and are not very good). He has even occasionally brought the sermon book itself up to the lectern and has read the sermon, word for word from the book, to his benumbed congregation. He and I had a good chuckle over this.

Someone recently moved to our community from that rabbi's synagogue. Reminiscing about the rabbi, he said: "I really loved Rabbi _____. He is a very good man. And his sermons! Rabbi, they are absolutely eloquent."

If Rabbi _____ was able to pull this off, I should be chuckling at myself instead of at him. Because I, who supposedly can organize my thoughts, still work inordinately long hours at preparing sermons.

The truth is that even the simplest talk requires careful preparation. It is relatively easy to package and deliver a popular, well-liked sermon: take a current headline, stir in a biblical verse, mix in a light anecdote, blend quickly, and out pops a fluffy and frothy sermon which everyone "enjoys" — mental and religious junk food. It is all fat, with no food value and no spiritual energy.

It is not easy to resist the temptation to be a crowd pleaser, to make the listeners happy and send them off in a good mood. The only hope is that the countervailing desire to shake them up, to challenge their assumptions, and to stir their souls will triumph.

If one wants to lift the flock spiritually, move them forward intellectually, bring them closer to themselves and to their roots, fluff simply will not do. Good weekly sermons require serious planning, changes in approaches, and a variety of subjects. One week the rabbi can preach and exhort; the second, he can simply teach a text; sometimes he should be extremely brief; and occasionally he should not speak at all. What can be more stupefying than the same type of talk week after week after week?

I once gave a sermon dealing with the sin of *lashon hara*, gossip and slander, and tried to point out how heinous an offense this is in the Jewish scheme of things, and how we normally overlook it. What can be more entertaining than a juicy bit of gossip about someone?

On the next Shabbat I spoke about the practice of *taharat hamishpacha*, discussing the laws of *mikveh* and abstinence between husband and wife.

On the third Shabbat, I discussed the Ramban's famous commentary on *Vayikra* 19, "You shall be holy." Ramban says that this overarching commandment is meant to prohibit all the excesses that one might theoretically perform even within the framework of Torah. For example, the Torah does not forbid eating per se, as long as the food is kosher and is prepared in the proper way. Technically, one could be a glutton and still not be in literal violation of a Torah law. "You shall be holy" thus puts us on notice that even in those things that are permissible to us we are required to behave in a holy way. I then took as my point of departure the inordinate contemporary emphasis on food.

After this sermon, Sam Kohn approached me during *kiddush*. "Rabbi, you've got to let up on us. First you took away the pleasure of gossip. Then you started interfering with our marriages. Now you're meddling in our eating. Rabbi, we love you dearly, but we're all scared to come to shul next week. Who knows what else you're going to take away from us?"

the briefest sermon on record

One of my most effective sermons took exactly thirty seconds. It consisted simply of one question: if we recite *berachot* prior to the performance of *mitzvot*, such as wearing *tefillin* or lighting candles, why do we not recite a *berachah* prior to the giving of *tzedakah* or visiting the sick? Think about it, I said, and then I sat down.

The congregation was so stunned by the brevity of the sermon that they buzzed about it during the entire *Mussaf*. And they discussed the question for the entire week. On the next Shabbat I proposed several answers. My favorite answer, ascribed to one of the *Rishonim*: we give *tzedakah* or visit the sick or perform any deed of compassion only because someone is in need of our help. To recite a blessing to God over a *mitzvah* which is being performed because someone else is in need is inappropriate. It's as if we were praising God for the poor man's poverty or the sick man's illness. This is why in general there are no *berachot* for *mitzvot* between man and his fellow man.

speaking vs writing

With all this talk about sermons, I must confess that I do not have that fire in the belly about public speaking. I would much rather write than speak, even though I find writing much more demanding.

In a speech, not every word must be written out and not every phrase carefully worded. Once the speaker has clarified in his mind the essential ideas and their sequence, he is ready to speak. His use of particular words or phrases will depend on the mood of the speaking moment.

In an essay, however, nuance and phrasing must be on target the first time. Each word must be precise; there is only one right word, not two. The writer cannot clarify an idea by repeating it from a different perspective if the first attempt is unsuccessful. Nor does he have the luxury of an audience that can generate within him energy and excitement. He faces the stark, lonely, empty page, waiting to be filled. And the reader, confronting black typeface on white paper, cannot be persuaded by inflection of voice or pauses or eye contact or gestures. In writing there are no second chances.

True, the writer is not required to think on his feet, and he has the luxury of refining and restructuring. But once the final draft is published, it stands alone on the printed page, isolated and vulnerable. If the words are unfocused and the tone unsteady, the reader closes the book and the writer has no further opportunities to recapture him.

It is no wonder that Maimonides writes in his "Letter on Apostasy" that before a person speaks in public he should review "two or three times that which he desires to say, and should learn it exceedingly well." But when it comes to writing, "it would be proper for the writer to review his words one thousand times if at all possible."

Despite all this, however, I realize that a good sermon can be an effective teaching medium, and that is what I have always tried to do with sermons: teach and educate, and if possible, make us more ambitious religiously.

the high holiday sermon: the crucial tool

As important as the sermon is, it is, after all, only a tool. If the rabbi is not careful, the sermon can dominate everything else he does, particularly around the High Holiday season. The classic dilemma operates here, but it is magnified tenfold. On a practical level, the rabbi wants to be judged well by his people, so many of whom are in shul on these days; and on an idealistic level, he wants his sermon to move his people forward.

During this season of the year, thoughts of the sermon were never far from my mind. Will there be a rapport between the listeners and me? Will it be understood? Will it inspire the people or leave them flat? Even as I performed all the obligatory pre-Yom Kippur duties — immersing in the *mikveh,* reciting the *Kapparos* and the *Al chet,* giving extra *tzedakah, davening* the special *Minchah,* reading the *Tefillah zakah* and expressing contrition before the Creator and begging for another year of life for this undeserving me — hovering above it all, and never quite leaving my consciousness, was the sermon.

But then again, I would say to myself, it should be front and center. If you don't inspire them, who will? This is your task in this life — to pierce the thick, protective armor that people build around themselves; somehow to touch them, to move them; somehow to persuade them to reevaluate their lives, to sense the glory and the majesty of Torah and Judaism, and to lift them up from the abyss of self-centeredness and physicality which life in the comfortable West has created for all of us.

The sermon is the vehicle through which the rabbi challenges and leads. And Yom Kippur night is when the hearts of Jews are wide open, when the curtain within them, tightly closed the entire year, begins to part. It is the rabbi's sacred duty to do the best he possibly can. For the sermon to be uppermost in his mind is thus perfectly acceptable.

sermonic lead

Trying hard, however, is not always enough. One Rosh Hashanah I spoke on the first day about the hidden meaning of the shofar blasts, and how and why they represent the sounds of groaning, sighing, and sobbing. I had invested in the sermon an inordinate amount of thought and work.

But as I began, it quickly became apparent that I was delivering a sermonic lead balloon. Nothing is as depressing and as frustrating, and no experience can be more harrowing, than a rabbi's gradual realization that the idea he has worked on for so long is not getting across.

By contrast, the second day's sermon, on which I had worked very little, was extremely effective. It was more emotional than the first sermon, and contained drama and narratives and human interest and humor. The first, which contained many more ideas, was apparently too cerebral and lacked excitement and passion.

After the second day's *davening* a lady whom I know very well said to me: "Today was a 'ten.' It more than made up for yesterday." It was a rather tactless comment, but the fact was that only a handful of people had anything positive to say about that first day's sermon, even though I thought it was a far superior talk.

On the following Shabbat in shul the same lady tried to apologize for her remark. "I probably should not have said it quite that way," she said.

With a polite smile I responded, "No need to apologize — the first day's sermon was really too intellectual, and it went far over the heads of almost everyone."

She smiled, but she got the message.

* * *

Sometimes, I must confess, I feel a bit foolish stressing the overriding *Yamim Noraim* themes of Jewish sacrifice and the Jewish ability to surrender the now for the future. I suspect that the prevailing mood, particularly for the occasional High Holiday visitors, is: Yes, we come primarily to hear the sermon, but please, make it short, tell us a good story, be upbeat, be witty, and send us home happy, Rabbi. Life is tough enough.

It is a depressing thought, and hopefully a distorted one. But Zack Kronish's advice about sermons depressed me even more. Zack has been a member for many years, but he has not moved Jewishly at all. What he knew about Judaism twenty years ago, he knows now — very little. What he observed twenty years ago, he observes now — again very little. He is a very amiable man and I enjoy talking to him, but the fact is that he grew up Jewishly deprived.

Once, just before Rosh Hashanah, he said to me, "Rabbi, you ought to start giving sermons about contemporary events. Talk about liberals and conservatives in Congress, or about the elections, or about current issues — you know, about the real things in life. You gotta stop talking about guys like Abraham and Isaac and Jacob and all. Those guys been long dead, Rabbi."

Nevertheless, on a deeper level I am convinced that even for the tourists whom we never see from year to year, Rosh Hashanah and Yom Kippur *davening* and sermons can make an impact and begin to turn them around. Yes, their hearts are perhaps more difficult to penetrate, their minds may be harder to reach, but deep inside they, like everyone else, yearn for meaning and purpose. The Jewish spark within them brings them to shul, and they can be touched.

I think of Rabbi Yehudah Sandberg, who is today a superb yeshivah *rebbe*. Yehudah — his name was then Jerome — is from Atlanta, from a family that initially observed neither Shabbat nor kashrut, and attended shul only on Yom Kippur. His parents once told me that the catalyst for the family's turn back towards Jewish practice — they instituted kashrut, Shabbat, and everything else over the years, and sent their children to study in yeshivot in other cities — was a chance remark of mine in a Yom Kippur sermon: something about the self-inflicted Holocaust within American Jewry, that we are destroying ourselves faster and more effectively than our enemies were ever able to do.

The remark was not particularly original, but it so touched them that they decided to make a change in their Jewish lives. They ultimately sent Jerry/Yehudah off to a major yeshivah in Israel, and he blossomed into an outstanding young scholar.

Oddly, it is the chance remark that sometimes has the most serious impact. In the early years, when Shabbat observance was still a rarity, I concluded a Rosh Hashanah sermon by asking off the cuff why people have to make hairdresser appointments or go shopping on Shabbat. After all, there are six other days in the week.

Years later, Pearl Weisman told me that that simple question started her and her family on the road to Jewish observance. Why indeed? she asked herself, and she canceled her hairdresser appointment for that Shabbat. Kashrut and the rest followed shortly thereafter, and today she, her husband, children, and even grandchildren are all committed to a full Torah life. Abstract and convoluted persuasion were not the catalyst; just a simple question that happened to strike a chord within her Jewish soul.

* * *

Sometimes the effectiveness of a sermon is expressed in the most unexpected ways. After services one Rosh Hashanah my wife and I were standing in the lobby of the shul, wishing a *Shanah Tovah* to the hundreds of people on their way out. Esther Gottstein was there, holding her newborn infant. When she spotted me across the length of the lobby, she called out with a big smile, "Rabbi, come say hello to your baby."

I smiled politely and continued on my way, but she persisted. "Rabbi, this baby is yours." A crowd began to gather around her when finally she explained: "You remember last Yom Kippur? You told us that it's a shame that after losing all those people in the Holocaust the Jewish rate of reproduction is the lowest of any group in America. You suggested that any family that has decided it has had enough children should reconsider and have at least one more child. Rabbi, this little boy is my answer to that sermon."

out-of-town lecturing: pitfalls

Many rabbis do a great deal of guest lecturing in various communities. In the early years I used to accept with alacrity any invitation to speak in another city.

My very first out-of-town guest appearance took place in Chattanooga, Tennessee, about one hundred miles from Atlanta. The turnout to hear the new young rabbi from Atlanta was less than thirty people, including the host rabbi, his wife, and their two children. It didn't matter. I had become a celebrity: I was a guest speaker in another town.

The rabbi of the little shul, who was even younger than I, introduced me. "Tonight I have the great honor to present to you one of the most learned (*I breathed in deeply*), most dynamic and charismatic (*a favorite adjectives for rabbis — no one is quite certain what dynamic and charismatic rabbis are, but they are wondrous adjectives when they are used about you*), most beloved, most influential (*I inhaled the lovely rhetoric; it was all cliche, but it was being said about me, and surely there was a modicum of truth in his words, for would a rabbi lie or flatter?*) in all of Atlanta Orthodoxy."

In all of Atlanta Orthodoxy? I was at that time the only Orthodox rabbi in Atlanta, and there was then no Atlanta Orthodoxy at all! Was he serious? He was. Never having been to Atlanta, he thought he was praising me. For this I had inhaled the intoxicating fumes of flattery? I exhaled and mounted the pulpit and, chastened and deflated but a bit wiser, gave my speech.

As the years went by, the excitement of out-of-town speaking began to dissipate. I began to feel that these engagements were not the most productive use of time. It was flattering to be the out-of-town expert, but I felt that I was more like a guest entertainer than a guest teacher — especially since I could provide no follow-up. I would come into a strange community, address people whose background and capacity to absorb and understand I knew nothing about, speak either above or below their heads, answer a few questions, enjoy the change of scenery, spend the evening with the host rabbi, and then leave town the next morning.

For this I would abandon my wife and children, who were already receiving too little of my time. So these past years, with the exception of situations where I thought I could really be of concrete help to a rabbi or his community, I have not accepted such invitations.

Normally, of course, one is invited at least three to six months in advance. Occasionally I would receive an invitation with just a few weeks' notice. This is an immediate indication that either the host community is hopelessly inefficient, or that the original invitee had to cancel. I would politely decline, and was always able to cite a conflicting obligation. If, however, the caller was a rabbi friend, I developed this routine over the years: "My dear Chaim, with such short notice you obviously are in a bind, and I'll try to help you — but on one condition. Tell me the name of the person you invited first and why he canceled."

After a few hems and haws the truth would emerge, and I would agree to be the pinch hitter. Coming off the bench like that is not easy, and to make things worse for the ego, the audience knows that you were not the first choice. But it is very good for one's humility.

During the course of one particular year I turned down speaking engagements in a number of cities, including one in Australia that I wanted to accept but did not because of a synagogue commitment. So I was not amused when one of my members complained to me, "You do so much traveling, you're hardly ever here when I need you." He had tried to contact me during the one assignment I had accepted this year. My instinct was to inform him, in righteous indignation, of all the invitations I had turned down, but I thought better of it. Sometimes too much explaining is worse than none at all.

the Pesach humiliation

Many years ago, before people started coming to shul in respectable numbers, I severely castigated the congregation on the first day of Pesach. It happened to coincide with Easter Sunday, and I had noticed that the small Baptist church down the street was packed with hundreds of worshipers. Our shul, which by then had one hundred fifty members, had twenty-five. On Pesach! On a Sunday! I was humiliated for God, Torah, Judaism, and myself. I unleashed a barrage of criticism at the lethargy and the casualness which marks Jewish life. "Where are our people on this Passover Sunday morning when no one goes to work!" I thundered. "Are they still asleep? Are they reading the Sunday comics? Are they out playing golf? If we are not ashamed before God, should we not be ashamed before our Christian neighbors?"

For good measure, I added that since American Jews are so obsessed with imitating the non-Jews, why is it that we don't imitate their positive qualities, like loyalty to their religion? "Those of you who are here do not need to be castigated," I concluded, "but I am asking each one of you to tell your absentee friends exactly and precisely what I am saying here today." I was deeply upset, and I hoped that it showed.

During *Mussaf* I wondered how the congregation would react. I didn't have to wait long. They congratulated me after the *davening*, and I received positive comments all week. They loved it. I anticipated that on the last day of Pesach, also on a Sunday, we would have a packed sanctuary. But on the last day of Pesach the same twenty-five people were present.

Thank God that shul attendance and *mitzvah* observance in general are today on a much higher level. A normal Shabbat *davening* brings over four hundred people, and a Yom Tov can bring out six hundred people.

The change was slow and gradual over the years, but it was not effected by sermons alone. Sermons are an important teaching tool, but without follow-up, the momentary inspiration dissipates quickly. Even when everybody nods in agreement and the congregants tell one another at the *kiddush* after services, "You know, the rabbi's right. He really has a point there," I fear that the effect is short-lived. Shabbat or Yom Tov ends, life returns to its normal rhythms, and the authentic Jewish soul is placed on hold once again

There is only one proven way to maintain the level of inspiration that sermons occasionally provide, and that is through continuing Jewish study and learning: classes, discussion groups, one-on-one learning sessions, lectures, courses, textual study. Once in a while a sermon on its own will hit a bullseye in the soul, but by and large even the best sermons require follow-up. Without this, it is all pretty theory and pleasant entertainment, with little consequence for daily living.

dear mr. president

This is the story of the sermon heard round the world: I was preparing my Pesach sermon one Erev Pesach, desperately behind schedule in all the frenetic pre-Pesach duties. The phone rang. It was the White House. (This is the ultimate name-drop, I realize, but it was the White House, during the time when Jimmy Carter, he of Plains, Georgia, was president.) One of his assistants was on the phone. He had been assigned to draw up some ideas for a speech the President would be delivering at a reception to mark the thirtieth anniversary of the founding of the State of Israel. Prime Minister Menachem Begin would be there, and a thousand rabbis were being invited. The assistant, a fellow Atlantan, knew me and asked me for some speech ideas.

Looking at the clock, I asked him when he needed to hear from me. "I apologize for the short notice," he said, "but the boss's staff wants it before tonight so they can begin working on it immediately."

Command performance. I put everything aside and began to think. Services were to begin in two hours. I was frantic and the clock was ticking. It occurred to me that the best idea would be to base the theme on the concept of the number thirty and what it means in Jewish tradition. The most obvious source was the listing of the various ages of man in *Avot* 5:25, in which it is stated, *"Ben sheloshim lekoach,* a thirty-year-old attains full strength."

I jotted down some hasty notes about the spiritual and moral strength of Israel at this juncture of thirty years, about its adherence to human rights and democratic ideals, about the close ties between the United States and Israel, and wound it all around the number thirty. I got the assistant on the phone and dictated the concept to his secretary. He liked it and said he would relay it to the President's speech writers.

Four weeks later, on a bright, sunlit afternoon, I stood on the packed White House lawn together, it seemed, with every rabbi in America. On a specially constructed platform in the center of the lawn stood President and Mrs. Carter and Prime Minister and Mrs. Begin.

Mr. Carter began his speech. He spoke eloquently (of course, eloquently; they were my words) about the spiritual and moral strength of the State of Israel, about its adherence to human rights and democratic ideals, about the close ties between America and Israel. In his final peroration he cited the Mishnah in *Avot* that the age of thirty represents full strength, and wished Israel continued spiritual and physical strength in its life as a nation.

Never in my life did I enjoy a speech as much as this one.

As the President elaborated on the concept of thirty and strength, a rabbi standing beside me murmured to no one in particular: "He's got it all wrong. The Mishnah doesn't say that thirty is strength. It says that thirty is understanding. Forty is strength. But what can you expect from a *goyishe* president?"

I leaned over and whispered to him: "When you get home, look it up and check it out. You'll find that this *goyishe* president knows exactly what he's talking about."

And while dropping names, let me relate the time when a game of tennis could have changed the course of history. I was visiting the Carter White House on a special mission dealing with Iranian Jews during the Iranian hostage crisis, and had been given a few minutes to meet with the President's Chief of Staff, Hamilton Jordan. After our meeting ended and he was walking me to the door, I noticed a tennis racket and an old pair of sneakers in the corner of the room. "Do you play tennis?" I asked.

"Sure do," said Jordan. "Do you?"

"Yes, I do. How about playing some time?"

Always the affable Southerner, he said, "Any time. Just give me a call."

"How about right now?"

Without any hesitation he said, "That's fine. I can supply you with a racket and tennis clothes."

"But Mr. Jordan," I said, "I play for high stakes."

He smiled. "A rabbi gambles? I don't believe it."

"A very serious gamble. If you win, you do with Israel's West Bank what you want, and I will drum up support for the administration. If I win, you recommend to the President to do what I want."

"You weren't kidding, were you? Them's really high stakes. Wait a minute, now, let me check you out." He reached over and patted my stomach and poked my arm muscles. "I don't know, Rabbi. You seem to be in fairly good shape. Plus you're taller and you have a longer reach. Sorry, Rabbi, no go."

We had a good laugh. As I left I remarked that since he basically admitted that I could beat him, he was morally bound to behave as if he had lost the bet and to write that memo to his boss anyway.

He smiled, and in his best Georgia accent he said, "Ah didn't promise nuthin'."

can sermons be deleted?

Speaking in public can be dangerous to one's health. Two hundred listeners sometimes hear two hundred different messages.

Case in point: I once spoke about the incident in Genesis 9 concerning the drunkenness of Noah, how his son Ham "gazed at his father's nakedness," while the other sons, Shem and Jephet, "covered their father with a cloak." Many of the Midrashim indicate that Ham was guilty of a much more serious transgression. The Sages suggest that because Shem initiated the covering of his father, Shem's descendants — the people

Israel — were rewarded with the privilege of wearing *tallis* and *tzitzis* (Sanhedrin 70a).

My sermon dealt with the relationship between what the sons did to their father and the *mitzvah* of *tzitzis*. I suggested that it is clear that the Noah incident contains certain sexual overtones, and that apparently one of the purposes of *tzitzis* — since they are conceptually connected with that incident — is to guide and control man's sexuality in a framework of sanctity, and cited numerous Talmudic incidents about *tzitzis* serving as an antidote to unbridled physical temptation. There is also the crucial passage in the *Shema*: immediately following the commandment to wear *tzitzis* we read: "And you shall not wander after your hearts and after your eyes, after which you go astray . . ." — which, among other things, refers to sexual temptation.

I then tried to address myself to the difficult question of why women are not required to wear *tzitzis*. Perhaps, I suggested — tentatively and with many caveats — this is because the male is by nature the initiator in sexual matters. Therefore, it is possible that he, more than the female, requires the greater safeguards represented by the *tzitzis*.

Jeff and Fran Singer's preteen children came home from shul that Shabbat morning one by one. Fran was home with the baby, and as always she asked the kids what the rabbi spoke about.

"I don't know," said the first child, "something about castration. Mommy, what's castration?"

When the second child walked in Fran asked the same question, and he replied, "Something about sodomy. Mommy, what's sodomy?"

The third child said, "Mommy, he spoke about sexuality. What's sexuality?"

Finally, the husband walked through the door. Fran, by now exploding with curiosity, said, "My God, Jeff, what in the world did the rabbi speak about today?"

Jeff replied, "Oh, nothing unusual. He talked about the commandment to wear *tzitzis*."

But while all that was taking place, a less amusing incident was occurring in the social hall after services. During the *kiddush,* Gertrude Kohl approached me. Gertrude is rather intelligent, well read, has a smattering of Jewish education, and considers herself very learned Jewishly. She has not had an easy life, was widowed in her forties, never had children, feels unappreciated, and is rather bitter. I try very hard to be nice to her even when her Judaic theories are the results of dangerously little learning. She still gives credence, for example, to Wellhausen's Documentary Hypothesis, not realizing that it was only an hypothesis and that much of it has long since been discredited. Then again, most people never heard of Wellhausen in the first place.

Gertrude was obviously very agitated. She didn't give me her usual "Shabbat Shalom," but attacked at once, eyes narrow with rage: "You have no regard for women. You split the synagogue in two with this sermon. I am fuming. You call us passive. For you we don't exist at all. We are just things, objects with no feelings." The lava flowed over as she raged on and on.

I told her that while she was entitled to her views, she had misunderstood what I was trying to get across; that I had not claimed that what I was suggesting about male and female sexuality was the final word; that I was simply trying to help the congregation understand the subtleties that lie beneath the surface of biblical narratives.

She would not be mollified: "You deliberately chose that subject to embarrass women. You have ruined my Shabbat." And she erupted into tears and left the building.

By Saturday night I was beginning to feel very sorry for her. I imagined her fuming and crying all day. So that night I called her and told her, half in jest, that I was sorry that I had "ruined her Shabbat," and invited her to come in whenever she had a chance to discuss the issues raised in the sermon. She was by now quite calm and said that she appreciated my call very much, that she hadn't meant to create a scene, and that she would see me during the week.

On Sunday afternoon it became evident that my call to her, while well intended, was misguided. Frank Efrat, one of her colleagues at work, told me in confidence that she had called him on Sunday morning and declared rather triumphantly, "At 8:25 last night, Rabbi Feldman called me to apologize for his sermon." He was incredulous and wanted to know whether it was true. I was just as incredulous.

Were it not for the amusing results in the Singer family, I would be tempted to press very hard on the Delete button on that particular sermon.

Chapter 9:
The Ritual of the
Red Pepper

Why-rabbis-don't-get-swelled-heads department: One of my good members told me a few months ago, "My wife and I were talking about your sermons. They've gotten much better lately."

A chance remark like that gives a rabbi an insight into what transpires behind the sweet facade of rapt attention.

The comment reminded me of Fannie Pearlman, a good soul who never means any harm, who said to me quite innocently one Shabbat morning, "I enjoyed your sermon very much today. It was much better than the one you gave last week."

From Fannie — simple, naive, fully honest — one always gets it straight, without frills or decoration. But I must confess to a rather unkind thought: when Fannie, who through no fault of her own is not an intellectual giant, finds a sermon "enjoyable," I begin to worry. When she finds the sermon over her head, at least I know I wasn't too elementary.

But such thoughts are not only unkind but untrue. Does God love only the great minds of humanity? Are not unlettered and simple folks an integral part of His creation? Are the souls of the unlearned any less in need of inspiration than those of the brilliant congregants? A rabbi's job is to appreciate the soul of every single Jew.

Which is easier said than done. The wall-to-wall nature of our synagogue — from the very learned to the very unlearned, and from the very observant to the very unobservant — adds a certain spice to the preparation of the weekly sermon: the scholar will comprehend this, but will it hold the attention of the newcomer? Or: the newcomer will be moved by this idea, but will I lose the attention of the veteran? For the selfsame words to touch the souls of the learned and the unlearned simultaneously is not easy. The last time this occurred was when God gave the Torah at Sinai.

painful reactions

I am nevertheless blessed with a congregation whose perception and intelligence, by and large, is far above average, and who demand and expect sermons that will make them think. In fact, when out-of-town lecturers come to our shul, I always caution them not to talk down to our people. I urge them not to hold back any ideas or concepts, but to give our people all the depth and profundity the speakers can muster. Some of my own best work has been done because I know that the congregation will not accept pap and expects the rabbi to dig far beneath the surface.

No one ever taught me how to respond to this type of praise: a young woman tells me after *davening* one Shabbat, "I love to hear your sermons, because you're so easy to listen to. Your material is clear and you speak directly to us. And, Rabbi, the most amazing thing: if my mind wanders during your sermon or if I doze off for a while, when I get back to you I find I haven't missed a thing."

She was not trying to be clever. She meant it as a compliment. We were neither flattered nor amused.

Sometimes the most painful reactions to a sermon occur after Shabbat, particularly at Bar Mitzvah receptions. "Rabbi, I just adored your sermon this morning. Just marvelous, simply marvelous. I'm going to come every week from now on." The lady from whom all this gushed forth was someone whom I'd never seen before and would probably never see again — certainly not in this synagogue. She knew it, I knew it, and she knew that I knew it. I suppose she was merely trying to be nice to me, and that this was the only way she knew to be polite to a rabbi. Unable to think of an appropriate response, I nodded politely and thanked her, thus playing my part in the charade.

One Shabbat morning my sermon dealt with the two famous biblical cows: the Red Heifer and the Golden Calf. According to the Sages there is a conceptual connection between the two: the Red Heifer is considered to be an atonement for the sin of the Calf.

I tried to explain that the underlying cause of the sin of the Golden Calf was the inability of the people to accept something which they could not comprehend with their rational faculties; that is, that there could be a God without intermediaries. They reverted back to an idolatrous intermediary, the Calf, as soon as they were convinced that Moses had died.

Because of this, God gave them a law which is the embodiment of the nonrational and which no mortal mind can comprehend. Even King Solomon, the wisest of all men, could not fathom the laws of the Red Heifer, in which the one who initiates the purifying sprinkling rites, though he was previously undefiled, becomes defiled, while the recipient of the sprinkling, until now defiled, becomes undefiled. It is an assault on all rationality.

The fulfillment of this Red Heifer rite serves as an atonement for the transgression of the Calf. "Let the mother (the Heifer) come and clean up the dirt which the Calf made," says the Midrash.

In other words, by making this rite inaccessible to the probing of our minds, God creates a correction and a mending of the sin of the Calf, which had as its root cause the idea that our mortal minds are the final arbiter of our behavior. My point in the sermon was this: the Red Heifer laws teach us that service of God is not subject to mere rationality; the service of God possesses a rationality of its own.

Later, in the social hall during *kiddush*, an out-of-town guest, trying to be pleasant, gushed about how he really loved and was uplifted by the sermon. "There's only one thing that puzzles me," he said. "What exactly is the ritual of the Red Pepper?"

make the sermon dull

Questions for which no training can prepare you: Sarah Winbaum, a highly intelligent and perceptive forty-year-old single woman, asked me just before Yom Kippur: "Rabbi, do you think I'm sort of attractive?"

I have counseled Sarah with many of her problems over the years. Whether she is or is not attractive had never occurred to me, and her sudden question unnerved me. What was the appropriate answer? I dodged and weaved and hedged, but did not respond.

She laughed at my discomfort. "Well, if I am at all attractive, it's primarily because I pickle my eyes for days in mascara."

"Fine," I said, waiting for the point.

"Your Rosh Hashanah sermons absolutely destroyed my

mascara. I was totally broken up. I was so moved, I wept throughout."

"I am sorry about that, but I am truly gratified."

"I am calling to ask that you not do such a good job on Yom Kippur. Kindly make your sermons dull and drab, so I can continue to look attractive. You realize you are ruining my chances of making a good impression on any eligible man."

It was probably the most original sermon reaction I had ever received, and I enjoyed it immensely — particularly when she told me that mascara was also running from the eyes of other women around her. Their mascara runneth over.

* * *

No one is ever insulted by a compliment. The day after Yom Kippur an elderly woman said to me in the synagogue office, "I don't want to swell your head, but I thought your holiday sermons were magnificent." I thanked her graciously, because I truly appreciated her words.

Later in the afternoon she called me to apologize. She should not have been so flippant with the rabbi. She asked my forgiveness for not having been respectful enough to me. I assured her that her comments were very respectful and were very much valued.

All my congregants should be so disrespectful.

Now, Jonathan Sykes is another story. He is intelligent, smart — they don't always go together — and well read. And he is totally honest. When he avoids me after a sermon I know that I was well below par. When he tells me that something was good, I know it was good. And unlike almost everyone else, he never uses the word "enjoy" to describe his reaction to a sermon.

* * *

No matter how profound or original a sermon of mine might occasionally be, Herman Roth, who knows no Hebrew and little about Judaism, will invariably sidle up to me and

say, "That was a very nice concept, Rabbi. In fact, we discussed that very idea last night at our Friday-night dinner."
Whatever I say, he always finds a way to tell me that the same
thought occurred to him a few weeks earlier.

He has no malicious intent; he is really a very decent human
being. But he does not grasp the nuances of abstract ideas, sim-
plifies them and brings them down to his own level of Jewish
understanding. For him it is perfectly normal that he and the
rabbi should be thinking along the same scholarly lines.
Sometimes I wonder why I have to work so hard to produce an
idea that he can concoct over his Friday-night chicken soup.

when thou liest down

Whenever I begin to speak, several men — always the
same ones — nod off within the first two minutes. (For an
inexplicable reason, I rarely see women dozing off.) They
have become an integral part of my sermon life. They always
— without exception — take an involuntary nap (who knows,
perhaps it is voluntary) when I speak. They have been doing
it for twenty years, and will do it, please God, until one hundred twenty. It doesn't matter whether it's a lecture, a talk at
shalosh seudos, or a Shabbat sermon; at the sound of my
voice, the eyes begin to glaze over, and before I end my intro-
ductory remarks they are in deep slumber. Those sitting next
to one of these men have confided in me that from time to
time they have even heard a snore. (That's only when I was
delivering a particularly deep sermon.)

There was a time when this made me worry about what
might be wrong with my sermons. But I once happened to
glance in their direction while I was chanting an Haftarah, and
they were sound asleep then, too. So I realized that at least it
was not my content which was responsible — after all, the
words of Isaiah are not boring — but the sound of my voice
that had such a soporific effect.

Then I began taking it as a challenge. If I couldn't wake

them up by the end of the sermon, they won and I lost. I varied my pitch; I tried long and pregnant pauses; I raised and lowered my voice. I tried everything I legally could, but rarely did I succeed in waking them up. Only when I finished and the *chazzan* intoned the *Mussaf Kaddish* would they bestir themselves, rise to their feet, and recite *Mussaf.*

But they were always gracious. After services the sleepers would invariably tell me how much they enjoyed the sermon. I always thanked them and, in a model of self-restraint, never ever suggested to them that perhaps what they really meant was that they enjoyed their nap. One thing can be said for these folks: for them, no sermon could ever be too long.

Snoozers are good for the soul. A rabbi keeps hearing how great he is, that he is God's gift to the Jewish people, that he is the most learned and the wisest, and if he is not careful he begins to believe it all. A regular and reliable snoozer is an invaluable antidote. And beyond all the philosophy, over the years I developed a real affection for these folks. I knew they were sleepers, they knew that I knew, and those were the facts of life. I also knew that they made valiant efforts to stay awake. Was it their fault that my voice so tranquilized them?

A few months ago I spoke at a Jewish forum in an outlying area at least one hour's drive from the shul. It was open to the public, but I really expected no one from my synagogue to come, especially since it was a cold, rainy night. After all, my congregants can hear me any time they want to.

To my great surprise and pleasure, my members Sam and Susan Rosen were in the hallway as I came in from the parking lot. "How nice of you to come," I said, "but this is a long haul. You really didn't have to come out all this distance. You can hear me every week."

Sam smiled sweetly and said, "We would drive to the ends of the earth to hear you, you know that."

They are very gentle and thoughtful people and I like them, but I could not help remembering that Sam, though he attends all my classes and comes to all services, is also a catnapper who frequently nods off when I lecture or teach. He is not as dependable as the others, but a close second.

Susan and Sam had front-row seats. Four minutes into my remarks — surely not more — Sam's eyes began to close slowly, surely, inexorably. *Sam, not now, not after shlepping all the way out here on a rainy night, surely you're not going to fall asleep once again. To sleep you could have stayed at home snug in your bed.*

Two minutes later I glanced at him again. He was sound asleep, his mouth agape, chin on neck, his head bobbing ever so gently up and down. And he slept soundly for the next thirty minutes. He would go to the ends of the earth to enjoy a good, solid nap.

a congregant takes revenge; so does the rabbi

There are many ways not to listen to a sermon. Some close their eyes. Some look at a *Chumash* or *Mishnayos*. The act that Irving Seemans puts on during sermons is probably the best I have ever seen.

It all began some years ago when, after a number of provocations, I told him privately that his constant talking during services disturbed me and everyone around him. "Who are you to tell me how to behave?" was his response.

"Well," I said, "this is certainly the responsibility of the rabbi."

"Not even a rabbi tells me what to do."

I realized then that I was dealing with someone who was extremely angry at life, so I dropped the subject. Ever since that pleasant exchange he was implacably hostile, and whenever I delivered a sermon, he made his displeasure known by folding his arms across his chest, throwing his head back, and staring at the ceiling — making it clear that he was not listening.

In time, he received his recompense. After not having spoken to me for a year, his son's forthcoming Bar Mitzvah forced him to come into my study to discuss certain study requirements. He was clearly ill at ease during the meeting. As he was leaving, he turned to me and said, "You probably have been wondering why I stare at the ceiling during your sermons. I wanted you to know why I do that."

"You stare at the ceiling? Really? I hadn't noticed."

"You don't see me doing that during every sermon?"

"No. I guess I'm too busy thinking about what I'm going to say next."

He was completely nonplussed. "Well, just forget it," he mumbled, and left.

Nothing could have disappointed him more than the thought that I hadn't noticed.

Thank God that for every Seemans there is a Jan Gordon. For Jan I can do no wrong. Always smiling, always with an encouraging word — I could use ten Jans in the congregation. One Shabbat morning after services he said to me, "Rabbi, your sermon was terrific today. Terrific."

"But Jan," I blurted out, "I didn't even speak today."

Jan didn't skip a beat. "Don't matter, Rabbi. You were still terrific."

The faces of people during sermons: most make a serious effort to listen, seem to hang on every word, and their faces show that they are absorbing what I am trying to get across. Some are clearly not aware of what I am saying, but make a valiant effort. Others yawn. Others glance furtively at their watches. A few look at their watches only twice: precisely when I begin, and precisely when I end. These are the time-keepers. (Last Rosh Hashanah, after having spent weeks preparing the sermon, I was eager for some reaction from somebody. No one said anything — always an ominous sign. Finally, Joe Kramer came over to me. "Rabbi, that sermon you gave today . . ." "Yes?" I said, eagerly awaiting some vindication. "It took exactly twenty-nine minutes. Not bad for a High Holiday sermon, Rabbi.") As a group, they are an excellent audience: intelligent, responsive, expressive. The sleepers are there, yes, but they are a necessary ingredient in the audience mix. Ironically, they keep me alert.

Audiences: Emil Fackenheim, the noted Jewish philosopher, is in town lecturing on the Holocaust. In the audience a woman glances into her mirror and daubs her mouth with bright red lipstick.

He speaks of the awesome responsibility that befalls Jews today, now that one-third of our people have been decimated. She puckers her lips, smacks them together, rolls them in and out.

He says that each Jew must live an even more Jewish life. She puts away her lipstick.

We must not give Hitler a posthumous victory, he cries out. She checks her mascara.

better off without a sermon

It is good occasionally to see sermons from the layman's point of view. Last year the president of a small local congregation — not Orthodox — called me just before Rosh Hashanah. Their rabbi had suddenly been taken ill and was unable to speak on the High Holidays, and one of the members had been asked to give the sermon. Could I possibly suggest a theme? I was happy that they felt close enough to me, an Orthodox rabbi, to call for help, but I was nonetheless uncomfortable about the whole matter.

"Well," I said, "repentance is certainly the overall theme for the High Holidays. By the way, what are this gentleman's qualifications for delivering a sermon on Rosh Hashanah?"

"He gives seminars on public speaking. He is really very good."

"Yes, but what are his qualifications to speak on a religious theme to a Jewish congregation at the holiest time of the year?" I was unable to hide my annoyance.

"Well, to tell the truth, he probably doesn't have any special qualifications of that sort."

"Then what good would a theme be to him if he has no religious qualifications or background?"

"Well, he could read up on it."

My annoyance flowed over. I said to him, "What would you think of me if I were to prepare a talk on atomic physics, and though I have no backgound at all in it, I read up on it in a few days?"

"Well, you have a point, but they still want him to do it because they have no choice. They're stuck without a speaker."

"They would be better off if no one spoke at all. Let them take the time normally devoted to the sermon and sit quietly and pray by themselves, or study the Torah reading together, or meditate a bit about the meaning of Rosh Hashanah, or about God, or about our purpose in this world. That would be much more worthwhile than listening to a sermon from someone who really doesn't know his subject."

"Not have a sermon at all? How can you have a service without a sermon?"

I informed him that it is perfectly acceptable and proper to have a Jewish religious service without a sermon. "Please think about this," I said. "Rather than have a sermon delivered by someone who is totally unaware of anything Jewish, your congregation is better off without a sermon at all."

There was dead silence on the other end of the phone. Then he said to me: "With all due respect to you, sir, are you absolutely sure about that? In my entire life I have never heard of a Jewish service without a sermon."

So Christianized have we become in our thinking that my comments impressed this gentleman as some kind of radical deviation. I received the same reaction some time ago when I told a fellow Jew that the major service of the Jewish week is not on Friday night but Saturday morning. In his congregation this was unheard of, since they can get no attendance on Shabbat morning and therefore, like most non-Orthodox congregations, emphasize late Friday-night services.

I heard after Rosh Hashanah that this congregation really "enjoyed" the sermon given to them by one of their laymen.

His theme? Repentance.

The painful lesson of all this is that for many laymen the sermon is a part of the religious performance, and the fact that it takes place is more important than what is said. In their eyes, a rabbi is one who is trained to give the sermon; otherwise, there is no qualitative difference between a rabbi and a layman. In fact, when a layman "reads up" on subjects like repentance, he, too, can deliver sermons. Overnight, he is a rabbi.

he means them; he means me

There are two kinds of listeners: those who feel that nothing you say applies to them personally, and those who feel that everything you say applies to them personally.

An example of the first type surfaced when I spoke on the subject of *sin'at hinam,* causeless hatred, disliking people for no apparent reason, and the habit of ascribing evil motives and making negative assumptions about the things they do. I tied it in with the conflict between Joseph and his brothers. Joseph assumed that their actions were evil when they were not; the brothers could not see beneath the exterior surface of Joseph and assumed that his motives were evil as well. After the sermon, several people said to me: "The people who needed to hear it were not here."

It's humbling to see the kind of impact my sermons make.

Rachel Markowitz was type II; she took to heart every remark I ever made. If I spoke of spiritual incompetence, she was certain I was referring to her, felt that she deserved to be chastised, knew that everything I was saying about her was absolutely true, and would go into spiritual depression for a week.

If I discussed Jewish ignorance, she knew I was talking about her. Gossip? Intellectual dishonesty? Carelessness about one's Jewishness? The need to give more *tzedakah* and to be more concerned with our fellow human beings? Yes, Rabbi, you really opened my eyes to myself today. You are absolutely right. Those are my greatest weaknesses. I hope I'm not a hopeless case.

The fact is that I never ever had Rachel in mind. She was not a gossip, she was the epitome of consideration and kindness, she attended all my classes and was a good student, was serious about growing steadily as a Jewess, and instilled all these things in her family.

Chapter 10:
Two Kinds of
Processions

Two kinds of processions bring a lump to my throat.

One is the procession of a bride down the aisle on the way to the wedding canopy: slow, stately, triumphant, radiant, filled with the possibilities of life. She is flanked on both sides by loved ones, her walk is erect, her head held high, she glows in her flowing white gown.

The other is the procession of a bereaved wife behind the coffin on the way to the grave. Once again she and he are walking down the same path. Once again, he goes first. Once again, she follows him slowly, flanked on both sides by loved ones. But now she is not wearing radiant white garments. Now her clothes are dark, her shoulders bent, the smile vanished, her head held low.

Two processions, two paths.

Of all the duties that befall a rabbi, none is more painful and more difficult than to officiate at a funeral. When the angel of death pays a visit, there is no reprieve and no appeal. Finis. Not to be continued. Were it not for our belief in a life of the soul after death, life on this earth would have little meaning. Just to live the biblical threescore years and ten and then to die would be without sense or purpose.

At this moment of finitude and finality, people view the rabbi as the bearer of the keys to all the hidden answers. What is it all about? Why? Why me? The rabbi is expected to provide the healing and the soothing balm to help them through this searing moment.

afraid of the rabbi

It is strange: in the eulogy, a rabbi tries to uncover the essence of the life of the deceased, but very often it is the essence of the living people present that is revealed. Death and cemeteries often expose life in all of its pathos and comedy, crudity and refinement, compassion and selfishness.

I think of the funeral of Ida Blumfeld and the behavior of her oldest son Ronald, a thirty-year-old wheeler and dealer.

Ida was a gentle soul who had tried very hard to raise her children properly, but it was a losing battle. Her husband Sam was not a very refined person and was more interested in business, making good impressions on people, and gambling on athletic events than he was in her or in the children. She tried heroically to instill good values into the kids, but she was sickly all her life and it was a desperate struggle.

Ida once confided to me this account of an argument she had had with her husband.

> *Ida:* I want to go to *Selichos* Saturday night.
>
> *Sam:* I'm going to the football game Saturday night.
>
> *Ida:* Forget your football game. We're going to *Selichos*. Once a year it won't kill you.
>
> *Sam:* You want to go to *Selichos,* go. I'm going to the game, period.
>
> *Ida:* What kind of Jew are you, won't even go to *Selichos* one night a year!
>
> *Sam:* I'm not going to *Selichos.* You want to go, go. Am I keeping you from going?
>
> *Ida:* No wonder our kids are the way they are. Look at their example. I'm calling Rabbi Feldman to tell him about this.
>
> *Sam:* Don't you call the rabbi. It's none of his business.
>
> *Ida:* Well, if you're not afraid of God, at least you're afraid of the rabbi.

To Ida's everlasting credit, most of the children did not turn out badly. But she did not succeed with Ronald, who adored his father and grew up to be a carbon copy of him.

Ida had been very sick for a long time, and her death seemed to be a release of a heavy burden on the family. When I visited the children before the funeral — her husband had died years earlier — Ronald told me that he was comforted by the fact that his mother had died on Mother's Day. "That's meaningful to me," he said. "Now she'll be able to join my Pop on her day." I had never known Big Ron — at six-three and two hundred fifty pounds that was an appropriate name — to be comforted by anything that was not completely material, so I suppose this was for him a step forward, although I had never viewed Father's Day or Mother's Day as integral units of the religious life cycle. But all that was only a prologue to the funeral itself.

When I arrived at the cemetery, a number of people were already gathered beside the gaping, yawning grave, waiting for the service to begin. I could not help noticing that they were all chattering away as if they were at a party. Even the specter of death exerts no restraints on prattle.

The three daughters were all quite calm and self-possessed as we waited for the appointed hour. Ronald had not yet arrived. Only Jason, about twenty, displayed any signs of grief.

Just at the stroke of two, Ronald came tooling up in his glistening white Corvette, top down, radio blaring music — with a blond and clearly non-Jewish young lady sitting beside him.

My eulogy was devoted to the importance of doing something worthwhile with our lives, and to the tragedy of squandered lives. I urged those present to consider that every human being ultimately ends up in a grave, and that while God gives us life, we should be careful not to waste it on foolishness. Whether I made an impact on anyone I don't know, but on Ronald I certainly did not. He simply gazed at the sky and at the tops of the trees, not at me. His foot tapped up and down, up and down.

After the burial, with all the guests milling around and saying goodbye to one another, Ronald ostentatiously handed me an envelope filled with dollar bills, and said, loud enough for everyone to hear, "This is from the whole family, Rabbi, in appreciation for your help today, for you to do with as you please." It was obviously a well-rehearsed speech, and he did not mean to embarrass me, but he did. The net effect was that he was the employer paying off his laborer. I refused several times to take it. He insisted. People were taking notice of our little discussion.

"Please, Ron," I finally said, "I don't feel right taking this. You keep it and give it to the shul." This was not in the script and he was annoyed, but he agreed. I left the funeral very saddened by Ida's death and the insensitivity of her big boy — and not a little embarrassed by his girlfriend, his convertible, his music, his impatient feet, and his tastelessness.

on the day I get used to it . . .

Funerals also reveal something about rabbis. I remember one of the first funerals at which I officiated. A young father of thirty-five had died suddenly, without any warning, leaving behind a wife and three little ones. I co-officiated at the funeral with another rabbi, a veteran of many years. I was visibly shaken by the tragedy, and the older rabbi tried to comfort me. "You're young, you'll get used to it as time goes on." He was trying to be fatherly, but I remember saying to myself that the day I get used to it is the day I leave the rabbinate.

Funerals are by definition sad, but on rare occasions they can be ludicrous. Old Mrs. Greenblatt's funeral was one of the ludicrous ones. She was eight-five, her surviving husband ninety. The graveside service was sparsely attended; most of her friends had unfortunately preceded her to this place. In attendance were her husband, her sister, her daughter, some grandchildren, and a handful of aging friends.

As we lowered the casket into the ground, her husband broke the silence: "Rabbi, you don't have to sit *shivah* for a wife, do you?"

His wife wasn't even buried yet, and already he was concerned about his *shivah* obligations. "Yes," I managed to whisper to him, "there is *shivah* for a wife."

"Really? I didn't know that. Did you hear that?" he said to his daughter. "There is *shivah* for a wife."

I tried not to carry on a conversation with him during the service, but he was as casual as if he were asking the price of a suit of clothes. The casket thudded as it touched bottom.

"I always thought you only sit *shivah* for your parents."

"No, you definitely do sit *shivah* for a wife," I whispered.

"I never knew that." He was quite disappointed. "Rabbi, are you sure?"

At that point his sister leaned over to him and said in a loud whisper, "Jake, shhh! You know Rabbi Feldman is very Orthodox."

she died tomorrow

A man calls me: "Rabbi, you don't know me, but would you mind arranging for someone to say *Kaddish* for my mother? She died tomorrow."

"She died tomorrow?"

"Tomorrow's the anniversary of her death. I won't be able to make it to shul that early in the morning to say *Kaddish*. Could you get someone to say it in my place? I'll pay him."

"Well, the idea of having a total stranger say *Kaddish* for one's mother is not a very good one. Perhaps you could manage to come yourself. I'd be happy to help you with anything you need during the services."

"Well, the truth is that it's kind of tough for me to get up that early. I heard that it's possible to get someone to do it for you when you can't make it to shul."

"I'm sorry, but we don't routinely do that here."

The fellow was right: many years ago I used to permit this practice, but then decided to call a halt to it. I realized that I was helping sever the last, tenuous tie to a shul — the annual *yahrzeit* visit. You stay in bed and hire someone to handle for you the onerous chore of getting up early to pray for your loved one's soul. So even though the practice is technically permissible, I felt that a person's unwillingness to get out of bed was insufficient reason to arrange for a stranger to say the *Kaddish*.

I couldn't help wondering about this fellow's poor old mother: How many times a night had she gotten up for him when he was a child? Foolish woman; she should have hired someone else to do it.

Let me not give the wrong impression. There are those who won't get up early for their mother's *yahrzeit*, but there are many more who are serious about their obligations and attend morning and evening *minyan* daily, for the entire year of mourning. A nonobservant person, until now attending synagogue only a few times a year, who suddenly undertakes this obligation is in fact engaging in an impressive display of devotion and love — and determination.

We have had physicians, for example, who readjusted their entire office schedules in order to attend the daily *minyan*. The late afternoon *Minchah/Maariv* schedule and its summer-winter variations create more difficulties for a busy man than does the early morning *davening*. In December, *Minchah* takes place at about five P.M., making it necessary to make radical adjustments in one's daily routine. In June, it takes place at eight P.M., making it difficult to plan any evening activities.

And yet, this year-long regimen is commonly undertaken and fulfilled. To a man, literally, they have told me that what started out as a burden became something to which they looked forward every day and which they felt had contributed something permanent to their lives.

duel at the cemetery

When a rabbi is asked to officiate at a funeral of someone he has never met, strange things can happen.

At one such service, I was delivering the eulogy in glittering generalities, based on the few snippets the deceased's family was able to tell me: he was a "nice person, had a good heart, and belonged to charitable organizations." They were hard pressed to give me any specifics, so I was on my own.

I tried to expand a bit on these tenuous themes without overdoing it. But whenever I opened up a new subject, one elderly woman among the guests would involuntarily shake her head sternly from side to side, clearly disagreeing with me.

I spoke of how he had supported charities; she shook her head and whispered disapprovingly to her neighbor.

I switched to loyalty to the Jewish people and supporter of Israel, which applies to almost anyone. No good.

A loving, gentle person? She rolled her eyes. A good father? Forget it.

It was a silent debate between the two of us, I proposing new themes, she vetoing them. It was a dance of opposites, she pulling in one direction, I in another. I was on stage center, but she was the choreographer, correcting my every step.

Why, I asked myself, was I allowing this anonymous woman to control what I wanted to say? Because, I answered myself, I don't know this man and therefore don't know what I want to say. She obviously knew him only too well.

I was by now badly unnerved. Would she like it if someone were to do this to her at her own funeral as she lay there unable to defend herself?

In desperation I concluded my eulogy with a prayer for eternal life under the protection of the Almighty, and proceeded to read *Psalm* 23: "The Lord is my shepherd, I shall not want . . ."

It was my only good move of the day. She nodded her head approvingly.

This brought to mind the time I was fifteen years old and my father was confiding in me. "My luck," he said. "Of all the rabbis in Baltimore, they have to ask me to do the funeral of Joe_____. Everyone knows he was a low-life, a swindler, and an adulterer. What can I say at his eulogy?"

"Well," I teased, "you could always lie."

"Don't be silly," he teased back. "When is a lie effective? When no one knows you're lying. But in this case, if I say something positive everyone will know I'm lying. "

When he returned from the funeral, I asked him what he had said. He had an odd glint in his eye: "I said that for forty years Joe passed a church every morning on his way to work, and not once in those forty years did he ever enter that church and become an apostate."

"Come on," I pleaded, "what did you really say?"

"You can always find something positive to say about any-one. So I said he was loyal to the Jewish people, that he was fond of little children, that he had a zest for living, that there was always a smile on his face. It was not my greatest eulo-gy, but it was okay."

I'm sure it was okay — as long as someone was not in front of him rejecting his every word.

✳ ✳ ✳

There was another lady who was the very opposite of this one. I never found out who she was, but for a period of sever-al years she appeared at every single funeral at which I offici-ated. At every funeral she would sit in the same seat. More remarkably, at every funeral she would weep. She appeared only in the funeral chapel; she would never come out to the cemetery.

At first I did not notice her, but after three or four funerals I realized that this woman was always in the audience. I looked for her at the fifth funeral, and there she was in the same seat in the middle of the chapel on the far left aisle. At the sixth she was there again, and at the seventh and eighth and ninth, eyes tearing, handkerchief at the ready. She must have attended ten or fifteen in a row.

Surely she could not have been related or even known all the people who had died in my synagogue, especially since she was not even a member. I even asked the other rabbis if a similar phenomenon was occurring to them, but they were not aware of anything unusual. And then she stopped com-ing and I never saw her again.

Why had she come? How could she cry at every funeral? Why did she sit in the same seat? Why did she never come out to the actual burial itself? Why did she start coming in the first place, and why did she stop? Why was she appear-ing at the services of my congregants and not those of the other synagogues?

visiting father

Embarrassing moments: I was officiating at a tombstone unveiling ceremony on a hot August afternoon. After the service ended and the crowd began to disperse, a gentleman greeted me and asked how the family and I were doing. He obviously knew me, but I could not remember him. I made some small talk, all the time trying to place him, but it was useless.

"I'm going over to visit Dad," he said.

"Oh," I said, hoping that I might find a clue when he told me about his father, "how is he?"

" 'How is he'! Rabbi, you buried him two years ago. His grave is right over there, behind you. I'm Leon Binstock."

Suddenly I remembered. "Leon! Of course! With those big sunglasses on you, how can anyone recognize you? Take those sunglasses off so people can see your face."

It was a desperate attempt to squeeze out of a jam, but he was a very gracious man and made light of it. Would I accompany him to his father's grave and say a prayer for him? I went readily, greatly relieved that he was not offended by my blunder.

Somehow, I chose Psalm 27 as one of the readings: "Conceal not Thy face before me . . ." It was only in retrospect that I understood why Leon seemed to smile at that point.

a funeral all our own

People often forget the significance of a funeral and of mourning, which is designed not only to pay tribute to the dead, but also to remind us of our own mortality. Therefore, when I deliver eulogies, I refer to the graves that lie all around us, pointing out that every single one of us will, sooner or later, be the featured player in a funeral all his own. We pray that it will not take place until the biblical 120 years, but no one, no matter how rich or powerful, escapes the grave.

Fortunately, God has given us the ability to forget this crucial fact of life, but on occasion, such as at a funeral, it is valuable and sobering to call it to mind. Merely to attend a funeral, I tell them, to offer condolences to the mourners, and then to proceed on our merry way, is to waste an opportunity to reflect on the meaning of life and the purpose of what we are doing.

That's why King Solomon says that it is better to go to the house of mourning than to the house of feasting (Ecclesiastes 7:2). Solomon was not being morbid, but wise. He knew that life can only be enriched when we recall that the material and physical aspects of life are limited and finite. If we are able to put this in perspective, our lives can take on some higher purpose and meaning. We might then be able to pause in our relentless pursuit of ephemeral things and pleasures to consider where we are now, why we are here, and where we are going. And then we might resolve to put meaning and purpose into our lives by allowing God to enter it, by following His teachings, and by living considerately, lovingly, and givingly.

Jerry Reinman's funeral is illustrative. Jerry, a non-member in his late thirties, was not at all observant, and those who attended the funeral — none of whom I had ever met before — were all youngish people from apparently minimal Jewish backgrounds.

I spoke informally and conversationally. My theme was plain: at a funeral it is appropriate not only to think about the life of the departed one, but also to evaluate our own lives, and to ask what will be said of us at our own funerals when our own time comes.

What kind of legacy are we leaving behind? What do we consider most important in our lives? Making money? Acquiring playthings and gadgets? Where in our scale of priorities stands the idea of living as a Jew and as a bearer of the world's oldest and richest religious tradition? Do we really think that we will be satisfied by running after even more goodies and more possessions — all the while neglecting our own souls and our own spiritual development as members of a holy people?

It was all said in a low-key and casual tone, as the small group of us stood around the open grave.

Afterwards, a young man I had never met approached me. "I've been to lots of funerals, but this is the first time it ever meant anything." I told him I was gratified to hear that. He continued: "Rabbis most of the time just read what's written in the book, but you said it like it is. It was like you were speaking to me personally."

Here was a sensitive soul ready to be touched, if only someone reached out to him with an authentic Jewish message about the demands that Torah makes, the discipline it requires, the joys it engenders.

for you, Mama

Of course, it doesn't always work out as I plan, and people are not always moved to greater sensitivity or thoughtfulness.

We were dedicating a tombstone of an elderly gentleman who had died a year before. His middle-aged daughter and his aged widow were in attendance. After the service, the old woman asked her daughter, "Molly dear, look at Daddy's stone — it's twice as wide as the grave. Why such a big stone?"

"The stone is big so we can get your name on it also. See this part over here?" she asked, pointing to the untouched area of ground alongside her father's grave. "This part over here is for you, Mama."

✳ ✳ ✳

When Mrs. Zonfeld passed away, I met with her three sons prior to the funeral. They are now in their forties, but I remember them from the time they were children. I used to walk to shul with them on Shabbat when they were very young, but have not seen them since their respective Bar

Mitzvahs. Their widowed mother retained her membership, but the boys drifted away.

They were particularly anxious that I do justice to their mother in my eulogy. They asked me explicitly to say that she was an excellent mother who did more than was humanly possible for them, even though she was widowed at a young age. They were very concerned that I not omit anything complimentary. They obviously felt unusually close to her, and they wept profusely during our discussion. Somehow, however, I found their concern about my eulogy rather unsettling.

At the funeral, I did try to do justice to her. It was not difficult to speak of her kindness and selflessness, for these were accurate descriptions of her. I mentioned how happy she was that her three sons used to walk to shul with me every Shabbat; how she always wanted them to become committed and loyal Jews, just as she herself was. And I added that in fact they did grow up to be a pride and joy to our people.

As I spoke this last sentence I knew I had overstepped my bounds. They had not been in shul for twenty-five years, and it was obvious from my earlier conversation with them that they were far removed from most things Jewish. I was clearly teetering on the edge between permissible funeral exaggerations and outright untruths.

To add to my sense of unease, as I glanced at them at that moment it became apparent to me that not one of their wives was Jewish.

So much for their commitment to Judaism. So much for the pride and joy they had become to their mother and to Judaism. So much for my own influence on them as kids.

As the casket was lowered, the boys lovingly touched it as it sank beneath ground level. One of them whispered, "We're sorry, Mama."

I wondered all day what they might have been sorry for. Had they had some strong disagreements? Or were they apologizing for the anguish they had undoubtedly caused Mama when they each married out of the faith? Was this why they had been so insistent that I say good things about her — to compensate for her shattered dreams, with three non-Jewish daughters-in-law and eight non-Jewish grandchildren?

dust to dust

Laymen are often far ahead of their rabbis in their sense of what is authentic and genuine. Our neighbor, Mr. Soberman, died, and since he was a member of one of the Reform congregations, their rabbi officiated at the funeral. The services were, of course, nontraditional: expensive metal casket, lots of flower wreaths, and everything dignified and antiseptic. At the graveside, the casket was not lowered into the grave and covered with earth as the halachah requires, but was laid to rest on two slats of wood on top of the grave — to be lowered and covered after the family left, and that to be done not by fellow Jews but by the anonymous cemetery workers.

Some people consider the halachic requirements insensitive because of its insistence that the casket be lowered into the earth — "dust to dust " — and be covered entirely with earth. In this way, the physical body is truly returned to its source, and the community participates in the final farewell. It is much more sensitive, they say, to ask the family to leave the gravesite and then do the actual burial in their absence, in order to spare them the pain. But halachah stresses that the honor and respect due the dead is the overriding consideration. (The family is suffering their own profound pain at their loss, and closing their eyes to the actual burial will not diminish that pain at all. On the contrary, to be a participant in the burial itself gives the living what they need most: a sense of finality and closing to the individual now being interred.) What could be more insensitive to the deceased than to leave the body alone, unburied, at the top of the grave, while loved ones, family, and friends turn their backs and go away — and then have complete strangers unceremoniously do the actual burial?

Mrs. Soberman understood all this instinctively. As the guests began leaving the graveside, she lingered behind. When they disappeared, she turned back to the grave and helped lower the casket into the ground. Then she began throwing fistfuls of earth onto the casket until the entire lid of the casket had some earth on it. She confided later to a friend that she had even convinced the mortician to permit the Orthodox Burial Society — the *Chevra Kadisha* — to prepare the body properly for burial: the ritual washing, the *tallis,* the traditional shrouds. All this without her rabbi's knowledge. She was certain he would have objected. Perhaps. Perhaps not.

a different universe

The men and women of the *Chevra Kadisha* do magnificent work. At any time of the day or night, on very short notice, they are prepared to go to the mortuary to prepare a body for burial. This includes loving and painstaking ritual washing and dressing, and the recitation of special prayers for the soul. In addition, Jewish law requires that between death and burial the body never be left alone, and so someone must always be in attendance, frequently overnight. All those who perform this final kindness are volunteers. Their only reward is a great *mitzvah* and the knowledge that they are performing a *chesed shel emet,* the ultimate in lovingkindness.

It is a difficult assignment, and that is why not very many people volunteer for this work. But those who do find it unusually fulfilling and rewarding. Our shul is blessed that we have enough truly dedicated men and women who are prepared to do what needs to be done as a labor of love — literally.

It was not always thus. In the early years, before the formal *chevra kadisha* society was organized, only one aged man and one aged woman were prepared to do this. When they themselves became too old to continue, we were unable to find anyone willing to replace them. Every death meant not only a funeral, but also the painful process of finding someone and begging him or her to do the required preparation just this one time.

Finally, we addressed the problem head on and called a mass meeting of our members to acquaint them with the facts of death. We presented the case for forming a *Chevra Kadisha* in our synagogue, underscoring the urgency of the matter and the great *chesed* involved — and were very pleased by the overwhelmingly positive response. By the end of the meeting, we had enough men and women volunteers to staff several teams of workers. We began training them and purchasing the necessary equipment — and prayed that they would not be needed for a very long time.

When the first death occurred, the women's team was mobilized. One woman, on her way down to the mortuary, called to tell me about her fears: "I have never seen a dead body, Rabbi. I'm really scared. I don't think I'm going to make it through the evening."

I assured her that she would be fine, that the good Lord would give her strength, and that I would say a prayer for her.

She called me the next morning."Rabbi, it was the most exhilarating experience of my life. I felt like I was in contact with a totally different universe. You can't use the word 'beautiful' about death, but that's what it was last night: beautiful. All four of us felt the same way. Thanks for encouraging us to do it." This was the general reaction of all the participants.

Similarly gratifying was the overwhelming appreciation of the families of the departed. The knowledge that their loved one was being prepared for burial by tender and caring hands was a tremendous source of comfort to them.

Our little Orthodox shul was the first to make the breakthrough. For several years, our teams even assisted the other synagogues in the community. Today even the Conservative synagogues have their own *chevra kadisha*, and I am confident that before very long the Reform congregations will organize their own groups as well.

Now, if we could only devise a way never to have to use these good people . . .

the sound of the shovel

A call from Mrs. Samuels, a prominent member of the Reform Temple. Her aged father, a long-time member of ours, had died, and she wanted me to officiate at his funeral because she knew that her father would have wanted that. But she had two requests. "I know that the Orthodox cover the casket with earth after it is lowered into the ground, and with all due respect I find that frankly a little barbaric. Is that an absolute must, or would it be possible not to do it this one time?"

I explained to her that it was an integral aspect of Jewish burial practice and could not be eliminated. I added that only a century ago people were referring to Jewish circumcision practices as "barbaric," and yet today it is universally accepted, so perhaps she should be careful before using such epithets about Jewish law. Absolutely nothing in Judaism is barbaric, I added.

"You're absolutely right, and I apologize for using that word. What I meant was that I personally find it unbearably painful. If you have to do it, fine. But if possible I would like to be excused from that part of the ritual. My second request is that since my father outlived all his friends, the only people at the funeral will be my own friends, and they're all Reform. Therefore, would it be okay with you if my own rabbi delivers a eulogy in addition to your eulogy?"

I replied that if she wanted to leave before the actual burial I would not stand in her way, but that I thought it would be more respectful to her father and to Jewish tradition to stay. I told her that I realized it would be painful, but every funeral of a loved one is painful. In the final analysis, this would be the proper tribute to her father, who had been a fully observant Jew. And then, in a bid to her own self-interest, I added, "In the long run, you yourself will feel better about it if you say goodbye to your father in the old-fashioned way."

"Well, I'll think about it," she said.

I went on to tell her that I had no problems with her rabbi delivering the eulogy, but I asked her to inform him in advance that the entire service would be conducted in keeping with Orthodox Jewish law. I also informed her about the required rending of her garment, which she readily accepted.

The graveside funeral was sparsely attended, and it was obvious that everyone present was from the Temple. After the eulogies and psalm readings, as we prepared to lower the casket and to cover it, I made my customary announcement that we would now proceed to cover the remains with the earth from which the body was created, in accordance with hallowed Jewish tradition and in keeping with the biblical expression "dust to dust." And, as I do at every funeral, I said, "Any of the pallbearers, as well as anyone else who wishes to join me in this holy task, is invited to do so." Mrs. Samuels had not left and was still in her place.

I took the shovel, dug into the loose earth, and placed the earth gently onto the casket, careful as always not to let it thud down harshly. I placed more earth and more earth, again and once again. None of the guests moved forward to participate. They stood immobile, as if frozen in place. As I worked back and forth, back and forth, the shovel moving in and out of the grave, I saw from my stooped vantage point only feet and shoes firmly planted on the ground. There was utter stillness in the air. The only sound was the sound of my shovel working back and forth, up and down. The family, the guests, everyone, stood stubbornly in place, watching me slowly fill the grave. I was puzzled. Were they trying to tell me that this was a barbaric rite, or were they simply embarrassed about engaging in a practice they had never seen?

Suddenly a figure appeared alongside me and began shoveling with me. I looked up. It was the Reform rabbi himself.

The two of us finished the task together, and I concluded the service with Psalm 23 and the *Kaddish*.

As we walked away from the grave, I turned to him and thanked him for his assistance. "Let me tell you something," he said. "Reform ritual doesn't require that you fill in the grave, and I never do it. But I couldn't stand seeing you doing all that by yourself. Someone should have stepped forward. I am very disappointed in them. It just wasn't right."

the old socialist's funeral

In the fifties, there still remained in Atlanta some remnants of the old Arbeiter Ring/Workmen's Circle organization. In the twenties and thirties this national council had branches in cities all across America. Primarily immigrants from Eastern Europe, their members were proudly Jewish and strove mightily to maintain the secular Yiddish culture of Eastern Europe. As indicated in their name, they were under the influence of socialism, and in their prime were militantly antireligious. They would not attend synagogue even on the High Holidays. Instead, on Rosh Hashanah and Yom Kippur they and their children would drop in on all the community's synagogues and temples, so that the kids would have a taste of Jewish culture, hear a real shofar, and learn how Jews used to pray and fast in ancient times. They had their own cemetery grounds, and I was told that their funerals were conducted without benefit of rabbi, without *Kaddish, El Molei Rachammim,* reference to God, or the world-to-come. Often the burial service included readings from great Yiddish writers like Y .L. Peretz and Shalom Aleichem.

By the fifties, however, the Arbeiter Ring had simply petered out. They had been unable to generate much enthusiasm in their offspring who, children of America, grew up apathetic to socialism, Judaism, and Yiddish. In addition, history, as it often does, played a mean trick on them and made an anachronism of their ideology.

The several aging veterans of the group whom I encountered in Atlanta were very literate and intelligent. They still maintained some idealism about Yiddish culture, which, at a time when idealism was so rare a commodity, I found refreshing despite the antireligious background from which it emanated. Their antireligious views had in any case mellowed considerably over the years. In fact, I discovered that they still had a vestigial attraction to classical Judaism. They were intrigued by this young Orthodox rabbi who actually spoke Yiddish fluently and even delivered an occasional Shabbos morning sermon in Yiddish to his nine old men. That this same rabbi was also a living embodiment of the old Judaism they had fought against in their prime did not seem to perturb them. They were, of course, not members in any synagogue, but I treated them with great deference and enjoyed our Yiddish conversations.

One day I received a call from the daughter of the old gentleman who for decades had been the most respected member of the Atlanta Yiddishists. He was an articulate, cultured, and learned person with whom I had had many discussions about God and Jewish tradition. Even though he consistently claimed to be an unbeliever, I had always found him highly intelligent, widely read — and irretrievably, but respectfully, antireligious. Without quite saying so explicitly, he still believed that religion was the opiate of the masses.

"Poppa died last night," said his daughter. "Before he died he made one request: he told me that he wants you to officiate at his funeral."

"Me?" I was stunned.

"Yes. You know how he felt about you."

"Thank you, but you know that if I officiate, I can only do it one way. We will need to use the *Chevra Kadisha,* of course, and I will conduct the service in the traditional manner. Are you sure that's all right with the family?"

"Rabbi, I've thought about that. I'm sure that if he asked for you, he knew that you would only do the funeral one way. So do what you have to do, and that's fine with all of us."

And so it was that this dedicated member of the Arbeiter Ring was buried in strict accordance with *halachic* requirements. The *Chevra Kadisha* dressed him in the traditional *kittel,* the funeral service contained the traditional *Kaddish,* the traditional memorial prayer, and the traditional readings from Psalms. I deviated from my normal practice in one major respect. Out of deference to him, I delivered the eulogy in Yiddish.

Chapter 11:
Please Make the
Ceremony Brief

f the funeral is the most painful of the rabbi's tasks, the wedding is certainly the most joyous. For one thing, no one at a wedding asks difficult questions about theodicy. How interesting that at the moment of a person's greatest joy no one asks the question: Why me? It occurs to no one to ask, Why was I chosen to be the recipient of such joy? What did I do to deserve this? Joy and good things are accepted as our due and our right; it is only when our joy is not unalloyed that we question the Creator.

But weddings do have this in common with funerals: as in all great rites of passage, they reveal our essential selves.

not the A&P

A telephone call from a woman, not a member: "You did my religious divorce last year, and now I wanted you to know that I'm getting married." I had never met her before her Jewish divorce, and was pleased that she had bothered to call.

"Would you be able to officiate at my wedding?"

I tell her I'd be delighted to do it, adding that I'd much rather do weddings than divorces.

Before I can ask her about the date and other particulars, she blurts out, "Rabbi, we'll have a lot of gentiles there. Can the ceremony be all in English so they'll understand, and could you make it, you know, not too long?"

I reply that I cannot change the service and cannot abbreviate it, but that I do normally translate certain key prayers.

"I want to make sure these people are able to follow everything," she says. "I want as much as possible of the service in English. I want you to explain every step of the ritual, so it will all be clear to everyone. Is Hebrew really a must?" ("I want" to the third power: modern life applied to religion.)

I tell her that while I, too, would like everyone to be able to follow, I cannot turn a religious service into a classroom exercise, and that I cannot change things to suit individual audiences. As gently as I can, I ask her: "Tell me, when a Catholic priest performs a wedding, and your Christian friends know that you and other Jews are going to be present, do they ask the priest to change the liturgy so that you will understand? Does the priest explain every step of the service as he performs it? Does he delete all the Latin phrases?"

She does not understand me. "Rabbi, all I want is for them

to follow the ceremony. I spoke to other rabbis and they said they would change it."

The proverbial cat is out of the proverbial bag. I resist the temptation to ask her why she does not invite one of the other rabbis to do the wedding. As if she had read my mind, she adds, "But I want you to do it because you treated me so nicely at my divorce. Besides, June is a very busy month for rabbis."

Obviously she has been shopping around, trying to make the best deal. But the best is yet to come: "Rabbi, may I ask what your fee is?"

(The question brings me back half a century. I am a little boy, and my father, a rabbi in Baltimore, is on the phone. I hear him saying with uncharacteristic annoyance: "Madam, I will not answer that question. This is not the A&P." When he gets off the phone, I ask him what that was all about. "She had the *chutzpah* to ask me what I charge for an unveiling ceremony. She is calling every rabbi in Baltimore and looking for the best price.")

Time contracts, and I find myself saying, "Really, now, this is not the A&P. Look, I will try to help you, but please discuss all this with your fiance, and tomorrow you can let me know what you decide. You are certainly not obligated to use me just because you called me. I want you to have the kind of wedding you will be happy with, but I can only give you the kind of ceremony that I know."

As soon as I hang up, I realize that with this pretty little speech I had embarrassed myself. I wanted her "to have the kind of wedding she will be happy with." Indeed! I sounded like the manager of an A&P that sells religious goods, and the customer is always right. What I should have told her was that I am not for hire, period.

The next morning I call her and inform her that I am not available to do her wedding, and wish her all the best. She is tenacious and asks me if perhaps I know a rabbi who will do it all in English. I tell her I don't know any. I do not add that she might be able to find the names of some rabbis in the Yellow Pages.

in what part of
the Bible is Gibran?

To have a wedding that is different, one that everyone will talk about — that is the goal of so many young couples. I know of a couple who wanted a genuine wedding, one that would be unencumbered by the phoniness and artificiality that marks so many wedding ceremonies. They would be married out of doors, under the heavens. Fine. That's in full keeping with Jewish tradition. Furthermore, instead of subjecting the guests to the customary pre-wedding songs — "O Promise Me," "Sunrise, Sunset," and other Irving Berlin or Fiddler-on-the-Roof banalities — they would offer "readings." Which readings? They would be from Khalil Gibran's *The Prophet.*

Gibran was *de rigeur* when I was in high school. Moody and introspective teenagers would memorize entire passages from it and carry the book around ostentatiously so that all might note how sensitive they were. Gibran, the Indian poet-philosopher of adolescence, who writes of love and trees and sky and earth: the poet of puberty. Next to Thomas Wolfe — before we became aware of his anti-Jewish prejudices — Gibran was the teenage pseudointellectual's status symbol and security blanket.

This sweet and sensitive young couple had rediscovered Gibran a generation later. The wedding was duly held, the readings took place, and the guests nodded approvingly to one another. I thanked the good Lord that I was not the officiant.

The whole business saddened me. If there are to be readings — and I'm not at all convinced that a wedding must be a literary soiree — do we have to go to India for our poets? Would Proverbs 31 about the "Woman of Valor" have been inappropriate? Or some of the Psalms?

Even more disheartening was the reaction of a nice lady who had been present at the wedding. She was very impressed and asked me in what part of the Bible Gibran could be found. The innocence of her request was touching in a way, but it demonstrated the many miles we still have to go in order to create a critical mass of knowledgeable Jews.

* * *

Although weddings are exalted moments, on occasion they have created great difficulties for me. For example, I refuse to officiate at weddings where nonkosher food will be served. There are, after all, excellent kosher facilities in our synagogue and in major hotels. Occasionally a nonobservant member family will insist on having a nonkosher menu, and the resultant negotiations between us are not very easy. I try to explain that a wedding is a religious event and not just a social function, and that it is inconsistent to have a religious ceremony with prayers to God and appeals for His blessings and then to turn right around and behave in a way that is in direct contradiction to God's requirements. (It is more than merely inconsistent; it is insulting, but I try to use the softer term.) There are no exceptions to my policy, and in most cases the family bends to the rules because they want me to officiate. But weddings are sensitive occasions, and the residue of resentment against the shul and its rabbi does not quickly dissipate.

The influence of New York Orthodox weddings, and a certain new affluence of our own, have not been a positive development for us. The simple Southern wedding of forty years ago has been transformed. Because of this influence and our own affluence, we too now experience the gaudy emphasis on food, flowers, and decorations.

Other New York wedding customs have made their way south as well. There, in order to distribute honors under the *chuppah* to as many people as possible, a number of different people are asked to recite the various *berachot*. My practice in Atlanta was to recite all the *berachot* myself or together with a second officiant, but never to have them distributed wholesale to friends and relatives. In this way we were able to avoid the delicate issue of vetoing certain people because they could not read Hebrew or were not conversant with the *berachah* or were simply not observant at all.

But the Northern custom has insinuated itself into our lives, and since it was not halachically forbidden, I was unable to keep it out. I tried to place certain restrictions on its practice, striving mightily to maintain a sense of the sanctity of the occasion — not always with great success.

the rabbi and the photographer

Of course, the true king of the wedding in New York is often the photographer/video man. He is in control of events; he is the producer and the director of the drama. He tells the rabbis where to stand, when they may speak, and quite literally pushes the rabbis around during the ceremony in order to get a close-up picture of the ring, or the wedding certificate, or the drinking of the wine, or the breaking of the glass. To many New York photographers, the rabbi at a wedding is simply one of the props, useful for certain pictures, but by and large an expendable potted plant. Everyone knows that if an event is not recorded on film, it never really took place.

At one particular New York wedding in which I participated, the photographer behaved like a middle linebacker, riding roughshod over everyone under the *chuppah*. As the groom was about to place the ring on the bride's finger, the photographer tried to shove me aside so he could bring his camera in close. I refused to budge. He shoved harder. I ignored him and literally stood my ground. "Rabbi," he hissed at me, "move over so I can get this shot."

I whispered back, "Sorry, you'll have to wait. I must be close in to say the next *berachah*."

"They'll be furious if I miss this shot."

"They'll be more furious if I don't say the *berachah*. So will

God. What's more important?"

He didn't answer, and I didn't budge.

This photographer tried to knock me off my feet, but I remember one wedding where the bride was literally unable to stand on her own two feet.

In the middle of the ceremony Ruth Fishman's groom whispered to me in alarm, "Rabbi, Ruth is about to faint."

I looked at her. Her eyes were half closed, her face was as white as her gown, she was swaying from side to side. Her mother grabbed Ruth's elbow and held it firm. I rapidly read the remaining *berachot,* gave a quick thirty-second speech, and wished them *Mazal Tov.* The groom grabbed the bride's elbow and escorted her back up the aisle.

Later, at the reception, one of the guests said to me politely: "Enjoyed the ceremony, rabbi. You did a good job. That's how I like wedding ceremonies — short and sweet."

marrying Sam

The lady on the other end of the phone asked, "Do you do weddings for non-members?"

"Occasionally, yes. It depends on a number of factors."

"Do you have a set fee for doing a wedding?"

Something about her questions mildly annoyed me, but I didn't quite know why. I responded, "You sound like you're shopping around."

"Well, not exactly."

"Are you the one who's getting married?"

Now it came out. "No, I'm calling for my boss."

"Is he marrying you?"

She giggled. "No."

"You mean he's asking you to call around town and find a rabbi for him?"

"Yes, I guess so."

"Please tell your boss that marriage is important enough

for him to call the rabbi himself and not to ask his secretary to do it for him." Obviously, the boss was too busy to worry about petty details like arranging for a rabbi. A secretary makes airline reservations, dinner reservations, theater reservations — so why shouldn't she do rabbi reservations?

"Yes, sir," she said. "I will have him call you. By the way, would you mind telling me your name?"

"On second thought," I said, "please tell your boss that he really ought to find someone else to do his wedding — maybe someone whose name he knows."

The poor woman, an innocent victim of her boss's insensitivity, mumbled an apology, and we said goodbye.

the document caused trembling

I once held in my hand a document that made me tremble. A young woman had come to see me with a strange question. Her great-grandparents were German Jews, but in the early nineteen-hundreds they had become apostates and abandoned Judaism to become Lutherans. Now the great-granddaughter, who was not raised as a Jewess, wanted to know whether she could still be considered a Jewess. She showed me the old German conversion certificate of her great-grandparents. The certificate, written in flowery German calligraphy on fine parchment paper, attested that on such and such a date, both husband and wife voluntarily became members of the Lutheran Church. (The pain, searing enough, was intensified by the document's German language and by the choice of the church of the virulently anti-Semitic Martin Luther.)

One can only speculate about what could have motivated two Jews to abandon their faith in such a formal and conscious way. Assimilation in their society was spreading rapidly; there was no identity whatsoever with Judaism, which was presumed dead; parents wanted to spare the children the pain of being a Jew; and perhaps there were economic considerations as well. Once they converted, Jews could join previously closed guilds or enter trades from which they had been barred. Who can know the complex motivations that contributed to this act of treason against the Jewish people?

As I held this document, I felt as if I were touching something loathsome. Here were Jews officially abandoning ship, turning their backs on themselves. But we triumphed. Here in front of me was the great-grandchild, a twenty-three-year-old woman who wanted to be considered a Jewess and who was rejecting the rejection of her own great-grandparents.

I like to think that her great-grandparents, after having had a century to think about it, are pleased by the return of their offspring to the ship of the Jews.

the inspiring Polish Catholic

Sometimes encouragement and strength come from unlikely places. I remember the woman who came in to talk to me this summer. Many years ago she had come over from Europe together with her husband and seven children. She was a Polish Catholic. During World War II, her parents had risked their lives to save a young Jewish boy from the Nazis. He had somehow escaped the roundup to Treblinka, and had come to their farm in search of food after wandering the countryside for weeks. They hid him in their barn, fed him, and tended to him for three full years. After the war, the Jewish boy and the Polish Catholic daughter were married.

The girl suffered many indignities from her townspeople. They called her a Jew-lover and prostitute, but she stuck with him. She did not convert to Judaism, nor he to Catholicism. When they came to America, they joined neither synagogue nor church. He observed none of the *mitzvot*, but did come to shul on Yom Kippur. Of course, neither she nor her children are Jews.

Now, thirty years later, she was wondering whether she should formally convert to Judaism. She told me that she was not sure she wanted to, but thought that perhaps it would be easier for her husband if she were to become Jewish. She was also concerned about burial because she knew that as a non-Jew she could not be buried in a Jewish cemetery. At the same time, deep inside her she did not feel it was right to take on a new religion just to make her husband feel better or to be buried next to him, and that even though she was no longer a religious Catholic, religion was too important a thing to be dealt with frivolously.

I did not attempt to persuade her to convert. I felt it wisest to maintain the status quo. We decided to discuss it further at a later date.

I remember how touched I was by her goodness and her integrity. Here was a woman who had her values straight. She had an instinctive appreciation for religion; she sensed deeply that changing one's religion involves more than changing outfits.

not a hypocrite

I was not touched at all by the question Gil Wolf asked me. Gil is a charming person, but he lacks what she had: religious principle. Gil, in his mid-forties, divorced his wife because of his non-Jewish girlfriend. He has three children, sends them to Jewish day schools, wants them to have a solid Jewish education. He keeps telling them to be proud Jews, to study hard.

One day Gil came in to see me. "I know it's not right, but I am going to marry this woman. Rabbi, give me some way to explain this to the kids. I don't want them to think I'm a hypocrite."

Rabbis are often confronted with questions they cannot possibly answer. Why do the righteous suffer, the wicked prosper? Why do innocent children die? These are the classic questions. According to the Sages, these are what Moses was referring to when he asked God: "Show me Thy essence." Rabbis learn to expect such unanswerable questions. But no one warned me about questions like Gil's.

I suggested to him that the best lesson he might give his children is to tell them that he loves this woman and wants very much to marry her, but he's giving her up because he is a Jew and she is not. That would be a very important signal for them, and they would never forget it. He refused to consider this. He wanted to have it both ways: he wanted both his non-Jewish girlfriend and the Jewish loyalty of his children. "Rabbis are supposed to know the answers. Can't you come up with something for me? I'm really in a bind, Rabbi."

After I convinced him that I had no answer for him that would please him, he asked me his second question: if he married out of the faith, could he still be buried in an Orthodox Jewish cemetery, and would an Orthodox rabbi officiate at his funeral — I, for example?

"Sure, Gil, and would you mind if I said the following in your eulogy? Gil was a great guy — sweet, loving, and charitable — except for one small thing: he divorced his wife of twenty years to marry a non-Jewish woman half her age."

Chapter 12:
Rabbi, Talk to My Son

Intermarriage is the kind of marriage that is really a funeral dirge for Judaism.

I was invited to participate in a panel discussion with a Protestant minister and a Catholic priest on the subject of intermarriage. Because it was taking place at the university, and because this is an issue for Jewish students — in truth, it is not really a live issue, but rather an accepted fact of life — I accepted the assignment.

The minister argued that such marriages violate the integrity of one's faith and uniqueness. I agreed, and added that from Judaism's point of view an intermarriage is often the final step into full assimilation for the Jewish participant.

The priest, however, thought intermarriage was a splendid idea, claiming that it is an "extension of one's community" with other peoples and faiths, and that one's own religion can be maintained even in the context of a mixed marriage. I was surprised to hear this from a Roman Catholic, and suspected he was merely playing for the gallery. Certainly his point of view was a big hit with the students.

But what disturbed me most was his attitude toward Judaism. "Why do you maintain your separatism so rigidly, why is your faith so parochial?" he asked me. Again, it was surprising to hear this from a Catholic; they are normally quite understanding and respectful of Jewish distinctiveness. I heard echoes of Haman's accusations against the Jews in the Book of Esther.

"On the contrary," I replied. "It is Judaism which has room in its heaven for the righteous of the world. From our perspective, you, a Roman Catholic priest, can theoretically have a share in the world-to-come. But until I accept Jesus, your Catholic heaven has no room whatsoever for me, no matter how exemplary a life I lead. I do not accept the divinity of Jesus; hence I am, from your point of view, an unbeliever and am eternally damned.

"That's why Christianity has missionaries — to save our souls from eternal damnation. Judaism has no missionaries. We do not claim that your soul is damned because you do not accept our faith. Furthermore, Catholicism claims that it is the new and the true Israel, that it has replaced Judaism, and that Judaism and the people Israel no longer exist because they have been subsumed into Christianity. Which one is rigid and parochial — Judaism or Catholicism?"

I must have spoken with considerable passion, because I received a round of applause from the Jewish students.

One of the student questioners, not Jewish, suggested that the Jewish insistence on remaining separate tended to make Christians dislike Jews. I asked her if she had ever been a victim of Jewish prejudice or discrimination or hatred. She had not. I told her that there were many Jews in this room who had been the object of Christian hatred, and that the "religion of love" had been burning Jews at one stake or another for two thousand years. I asked her if Jews had ever built crematoria or gas chambers in which to burn other human beings, and if those Germans and Poles who were involved in such things in Europe were Christians or Jews. I suggested that she contrast the historical treatment of Jews in Christian Europe with Jewish treatment of Arabs in Israel today, where Arabs can be citizens and vote, and even serve in the Israeli parliament.

The priest interrupted. "Why can't you forget about Germany and the crematoria? Jews ought to learn to forgive and forget. Love is all that matters."

Cliche, thy name is clergyman. "The crime in Europe was so heinous," I retorted heatedly, "that it is beyond the human power of forgiveness. Only God — or the victims themselves — can forgive something like that. And, by the way, the Jewish people is still waiting for an expression of Christian love that might include the Jews."

"If the Jews are always going to remain separate, how can you ever expect persecution to stop?" he persisted.

I was awestruck. "Are you justifying persecution because we are different?"

"You misunderstand. You simply have to become part of civilization again." He said it with a benevolent smile. I wanted to throw my chair at him.

"I'm not sure that I want to be part of a civilization that incinerated one-third of my people for no reason other than that they were Jews." Again the Jewish students applauded.

It was an agonizing evening, but in one respect it was a success; it vividly demonstrated to the Jews present that they have not as yet been accepted into the ranks of humanity. Perhaps this will give some of them pause before they abandon their Judaism in favor of marrying out of the faith.

it's my life, don't interfere

There are any number of causes for the skyrocketing rate of Jewish intermarriage: ignorance of Judaism, the open society in which we live, and our ethos of immediate gratification.

Steve Miller, all of twenty-five, just out of graduate school, is a case in point. His father called me last month and asked me to talk to Steve. As soon as he said, "Talk to Steve," I knew what the problem was: He was about to marry out of the faith. (These days, in what is surely a sign of our times, many non-observant parents tell me that they are relieved when a son comes home and informs them they are going to marry a non-Jewish girl. "It's a heckuva lot better than him telling me, 'Pa, I'm a homosexual.' At least he's normal.")

It's twenty-five years too late, but I "talk" to Steve. It is a non-starter; he is "in love," and besides, he doesn't see why religion should be a barrier between people — wasn't religion designed to bring people together?

My arguments about preserving the uniqueness of the Jewish people are meaningless. "What uniqueness? It's because we try to be different that we have anti-Semitism, Rabbi." (I didn't tell him that he sounded just like the priest.)

I talk about our mission in the world. "Mission? I didn't know we were missionaries."

I talk about loyalty to a way of life that has been battered by persecution and mass destruction, and yet has outlived its persecutors. "Would you abandon ship after all that your people has sacrificed to maintain this heritage of ours?"

"Well, maybe we have already fulfilled our historic function. Maybe it's time we amalgamated into the rest of the world. We have already made our contribution to civilization, and I'm very proud of that. Maybe it's time to say Enough."

I try a personal approach. "Marriages today are very risky. So many end in divorce even when the two partners come from the same background. In your case, with each of you stemming from totally different backgrounds, the chances of success are slim."

"Rabbi, she is just like me. She has no religious background. I go to shul once a year to please my father, and she goes to church once a year to please her mother. A perfect match. Besides, if it doesn't work out, we'll just call it quits."

I bring up the matter of children: how will they be raised?

"Rabbi, we don't believe in forcing them into any mold. We'll let them choose a religion when they grow up."

For an intelligent young man, he has swallowed every imaginable cliche. "What about your parents?" I ask. "This will all but kill them."

"I don't see why they're taking it so hard," he responds. "They want me to sacrifice this beautiful girl for Judaism. But what have they ever sacrificed for Judaism? They always lived their lives the way they wanted to and nothing stood in the way. Big deal — my father goes to shul on Rosh Hashanah and Yom Kippur, and conducts a Seder, and says *Kaddish* for his parents once a year, and my mother lights candles on Friday night — right on top of the TV set. They celebrate Friday night watching inane programs on TV, with the candles burning brightly! My dad doesn't keep Shabbat or kashrut and doesn't even own a set of *tefillin*, but he insists that I marry a Jewish girl. It's my life, and I am entitled to live it as I want it, in my own way. My parents are hypocrites, that's what they are, plain and simple."

So much for "talking" with Steve.

The truth is that by the time parents ask me to talk to their sons and daughters about intermarriage, it is too late, particularly when the youngsters have had only a fleeting relationship with Judaism, the synagogue, or with me, and the couple is already deeply involved with one another.

"Rabbi, talk to my son." It is the fathers and mothers who need to talk to their sons and daughters — as soon as they are born, they need to talk to them about being a Jew. And beyond talking about Judaism, they have to live Judaism.

Steve's parents are kind and sweet souls and mean well, but they know very little about Judaism, and have nothing religious to relay to their children. Poor things, they will soon have a non-Jewish grandchild to show for their neglect of Jewishness. Nevertheless, I know that they are terribly distraught over Steve. I wish I could have been of some help. My heart aches for them, and for us.

It is curious: Why should they really care about his marrying out? They have never demonstrated any concern about anything in Jewish life — in fact, about anything at all outside their own selves. If I wanted to write a manual on how to ensure that your son will marry out of the faith, Helen and Morty Miller would be the prime model: observe nothing Jewish in the home, give your child no Jewish learning at all, attend synagogue three days a year, demonstrate by your giving and living that Judaism is totally irrelevant in your life.

The fact is that the fear of intermarriage is nevertheless a real one even among nonpracticing Jews. Somehow it's a vestigial instinct that they themselves cannot articulate — an instinct that tells them that such things will destroy us as a people and write *finis* to Jewish history and destiny. But even this instinct, under the pressures of life in America, is beginning to wane, and the stigma and the fear of intermarriage has all but faded away.

I'd rather she marry a goy

At least Steve's parents were concerned. In some cases, Jewish parents have given up the ghost and bowed to the inevitable. I know one person who would prefer his daughter to marry out of the faith than to marry a certain kind of Jew.

A Hasidic young man came to town this year as a representative of a yeshivah in Brooklyn. He wore the traditional Hasidic garb: broad-brimmed black hat, long black *kappote*, black tie, side curls, full beard. He was about thirty, still single, very charming, very intelligent, and very handsome. He made the rounds of the various offices and business establishments in town, collecting the yearly contributions for his institution.

After he left town, one of his contributors, a prominent

member of the Jewish establishment, complained to me about the Hasid's visit to his office. "Rabbi," he said to me, "why does he have to dress like that? This is America. Let him dress like an American. I was embarrassed to tell my office staff that he was a Jew."

"But Hank," I said, "wasn't he a delightful person?"

"Yes. I have to admit that. Great personality. And good-looking, too."

I teased him a bit. "Hank, he's single. You have a single daughter. Would you like me to introduce him to her?"

"Rabbi, you gotta be kidding! A guy like that?"

"Listen, Hank, at least he's Jewish. It's hard to find a Jewish son-in-law these days."

"Rabbi, I'll be honest with you. Rather than have her bring home a fanatic like that, I'd rather she marry a nice *goy*. We'll get him converted and that's that."

"You can't be serious. You'd rather she marry a non-Jew than a Jew?"

"That's not my idea of a Jew. We left that stuff behind us long ago."

His words kept echoing in my ears: "That's not my idea of a Jew." I shudder to think what his idea of a Jew is.

Even more revealing was his "we'll get him converted and that's that." Everyone knows that when there is an impending intermarriage in the family, it is not difficult to find non-Orthodox rabbis, and occasionally Orthodox ones, who are ready and willing to give their imprimatur to quickie conversions for the non-Jewish spouse. Six or eight easy lessons, and presto! — out pops a Jew. No requirements or commitments to maintain *mitzvot,* or to observe Shabbat, to know even a minimum about Judaism or Jewish history, or even to be able to read Hebrew. With her new certificate she is entitled to a Jewish wedding, complete with caterer and smorgasbord and photographers and marriage consultants from the fancy stores, and she is now eligible to emulate the tens of thousands of born Jews who observe next to nothing, and to bear children who will be even less conscious of their

Jewishness than she — children who in any case will be halachically non-Jews.

mass conversions

These so-called converts are innocent dupes. The ones who will have to give an accounting are the rabbis who perform such conversions on a mass scale. By and large, they are engaging in this charade because they cannot resist the pressure from their congregants to do so. The fact that there are halachic standards as to who can and who cannot convert to Judaism, and requirements about *mitzvah* observance, is quickly rationalized away.

Judaism has always welcomed genuine converts, and we have been enriched by those who, for no ulterior motives, have chosen to accept the Covenant of Abraham. Our shul includes a number of authentic converts who accept the yoke and the privilege of being a Jew. They are truly in the spirit of Ruth the Moabite: "Your people is my people, and your God is my God . . . and only death shall separate us." Conversion requires more commitment than buying a new outfit; it is serious business. Those who possess this commitment, and the courage and faith and inner strength to forge a new path in their lives, are very special individuals.

I once proposed to the community rabbis that we should all agree on a one-year moratorium on conversions. Conversions, I argued, only encourage mixed marriages and are by and large merely a papering over of an intermarriage in order to keep peace in certain families.

All the non-Orthodox rabbis disagreed with me. It would be unjust, even authoritarian, they said. We have no right to bar the door to anyone. One Reform rabbi, who required nothing of his converts, said, "Conversion is a very good way to increase the population of the Jewish people. After all, we lost millions in the Holocaust." He, who himself was helping create a new, self-inflicted holocaust in America, was completely serious.

A Conservative rabbi asked me, "But what do you do when a member of yours has a child who is marrying a non-Jew?"

"I don't do conversions, period."

"But you have to do something for them when they come to you with this problem."

"I try very hard to do something. I try persuasion, pressure, whatever I think will help prevent the intermarriage. But I am not going to do a conversion that is on the face of it an insult to my intelligence — and to the intelligence of the convert, if he or she has any sensitivity at all. If I find a legitimate convert who is genuinely seeking to become a Jew without ulterior motives, without reasons of marriage, I will steer him or her to a proper Beth Din and help get it done. Otherwise, I am not in the rabbinate to aid and abet intermarriages."

Then he let the cat out of the bag: "What do you do if it's a very prominent family that needs the conversion for one of their children? If you don't do the conversion, you will lose them as members."

I retorted: "I know. Your congregation already has several of our families who left us because I wouldn't convert their children's girlfriends on demand."

the intermarried uncle

I will admit this: the pressures from congregants to convert their children's non-Jewish partners are overwhelming, and unless a rabbi establishes a clear policy about this he is going to find himself in serious trouble. In my case, from the very beginning I made it clear that I simply did not do conversions for purposes of marriage, and so the pressures upon me were lessened considerably. But not entirely. For example:

We have an unwritten rule in shul that we do not call to the Torah a Jew who has married out of the faith. (Nor do we offer honors to a man who has divorced his wife civilly but refuses to grant her a *get.*) In this small way we express our disapproval of an act which is a rejection of Judaism.

There is precious little a community can do today when a person intermarries; no sanctions can be imposed, no excommunication.

At the very least, however, a synagogue should not give public religious honors to a person who in effect publicly abandons Judaism and tosses overboard his future and that of his children. To give him a Torah *aliyah* in which he blesses God, "*Asher natan lanu Torat emet*/ Who has given us a Torah of truth . . . and chosen us from among the nations" is a mockery, and we simply do not permit it.

If a relative of a Bar Mitzvah is intermarried, as now happens all too frequently, the offending person comes to the Bar Mitzvah services, participates in the *davening*, but receives no special honors or recognition. We do not embarrass him, but neither do we go out of our way to honor him. This is so obvious that it has never been an issue — until one recent incident.

Lo and behold, it came to pass that the uncle of a forthcoming Bar Mitzvah, intermarried, expected an *aliyah*. I told the parents of the Bar Mitzvah family about our policy in such cases. They were not happy about it, but said they understood my position and would so inform him. But the uncle, who lives in another city, called me. He was very upset. Why was I singling him out? He loved his nephew and wanted to participate in his *simcha*.

I explained our policy.

"This is not just, it's not fair," he fumed. "How can Jews do such things to one another?"

I was in no mood to be subtle with him. "You speak of justice? Is it just for a Jew to do this to Judaism, to marry out of the faith and then to come back to that faith and demand that it honor him during religious services — and before the very Torah which this Jew has turned his back on? In Yiddish there's a word for that. It's called *chutzpah*, sir."

"I resent that. I haven't turned my back on any Judaism. Are you saying that I'm not a Jew?"

"I am not saying that at all. You are a Jew. But I can't say that you are a loyal Jew. Marrying out of the faith constitutes turning your back on the faith. You may not have thought of it that way because so many people are doing it, but surely you agree that intermarriage is not exactly an affirmation of our heritage. Besides which, the issue here is whether someone who has married out of the faith can be called to the Torah and recite the special *berachot* about the uniqueness and chosenness of the Torah and the Jewish people. We try to be honest with ourselves, and we do not permit it."

"But Rabbi, she is a very nice person. Why are you condemning her?"

"I am not condemning her at all. I'm sure that she is a fine person, but you know that that's not the point. You turned your back on Judaism, not she. I am sorry, sir, in more ways than you can ever know."

buying a rabbi

There was also the unhappy matter of Ludwig Katz's daughter, who was about to marry out of the faith. Ludwig and his wife were extremely upset about it. There were tears, screams, wailing — but Myrna was going to have her way, as she always did, and she was going to marry the fellow despite the turmoil she was creating.

This is how the parents, after all, had raised her. They had grown up in poverty, had become wealthy through sheer grit and hard labor, and were determined that their children would never have to suffer for want of anything. Whatever Myrna wanted, Myrna got. At her sixteenth birthday party, held at a fancy hotel at a cost of some twenty-five thousand dollars, her parents presented her with a simple little birthday gift: the keys to an expensive sports car. And when Myrna inevitably started accepting dates from non-Jews, the parents' objections were so tepid that Myrna got the message that it was not really a problem. And now, at age nineteen, she was all set to marry Jim.

Jim was willing to "become a Jew." We met together, and it was clear that, though he was a fine young man, he had no intention of changing his way of life in the slightest. He was forthright with me and told me clearly that he was not interested in the discipline of a traditional Jewish life. His Jewish friends kept nothing, and he would be just like his Jewish friends.

This was certainly his prerogative. But it was also my prerogative not to do his conversion, and I so informed him and Myrna's parents. In order to placate them, he began attending weekly conversion classes at one of the Reform temples.

Myrna's father knew that this was insufficient and asked me to reconsider. He was smart enough to know that Jim's primary motive in becoming a Jew was not Moses but Myrna, and so Ludwig did not try to convince me on those grounds. Instead, he put it on a personal basis, as a favor to him. His concern was what others would think. If I were to do the conversion, it would put a public *hechsher* on things and they could "have a big wedding" and not be embarrassed. Jim was such a nice boy, after all.

I was sympathetic with Ludwig's predicament, but I explained very patiently that Jewish law is very clear: we accept converts who sincerely desire to become part of the people Israel and who want to serve the God of Israel in every possible way. To be a "nice boy" is in itself insufficient.

Ludwig, however, was not listening. "Rabbi, it would make my wife and me so happy. Can't you help us just a little bit?"

"I wish I could help you, but you're asking something that's impossible for me to do in good conscience."

He persisted. "If you could only do this favor for us, I would be so grateful. I would do anything." His voice choked up and he began to weep. "It would mean so much to us. I'd do anything for you or the shul if you could help us. Anything. I'm ready to give ten thousand dollars to any cause at all — I would give it directly to you and you could do with it as you like — if you would reconsider." There was a strange look in Ludwig's eyes as he said this, but I couldn't quite decipher it.

"Ludwig, please don't press me. You know that my hands are tied."

"I know that, Rabbi, I know that. But I'm so miserable."

The vague sense of discomfort I felt during this conversation gradually turned to resentment and anger as the day went on. It began to dawn on me that although he had not, strictly speaking, made the offer, Ludwig had actually tried in his desperation to bribe me, to buy me: "You could do with it as you like."

In the world in which he functioned and in which he made all his money, everyone has his price: businessmen, lawyers, politicians. So why not rabbis?

Why not rabbis, indeed? Everyone is subject to the temptation of being bought off. That's why the Torah in Deuteronomy 16:19 warns that "bribery blinds the eyes of the wise, and distorts the words of the righteous." The righteous! The Torah here is referring to a righteous man who takes a bribe. That is to say, until the transaction of the bribe he was righteous. Everyone is warned about bribes; no one is considered immune.

saying yes and saying no

The historic strength and hallmark of the Jews has been our ability to say no to the world, but in my mind there swirl images of innocent, unlearned Jews who can only say yes to the world around them. I think of my encounter with the catering manager of one of the major local hotels. A Jewish woman, she was given the assignment of discussing with me the possibility of the hotel opening up a kosher kitchen.

As part of our discussions, we had to meet with the executive chef. As we walk towards his office, she tells me that she and the chef are planning to be married. I wish her *Mazal Tov.* She says, "He's not Jewish, he's a Catholic. I can't help it, Rabbi, I love him."

Her confession throws me a bit off balance, coming as it does in the context of burning out the ovens and kosherizing the utensils, so I tell her that whenever she wants to talk about the marriage more thoroughly, I would be happy to talk with her.

In the executive chef's office, in the midst of technical discussions about our kashrut requirements, the subject of marriage comes up again. Neither of them has ever discussed this with a rabbi, and since they have me captive in their office, they apparently want to make the most of it.

I tell them that Judaism is opposed to intermarriage, and I go through the entire well-known litany — to which they respond with the well-known deafness. I ask them what they will be doing about the religious upbringing of their children.

"I'm not that religious," he says. "It doesn't matter to me one way or the other." He is a smooth-talking, handsome, forty-year-old, the very model of a modern major hotel executive.

She: I would want to raise my children Jewish.

I: Why?

She: Because Jewish is so . . . good . . . so warm . . . so family oriented. It just gives you a good feeling. I love it.

I: If you love it, surely you realize that by marrying out of the faith you are in effect abandoning it.

She: Not really. I intend to maintain the warmth of Judaism in our home, and Ronnie here has no objections. I want my children to know the beauty of their religion.

She was mouthing all the right words, poor girl, but she knew not what she was saying. I point out that it will be impossible to impart Judaism to a child whose father is not Jewish and who therefore cannot participate in raising him in the traditions of the Jewish people.

She: Well, he's a very warm and good person, so he can definitely pass that part of Judaism on to the children.

I: But Judaism is more than being warm and good. It also makes demands.

She: What kind of demands? I never heard of demands besides kosher.

I: Listen, Judaism is not just sugary cotton candy. Judaism is a religion of deeds, of do's and don'ts — which we call Divine *mitzvot,* or commandments. Our commandments deal with food, with sex, with the intellect, with the way we eat and the way we talk. Wherever you turn in Judaism there are directions and demands. Judaism is not just lighting candles on Friday night and eating chicken soup. Jews sacrifice for their Judaism, they give up things, they always have. We have even given up our lives for our religion.

The executive chef says, "But isn't religion supposed to make you happy? Why should anyone want to die for it?"

It is obvious that I am making no inroads. I feel like a punchy, pummeled boxer in the fifteenth round. But I must keep trying, so I say, "A Jew certainly ends up a far more happy person when he follows his religion, but the purpose of Judaism is not just to make us happy. Its purpose is to make us holy, to teach us how to serve God and our fellow human beings. One of Judaism's demands is that we do what God wants us to do even if at that particular moment we would rather not do it. And that, in the final analysis, is the highest form of genuine happiness."

They shake their heads in disbelief. Clearly all this is totally new to them. The idea that religion makes demands, and that there is anything to life other than personal gratification is beyond belief — literally. As she escorts me down to the lobby, I raise the question of children again, and of how unrealistic it is to try to raise children as Jews when the father is a non-Jew.

"But he is willing," she says.

"Fine," I say, "but what happens on Christmas and Easter and Palm Sunday? What do you do with your child?"

"Well," says she, "my own parents had a Christmas tree in our home, with all the stockings and the trimmings. But we didn't go to church and all that. It was just a nice family holiday. Look at me, I turned out okay — so why can't I do the same with my children?"

Dear God above, Father of us all, You who answered Moses when even he had lost the strength to go on: Help me to maintain my sense of balance, my sanity and stability; let me not become cynical or bitter or angry. Save me from the depths of despair. Allow me to continue to hope for our future, to continue loving our Jewish people, to keep trying.

Chapter 13:
I've Hired and Fired
Dozens of Rabbis
Like You

Marriages, conversions, divorce: all are high on the rabbi's agenda. The word "divorce" used to be whispered; it stigmatized the couple. Today it has become fully acceptable. People put no more commitment into a marriage than they do into buying a new suit of clothing. In today's consciousness there is something glamorous about being divorced, something adventurous. Couples who stay married for several decades sometimes feel that there is something not entirely quite right with them. They are old-fashioned, out of tune, anachronisms. Newly engaged couples hold it out as a possibility even before they are married. At pre-marital counseling sessions with me they will say without any hesitation, "We wouldn't want it to happen, of course, but if it doesn't work out, we can always get a divorce."

Commitment and sacrifice through thick and thin for any cause or ideal is not part of today's life style.

if it doesn't work out

The weddings are lovely, the receptions joyous, the food and drink plentiful. But most worrisome to a rabbi is the cavalier attitude with which so many young couples seem to enter marriage. The overriding self-centeredness of contemporary life suffuses everything and makes it highly unlikely that there will be a successful marriage partnership. When the husband cares only for himself, and the wife cares only for herself, the marriage is headed nowhere. The irony of it all is that selflessness in marriage — as in all things — turns out to be the one guarantee of satisfying the self. But when I speak of such things in premarital interviews, I get the unmistakable feeling that I am not being understood.

A rabbi cannot play God and decide who may marry whom. If there are no halachic impediments to the couple marrying one another, I cannot refuse to officiate. But the truth is that I often wish I could. As these couples walk down the aisle, I say a silent prayer for them: Please, dear God, don't let them come back to me in a few years asking for a *get*.

* * *

Most American Jews — if they are aware of it at all — still do not take seriously the requirement for a *get*. Jewish law forbids either party to remarry without first obtaining the *get*. The consequences of remarriage without it are very serious. A man who marries a woman who is civilly divorced but has no *get* is, according to Jewish law, marrying a married woman, with obvious implications for adultery and the legitimacy of any future offspring. That's why rabbis move heaven and earth to make certain that when a couple is civilly divorced, they also obtain the *get*. But since divorce is frequently the result of a festering anger and resentment between the couple, this is not always an easy matter. A rabbi has to exercise all the persuasive powers and patience at his disposal when he encounters a recalcitrant and angry spouse.

it's none of your affair

One of our newer members, a divorcee of several years, had just learned about the importance of a *get*. She contacted her ex-husband, who now lived in another city, and asked his cooperation in obtaining the religious divorce. He saw no reason for it and refused her.

I called him up. I mentioned that it is advantageous both for him and for her to have the *get*; that in the eyes of God they are still married; and that since the marriage has been terminated civilly, why not terminate it in accordance with Jewish law?

He got very testy. "Listen, sir," he said coldly, "this is between my ex and I. It's a personal matter, and with all due respect it's really none of your affair."

This response irritated me, but in such situations one has to be certain not to antagonize the husband, or all is lost. "I realize that on the surface it may appear that way, but your ex is a member of my congregation, and since it is a religious matter I took it upon myself to try to help you both clean the slate."

"Listen, Rabbi, with all due respect, I was once a president of a synagogue, and I have hired and fired dozens of rabbis like you. I don't care what you say, I am not interested in the *get*, period."

I was seething inside and really wanted to lash out at him for his *chutzpah*. "With all due respect" indeed. But the situation did not afford me such luxuries. I told him that I hoped that he would think about it again and that we would be in touch.

The matter took months of painful and patient negotiations, but he finally agreed to cooperate. Upon completion of the *get* procedure, the ex-wife was so overcome with gratitude that she tried — unsuccessfully — to give me a bear hug in front of the stunned scribe and witnesses.

typical Orthodox discrimination

While Judaism requires a *get*, it is not a religious ceremony but a strictly legal one. Once husband and wife agree to a divorce, the document is written in Aramaic by a professional scribe, signed by competent witnesses, and handed by the husband to his wife — all under the supervision of a rabbi specially trained in this procedure. There are many old-wives' tales about what takes place during a *get*. Particularly prevalent is the myth that the wife is degraded and insulted. One woman was even told that the wife is spat upon as part of the ritual. Because of such unfortunate misimpressions, I have always taken special pains to ensure that the divorcing couple, especially the wife, is treated with extra sensitivity.

At the end of the procedure, after the husband presents the *get* document to his wife, one must always inform the wife that she may now marry any Jew she likes, but that there are several restrictions that devolve upon her. Firstly, a *kohen* may not marry a divorcee, and secondly, she is required to wait ninety days before remarrying.

One woman, upon hearing this second restriction, immediately asked, "Does my husband have to wait ninety days before he gets remarried?"

"No, " I said, "he can get married immediately if he wants to."

"Now isn't that just typical of the Orthodox! Everything is in favor of the man."

She was under great stress and I didn't want to upset her further, but I could not let this go unanswered.

"My dear," I said, "there is a simple biological reason for this."

"Sure," she said as she walked towards the door, "like everything else, Orthodoxy makes biology the key to everything."

"Can your husband have a baby?" I asked.

"No."

"Can you?"

"Yes."

"There's your answer." She looked at me, uncomprehending.

I explained to her that Jewish law insists on the ninety-day waiting period for this reason: if the wife should immediately remarry, and if later she turns out to be pregnant, it is important to know who the father is. Her eyes opened wide. "You know, I'll admit that makes sense. I never thought of that."

harei at

I have always been struck by the remarkable parallel between the operative words of the marriage ceremony and the operative words of the divorce ceremony. In the marriage ceremony the husband says to his bride as he places the ring on her finger, "*Harei at mekudeshet li* . . . / Behold, you are betrothed unto me . . ." In the divorce ceremony, the husband says to his wife as he hands her the *get* document, "*Harei at muteret lekhol adam* . . . / Behold, you are permitted to (marry) anyone . . ." The same cadence and almost the same words: *Harei at mekudeshet*, and *Harei at muteret*. Through one phrase she becomes his wife; through the other phrase she becomes his former wife. In the one case, the words are the cause of boundless joy; in the other, the words are the result of boundless sadness. In the one case, the future opens up with all of its possibilities; in the other, the past is closed with all of its pain. It is no wonder that the Sages tell us that when a man divorces his first wife, even the holy Altar itself sheds tears (*Gittin* 90a).

If people change their minds about their marriage and seek a divorce, halachah permits the reverse as well. In fact, one of the most pleasant tasks a rabbi can perform is to officiate at the remarriage of a divorced couple who want to be married again. I have officiated at two or three such remarriages, known as *mahzir gerushato*, "returning his divorcee." As long as the husband is not a *kohen*, and the divorced wife has remained unmarried, this is perfectly legal. A *kohen*, however, may not marry a divorced woman, even his own divorcee. Thus, when a *kohen* divorces his wife, it is truly final.

it's all in the translation

During a stay in Jerusalem, I was asked by my rabbinic organization to sit in as an observer on the *get* proceedings of the Jerusalem *Bet Din*/Rabbinic Court. After a few days, the presiding rabbi asked me to serve as interim translator for English-speaking Jews appearing before the *Bet Din*.

One morning an American gentleman appeared before them. He had been previously married, wanted now to get married again, but did not have the requisite Jewish divorce certificate with him. The presiding rabbi, a scholarly but rather crusty gentleman in his eighties, told him rather peremptorily that he must go back and bring documentation of his religious divorce, plus a letter from a rabbi that he had not been remarried since the date of the divorce.

The next day, the gentleman appeared again before the court, this time with the papers. The presiding rabbi looked at it and said that the letter was inadequate because it was written in English and not in Hebrew. "If your rabbi cannot write Hebrew, then his religious judgments are suspect," he snapped. "Find a Hebrew-speaking rabbi who can attest to your status."

The American, obviously unfamiliar with the labyrinthine ways of the Israeli bureaucracy and its impersonal demeanor (which in American terms is seen as rudeness but in Israel is considered a normal aspect of social intercourse) was very upset. He protested in English that he lived one hour from the court, had taken two buses to get here, had spent a great deal of time to obtain such a letter, and waited hours for his case to be heard. Before he left, I calmed him down a bit and reassured him that it would all work out.

The next day he appeared before us once again, angry even before he came in. He tossed the new letter on the desk of the presiding rabbi, itself a breach of good behavior, mumbling that he had to run all over Jerusalem to obtain it. "This better be it," he said to the rabbi.

The rabbi was in no mood to be trifled with. He examined the letter carefully and then turned to me. "Tell him," he said, "that the letter itself is fine, but it is not dated and therefore I cannot accept it. He has to go back to the rabbi and get it properly dated."

I so informed the American. He exploded. "This is nuts!" he shouted, "I am not going to go through this again and again! You people are impossible. Why don't you get your act together and tell me all these things in advance instead of springing new problems on me each time I show up?" He emphasized his point by pounding his fist on the desk of the presiding rabbi.

The rabbi was furious. He turned to me and said in Hebrew, "Tell him that for pounding on my desk in a courtroom I have the power to send him to jail. Tell him that for raising his voice at me I can also send him to jail. Tell him that if he says one more word I will summon the court officer and send him to jail at once! Tell him, tell him!"

I turned to the man and said, "Sir, the rabbi is extremely sorry that you have been inconvenienced, and he regrets the extra trouble you have been caused. But he has no choice in the matter because the documents you give him are entered in your permanent file, and for your own protection they must be absolutely perfect. He therefore asks for your indulgence and patience. He apologizes for the extra trouble you have gone through. Tomorrow, when you bring in the dated letter, just ask for me by name and we will see you without any waiting whatsoever. Please do understand."

Ma'aneh rach meishiv chemah, says Solomon in the Book of Proverbs: "A soft answer turneth away wrath." The man was so taken by the solicitous words of the rabbi that he broke into a smile and said, "Okay, I'll be back tomorrow. I'm sorry I blew my top."

The rabbi turned to me and demanded to know what he had said. "He said that he was sorry that he didn't get it right the first time, and that he would bring the dated letter tomorrow."

"You see?" said the rabbi to me. "If you're not firm with such people they do not take you seriously."

The power of translation . . .

it's still kosher

When Craig and Ethel Rothman were divorced, she moved to a small town in south Georgia, but they never bothered to obtain a *get*. I spoke to Ethel, and she was ready and willing. I spoke to Craig, and he too was amenable. But somehow, because she was living out of town and he was a traveling salesman, we were unable to effect the *get*.

Finally, I met with Craig and tried to pin him down on a specific date to have the document written. During our meeting he said, "Rabbi, I want to confess something to you. Every once in a while when I pass through the town where Ethel lives, I call her up, we go out together to eat something, and I spend the night with her in her home."

I said nothing.

He said, "I feel better now that I've told you about it."

Still I said nothing.

"Rabbi, you're not reacting."

"Craig," I said, "I have no problem at all with your meeting Ethel, because you and she are still husband and wife under Jewish law."

"Amazing! You're right! Now, isn't that interesting? In other words, it's all kosher."

Several weeks later I ran into Craig. "Rabbi," he said, "remember what you told me about me and Ethel being kosher and legal? Well, I still spend some time with her now and then, but you know something? You've taken all the joy out of it."

Chapter 14:
"Goodbye, God I'm Going Home Now"

My very first Yom Kippur sermon was unforgettable — to me, but not, unfortunately, to the community. I use the term "community" with poetic license: the combined living room-dining room in the ramshackle, converted old house that was our synagogue held one hundred fifty people, most of whom were not members but once-a-year visitors who had paid for their High Holiday seats. And I, nervous but well rehearsed and armed with some good stories and illustrations, appealed to them to return to their Jewish roots through study and practice.

I related the story of a young Jewish boy from a nonobservant home who was spending the summer with his pious grandparents. They take him to synagogue, observe Shabbat, and do all the Jewish things he had never seen at home. At the end of the summer, when his parents come to take him home, he kisses the mezuzah on the door and says, "Goodbye, God, I'm going home now."

My point was that although the High Holidays now come to a close, we should avoid the syndrome of saying goodbye to God until the next High Holidays. I urged them to make a real effort to remember their Jewishness throughout the year, to visit the synagogue occasionally, to add to their Jewishness by study, prayer, and the performance of *mitzvot.*

I actually had delusions that my first-ever Yom Kippur sermon had made an impact on them. But I learned the next day that right after the sermon, Mike Warner, one of our leading members, kissed the mezuzah on his way out of the synagogue and, to the accompaniment of the raucous laughter of everyone in the lobby, called out, "Goodbye, God, I'm going home now."

It was, in a way, funny and even clever, but it displayed a kind of religious imperviousness that, in Mike's case, I was never able to penetrate. And it taught me quickly that one good sermon doth not a good rabbi or a good Jew make.

the world's most gifted orator

An even more significant insight began to germinate inside me with that incident: a relentless, ongoing struggle takes place between rabbi and layman. Each tries to make the other over in his own image. It is a struggle about which the participants are not fully conscious, but it is a reality nevertheless.

The rabbi tries to create a layman who is religiously aware, knowledgeable, and is willing to place God, Torah, and Jewish destiny at the top of his priorities.

The layman tries to create a rabbi who does not take religion too seriously, who is a bit more casual about God, Torah, and Jewish destiny.

Look at how much more has to be done, says the rabbi to the layman.

Relax, says the layman to the rabbi.

The war goes on. Frequently, by dint of greater dedication to his cause — and also because of greater numbers — the layman is the victor. And, like the nature of the struggle itself, the rabbi is not fully aware that he has surrendered. He doesn't hoist a white flag. He continues through the motions of battle. But deep down he knows he has surrendered.

So does the layman.

I also learned early on that Southern audiences are unusually polite and courteous. A neophyte rabbi, unless he is warned about this in advance, can easily come to think that he is the world's most gifted orator. Whether or not a sermon holds their attention, they all seem to be listening. It is considered rude to appear disinterested. After some experience the rabbi can perceive who is listening and who is merely being polite — there is the occasional furtive glance at the wristwatch and other telltale signs — but if one is not careful it is quite easy to get the wrong impression about one's abilities from these sweet people. After every sermon, the graciousness of the Southerner comes to the fore and they volunteer to the rabbi their appreciation for a wonderful sermon, a great talk, a really inspiring idea.

same old rote

Strange: Mike Warner, who said goodbye to God, has remained a loyal supporter of the shul and me during all these years, and I have an excellent personal relationship with him. But his style of living has remained unchanged. No Shabbat, no kashrut, no prayer — nothing. He has served as a board member of the shul, attends every meeting and function faithfully, gives generously, but comes to shul only for *yahrzeit*,

Yizkor, and the High Holidays (first day Rosh Hashanah only, and a half day on Yom Kippur).

I once asked him why he doesn't come more often. "Same old rote," he blurted out. "Sit down, stand up; whisper this prayer, say that one out loud. Same old words, same old praising of God — does He need all this praise? It's just not very exciting, Rabbi."

I said, "Mike, look at you: same old getting up in the morning, same old going to work, same old eating, same old sleeping through the night, same old good health, same old wonderful family, same old making a fine living — don't you think you'd like to acknowledge the Author of all these good things? Praying is not a ball game — it doesn't have to be physically exciting. It's supposed to put you in touch with a higher power, and when that happens, it's more exciting than anything you ever experienced. But you don't give it half a chance. If you really thought about all the things that God does for you, 'all this praise' would hardly be enough."

He smiled his gracious smile and said, "Rabbi, don't try to convert me. I'm too far gone. But you know I love you and love the shul." Which was true and which he expressed in a hundred different ways. But the fact is that I could never move him off dead center religiously.

But God has His own ways. Somehow, Mike's daughter, Roberta, did not follow her father's model. Ever since childhood Roberta was very interested in Judaism. She was a leader in the synagogue youth groups, attended the day school and the Jewish high school, and had even spent a year in Israel in advanced Jewish study. As Mike was impenetrable when it came to Judaism, Roberta was open and sensitive.

Poor Mike — his daughter married a learned and observant young man who spent several years after marriage in full-time Jewish learning. "Study of Torah," Mike pontificated to his daughter and her husband, "is not the most productive use of the mind." This from a man who could not read a Hebrew sentence. Roberta was perceptive enough not to take his religious insights seriously. She recognized that he was sweet, generous and well-meaning, but basically an intellectual and spiritual philistine. When he had said, "Goodbye, God, I'm going home," he was not joking.

going back to Mississippi

One summer, many years after Mike said goodbye to God, that story became reified in a life-imitates-art situation. A ten-year-old Jewish boy from a small town in Mississippi came to stay for a month with his grandfather in Atlanta. Since the grandfather lived only a few doors away from us, Scott and our three little boys became fast friends.

Whenever they played together, Scott noticed that our three boys wore their *arba kanfos*, their *tzitzis* flapping in the breeze. He wanted *arba kanfos* for himself as well, so I bought a set for him. He was very proud and wore them every single day.

On Labor Day my doorbell rang. It was Scott. In his hand were the soiled, bedraggled *arba kanfos*, showing the evidence of faithful daily wear under the hot Georgia sun.

"I want to give these back to you," he said. "Thank you very much for letting me use them."

"Thank you, Scott, but you don't have to give them back. You can keep them if you want to."

"I don't need them anymore. I'm going back to Mississippi."

God the goodie dispenser

I think often of Mike Warner and the shock of reality he had provided me with his joke early on. It was a manifestation of a phenomenon that was to disturb me more and more as time went by — and that was the issue of whether, even for observant Jews, there is a consciousness of God's presence in our daily lives.

The truth is that rabbis do not speak of God often enough. It is ironic, but God is not an easy subject to discuss from the pulpit, which simply does not lend itself to detailed lessons concerning the meaning of One God, Providence, reward and punishment, the idea of a personal God, and the meaning of faith. The subject requires a classroom, the give-and-take of discussion. It calls for deep reflection and serious learning. And yet, most synagogue Jews today obtain their only Jewish education from the pulpit.

At a time when there is so little practice of Judaism, rabbis tend to stress doing rather than believing. Although belief would seem to precede practice — first I will find out who God is and then I will obey His commandments — very often the reverse is true. Sometimes a Jew begins to believe in God only after he practices.

For some reason even religious Jews are rather self-conscious when it comes to invoking the name of God. Perhaps this is because of a built-in sense of discretion and reserve about such things, or because we do not like to display our piety on our sleeves. Not so Christians or their ministers. Whenever I attend a conference with ministers, the contrast between their incessant use of the name of God and the Jewish reticence about it is palpable.

In any case, because God is rarely discussed seriously and in depth, most people end up with a distorted, simplistic view of God as a kind of heavenly vending machine dispensing goodies to those who behave themselves, and withholding those goodies from those who misbehave.

Judaism does believe in reward and punishment and accountability for our actions, but the matter is not simple. Why do the righteous suffer? Why do the wicked prosper? These are the eternal questions: If You are a just and merciful God, Moses asks, why do the righteous suffer?

God answers very cryptically — which one expects of God — and says that only his "back" can be seen, "but [His] face shall not be seen." This might mean that God's works are not always clear while events are unfolding, but often become clear only much later, that is to say, after He has passed by.

the rabbi and his God

If I wonder about the role that God plays in the lives of my people, I must also ask about the role that He plays in a rabbi's life. On the face of it, a rabbi lives with God constantly, but I am not sure if the reality is always so. There is the lurking danger that God will become a product that the rabbi is trying to sell, and not an integral part of his own life.

Yes, the rabbi prays regularly, but not always is his personal prayer up to par. There are forces mitigating against his focused concentration on prayer. Certainly the seat on the pulpit is not conducive to intensity in prayer. And he is always concerned lest his *Shema* or *Amidah* take too long, causing the congregants to wait and to become impatient. (One congregant to another: "You'd think that with all the studying he does the rabbi would be fluent enough in Hebrew to read a little faster.") There are distracting concerns on Shabbat and Yom Tov: will we finish on time, is the *chazzan* taking too long, are the people being uplifted, are the visitors being properly cared for, was my sermon effective, why are so many officers absent today, why is there so much talking?

Of course, a rabbi is closest to God in times of crisis, like everyone else. Before entering a hospital room or before a particularly difficult funeral, a rabbi asks Him for strength and for wisdom to say the right words. And when the inevitable low periods arrive and all looks bleak for the community, when very few want to listen and learn and be led, when the rabbi begins to wonder if he is wasting his time, prayer is his major source of strength and hope. Prayer and Torah study. God, after all, is the rabbi's Employer. Any prayer, however spontaneous and unprepared, will do. God's door is always open; even rabbis have entree and access. All that is required is the effort to push the door open a bit.

A rabbi learns soon enough that one of the essentials of the religious life is to learn to surrender to God. It is, when all is said and done, His world. A rabbi prays for the ability to do what he has to do in the most effective way that he can, and then the rest is up to His Master. As difficult as it is for a rabbi to admit it in the midst of the adulation and the beloved-great-wonderful-rabbi cliches he hears about himself, a rabbi must admit at the end of the day that he is not really God. In his daily contacts with people, a rabbi talks so much about belief in God, and faith in Him, and trust, and *bitachon* and *emunah*, that he is in danger of coming to believe that he himself need not work towards these qualities.

Praying with a *minyan* is the best way to reach out to Him. The presence of a *minyan,* which represents the community of Jews, lends strength and weight to each individual within the community. But occasionally I would deliberately not attend *minyan* on a weekday evening (never, of course, on a morning or on a Shabbat or Yom Tov) so that I could *daven* alone and renew my acquaintanceship with God without any pressures. A rabbi's task is a very lonely one; his motives are often misunderstood, he is judged by the standards of the marketplace, his goals are different from those of everyone else, laymen expect him to be "dynamic" or "charismatic." Therefore it is good now and then for a lonely rabbi to confront the lonely God in solitude, away from everyone else.

A well-meaning congregant once expressed his concern about not seeing me at the evening *minyan* the night before and asked if I was well. I didn't want to go into a long dissertation about the lonely addressing the Lonely, so I made a joke instead: "Milton, you don't expect me to pray every single day, do you?" Bad move. I later heard that Milton was very distressed that his rabbi doesn't *daven* every day.

an unorthodox Orthodox shul

Sometimes I look out at our Orthodox congregation and marvel at the variety of people in attendance. The fact is that this might well be America's most unique and diversified congregation, a very unorthodox Orthodox synagogue which counts among its membership men with pony tails who wear woolen *talleisim;* men with black *gartlach*; professional women in *sheitlach*; individuals and families who observe absolutely nothing; returnees to Judaism who have traveled a thousand spiritual miles; people who cannot read Hebrew and know nothing of their heritage; those who drive to shul on Shabbat while wearing a yarmulke; many who are just beginning to study Judaism; others who resist all religious growth and have remained religiously stationary and unmoved for the four decades of my rabbinate; and a number of ordained rabbis who are teaching in local Jewish schools.

We may even have our share of atheists. It was once reported to me that during my Yom Kippur sermon one woman whispered to her neighbor, "Promise you won't tell the rabbi, but I really don't believe in God at all."

During another High Holiday sermon, when I was attacking the casualness with which we approach Judaism and the generally cavalier attitude toward serious service of Him, one lady leaned over and said to her friend, "For this I had to get all dressed up to come to shul?"

the malleable God

God have mercy on the teacher of religion who even dares to suggest that the religious life is not always the easy life. To purvey religion successfully these days, one must demonstrate that it is as comfortable as a lounge chair, as pliant as a water bed, as malleable as silly putty; that it is adjustable, moves in any direction we determine, and is submissive to our every wish.

Even God Himself has to make us comfortable and must never disturb us, as witness this conversation with a Jewish young woman who was a university doctoral candidate.

She remarked, "We have a great religion, because God is very fair and never punishes us for the things we do."

I agreed that God is the very essence of fairness and justice, but suggested that fairness requires Him to punish His creatures for their misdeeds. If He punishes no one and treats the righteous and the wicked in the same way, where is His justice and fairness?

She was an intelligent woman, but neither logic nor theology were her forte, and my argument flew over her head. "Well," she said, "I heard it from a rabbi. God never punishes us, because He loves us."

"You ought to ask the rabbi whether it couldn't work the other way as well. God could punish us because He loves us."

But she could not grasp this. In her religious scheme everything goes. No matter what one does, it is acceptable. I'm okay, God's okay. All the rigor, discipline, and awe of the Creator of the universe gets washed away in this wishy-washiness. Not only may we do what we want to do; we have a god who does what we want him to do. (This kind of a god is deliberately a lower-case god.) "What," I asked her, "ever happened to Isaiah and Jeremiah and the admonitions in the Torah?"

"I don't really think they were serious. They were just trying to keep the Jews in line by frightening them. The difference between Christianity and Judaism is that Christianity is a religion where God punishes. In Judaism God does not punish anyone. That's why I'm proud to be a Jew."

This was at least a departure from the hackneyed idea of Christianity as the religion of love and Judaism as the religion of strict eye-for-an-eye justice, but it was nevertheless wrongheaded. What it represented was, once again, the human propensity to create a god in our own image, the kind of god we would create if we could write the specifications: an avuncular, white-bearded, heavenly *zeide* who tolerates anything and insists on nothing and always brings us gifts — a god with whom we can be comfortable.

God is indeed benevolent, but He is at the same time the awesome Creator of all things. We say three times daily in the *Amidah* that God is *gomel chasadim tovim*, "grants benevolent kindness," but in the very same breath He is addressed as "*gadol, gibor, v'nora*, "great, mighty, and awesome."

When we parted I gave her a reading assignment: chapter 28

of Leviticus; chapter 28 of Deuteronomy; and chapter 38 of the Book of Job, in which God speaks to Job out of the whirlwind: "Where were you when I laid the foundations of the earth?" These would definitely not make her comfortable.

Let's face it: everything else in contemporary life bends to the wishes of the consumer and is designed to be easy and fun, so why not religion? Why not God Himself?

Tiffany looks for God

Tiffany Stein, though, did have a theological problem of sorts. Tiffany is twelve years old and wants some sign from God that He really exists. Her mother tells me that her daughter prays every night for some clear indication from above, some unmistakable manifestation.

I know Mrs. Stein from her involvement in Jewish communal affairs. She is a dedicated worker for Jewish causes, but she and her family are religiously deprived. They are not members of any synagogue or Temple, and during our conversation it becomes clear that they have given their child no Jewish education whatsoever. They maintain what is in effect a Judaism-free home — not even candles on Friday night — and attend services only for Yom Kippur *Yizkor.*

She tells me that she has attempted to convince Tiffany that it is futile to ask God for any signs, since He never sends any signs to mortal man. As for all the stories in the Torah where God speaks to human beings, these, she tells her daughter, are only fables and never actually took place.

Tiffany is unhappy with her mother's theology, and in desperation her mother calls me. I ask Mrs. Stein why it is so important to her that her daughter believe in God.

"I don't want her growing up without faith in something," she says. "I don't really believe that God tells us what to do — He has more important things to worry about — but I do believe He protects us and watches over us." Would I kindly see Tiffany and try to help her? "If she's going to talk to a rabbi," she adds, "it might as well be an Orthodox rabbi."

I meet with Tiffany. Sweet, sensitive, intelligent, she might yet grow up into a fine Jewish woman, if only I can keep her mother from explaining Judaism to her. "I know God does wonderful things for everybody, like making the sun rise, and letting us see and hear and all that. But if God really is up there," says Tiffany, "why doesn't He prove it to me personally by making some little miracle for me? I pray every night for that, but He isn't listening to me."

I try to define for her what a miracle really is: God breaking the rules of nature He Himself established. God, I suggest to her, performs miracles for us when we perform miracles for Him.

She asks, "But how can a human being perform a miracle?"

"In our own small way, we can. Remember, a miracle is a change in the natural order of things. When we change our personal and natural order of things for the sake of God, when we go against our natural desires and instincts for His sake — that makes it possible for God to do the same thing for us, and to change the natural order of things for our sake."

I explain to her the concept of *middah k'neged middah*, the idea that God treats us in the way we treat Him, that our relationship with God is a two-way street.

"Well, how come so many miracles occurred to the people in the Bible? Were they so much better than we are?"

"They certainly were. They were not perfect, but they were willing to give up everything they had for the sake of God; they broke from the natural order of things, so God did the same for them. It wasn't natural for Abraham to be ready to sacrifice his son, for example, or for the Children of Israel to follow Moses into the Red Sea or into the Wilderness."

"So you're saying that unless I become a really outstanding person and a really deep believer in God, I'm not going to see any real signs from Him?"

"Once you get into the habit of breaking out of your natural ways for the sake of Judaism, then you're on your way. For example, you want to really hurt someone, but you don't. You want to steal something, but you don't. You want to eat on Yom

Kippur, but you don't. Of course, there's no guarantee, Tiffany. But one thing is guaranteed: if a person never makes himself or herself uncomfortable because of God's law, and never goes out of his way to please God or obey His Torah, that person can forget about seeing real signs from above."

I think Tiffany went away with a better understanding of the problem. Her mother may yet regret having sent her to me.

Were Tiffany a bit more mature, I would have put it this way: in the same way that we deal with God in our service of Him, so does He deal with us as His creatures. Whether He will deal with us according to the laws of nature — *teva* — or beyond the laws of nature — *lema'ala min hateva* — is really up to us. If we serve Him only in accordance with what is possible or feasible (we find it "impossible" to give charity, or to pray, or to act compassionately, or to do *mitzvot* in general), then God may find it "impossible" to deal with us in any way other than the natural *teva* way: He says to us that it is not possible to perform a miracle for us, not possible to save us from whatever distress threatens us. We are excluded from the orbit of the supernatural and remain in the orbit of the merely natural, where events take their normal course.

Similarly, to ascribe God's acts, which are supernatural, to ordinary nature is to demean God. Worse, this creates a measure-for-measure situation; since we do not have the understanding or perception of things above nature, and we insist on seeing everything as ordinary *teva*, then our perception actually creates a relationship between God and us that is based on mere *teva*, and God's dealings with us descend to the realm of ordinary nature.

It also occurs to me that faith in God does not take place in a vacuum. It cannot take root in a soul immersed in self-indulgence. Faith is co-extensive with holiness and purity, and with the surrender of the self before the Creator. The performance of *mitzvot* is not only an expression of one's service of God. It also builds faith within the soul. Hedonists and pleasure-seekers also wish they could develop some faith, but this faith-wish, I suspect, is also a reflection of their hedonism. They want something to lean on, something that will make life easier and more pleasant. They are not willing to pay the price for faith: to surrender oneself completely to God and His discipline. The sad fact is that once a person has placed his faith in false gods — material pleasure, thrills, enjoyment, fun — he is by definition unable to find faith in the Creator. Faith is not subject to hedging one's bets: I believe in God, but also in this and in that. A serene faith is a natural result of the decisive abandonment of all false gods, and the decisive acceptance of the true God and His ways.

justifying the ways of God

The really painful questions about God occur during times of tragedy: questions about His providence and love. That's when faith is on the line and belief is on the brink, and Why's are asked and Because's are insufficient.

I try to explain God's mysterious ways to the suffering and stricken families who ask Why, but I want to speak honestly and not offer them slogans and pap, so the words come haltingly and I end up saying very little, and I leave the hospital room or the house of mourning feeling diminished by my inability to be more comforting and by the difficulties of translating the ways of God to man. But every so often I will receive a note from someone: "Your presence was a comfort, your words were of great solace. Your being here meant a great deal to us. My faith in God is still strong."

It took a long time for me to realize that the mere presence of a rabbi is in itself a comfort for many. He does not have to say anything particularly profound. He just has to be there, show his genuine concern, and listen. Sometimes just a touch on the shoulder or a pat on the back are much more eloquent than words. Sickness and bereavement create a sense of deep loneliness, of being cast adrift. The presence of a trusted rabbi, who is perceived as nothing less than God's deputy, shows that he cares — and that God Himself also cares.

bending God to do our will

When all is said and done, the religious life is a titanic struggle between God and the self. The self wants to bend God to its will, while the major teaching of Judaism is that we must learn to bend the self to God's will. This is the bottom line. And this is why Judaism — the authentic kind — is such a hard sell in a society in which Me is king. The mere thought of bending ourselves to His will is enough to send some Jews scurrying to rabbis and congregations which offer less uncomfortable choices.

A second great impediment to service of God is God's essential unknowability. "For no man can see Me and live" (*Exodus* 33:20). No one who is mortal can fully comprehend the mysteries of the One Who created the universe and each one of us. And yet, it is a perfectly natural human desire to want to know more and understand more about God. Only pagan gods are knowable and immediately visible. The God of Israel is utterly unknowable, even though we are encouraged to expend every effort to know Him.

In general, the natural human desire to understand everything, to know the whys and wherefores of things, to comprehend why this is forbidden and that is permitted, to apprehend the logic that undergirds Judaism — all this is perfectly legitimate. But in matters of faith and belief, the mind and the intellect are inadequate.

This is the way God planned things: that He remain the Mysterious One, and that His conduct of the world remain hidden. In fact, hiddenness is an essential ingredient of God and His conduct of the world. It is built in to the universe. God is "He Who dwells in hiddenness," according to one reading of Psalm 91. When God says to Moses in the 32nd chapter of Exodus that "man cannot see Me and live," He is in fact saying that no mortal can "see" God in the sense of comprehending Him or His ways.

The Talmud says that the Hebrew word for "universe," *olam*, derives from the word *he'elem*, "hidden." In the Torah, God says to Moses, *"Zeh sh'mi l'olam,* This is My Name forever." The tradition points out that the word for "forever" in Hebrew, *l'olam*, is in this passage spelled as if it were *l'elem*, meaning "hidden." The hiddenness of God is not merely a result of our inability to comprehend Him; His hiddenness is an essential ingredient of Who He is.

In a way, religion is like poetry. Its power rests on being imperfectly understood. A God about Whom I understand everything and know everything is no longer a God. He is reduced to my level. It is perfectly reasonable that a finite mortal should not be able fully to comprehend the Infinite Creator.

But in this technological time we lack a sense of poetry and mystery, and therefore we insist on pedestrian clarity when it comes to God. This insistence on clarity has in the past resulted in the kind of worship where the deity himself becomes only too clear and manifest and tangible — in the forms of clay figurines, statues, idols — and in the form of gods who are born, walk the earth, and then die. Better that God and His demands be imperfectly understood.

Maybe some day Tiffany will understand that one has attained the heights of human understanding precisely at the point when one realizes that not every question must have an answer, that not everything needs to be crystal clear — especially matters dealing with God.

Amazing, the ferment in my mind created by that little twelve-year-old from a nonobservant home. My only fear is that, like Mike Warner, she is going home now.

Chapter 15:
When I Get Sick,
Nobody from the Shul
Comes to Visit

At 2:00 A.M. my phone rings. It is the chaplain at the hospital. "Sorry to disturb you at this hour, but there's a ninety-year-old Jewish woman here, and she may not make it through the night. She's fully conscious, and she asked to see an Orthodox rabbi even though she's not Orthodox. I'm afraid she needs to see you right away."

When I enter her room, she says in a faint voice, "Rabbi, I've been a member of the Reform Temple all my life, and so were my parents." She pauses for breath.

"May God give you many more years," I say.

"No, it's enough. But I wanted a rabbi to say the final prayers with me."

I am prepared to be by her side and to say the *vidui* with her, but an obvious question flits through my mind: if she is a long-time member of the Reform congregation, why did she call the Orthodox rabbi?

"Rabbi, you're probably wondering why I called you and not my own rabbi. Well, my rabbi has been here already. But I also wanted an Orthodox rabbi. I know I'm going, and I just don't want to take any chances."

* * *

The hospital visit to old Mr. Sachs was not unusual until I got up to leave. Although he was over ninety years old and his body frail and infirm, his mind was excellent. He had contracted pneumonia but was recovering. As I said goodbye to him, he said with pleading eyes, "Rabbi, please pray for me."

"Of course I will, Mr. Sachs. Three times each day. May God bless you and give you a *refuah shlemah*."

"Rabbi, you don't understand. I don't want to get well. I want to die. I have only enough money to get by for a few more months, and after that I will have to go on charity. I don't want charity. Pray for me. Pray that I don't get well. Ask God to take me soon." And he burst into bitter tears.

"Mr. Sachs, I will pray for two things: that you live a long life, and also that God make certain that you can support yourself as long as you have to. I promise you: you won't have to go on charity."

We spoke together for a while, and gradually he calmed down and seemed comforted. Driving back to my study, I began to work on the problem of raising the money to support him in a dignified way. I knew several people I could call on who would be happy to give financial help in confidence. And I knew that if and when Mr. Sachs was unable any longer to live alone, the Jewish Home would readily admit an aged gentleman who had no visible means of support.

When I got home, I checked into the *halachic* question of praying for someone's death when the person is suffering and beyond all hope. It is discussed in at least two places in the Talmud, in *Nedarim* 40a and in *Ketubot* 104a.

the goodness of Mordecai and Max

Mordecai Levy, eighty-seven years old and one of the most learned laymen in the community, is now infirm, having nearly wasted away during his most recent illness. Until then he would arise every morning at five to study *Chumash* for several hours before going to the daily *minyan* and then to work, as had been his practice for fifty years. Today he can hardly talk, cannot see, and is confined to his bed in the Jewish Home.

His roommate, by luck of the draw, is Max Dubinsky, a fellow who in his youth was a horse trainer, never quite earned a living, and who later became an alcoholic. He is probably the most unlettered person in the entire Jewish community, cannot read a word of Hebrew, but for some reason loved to come to the daily *minyan*. Now the two of them are sharing the same room, keeping each other company, waiting to die. The former alcoholic is very good-natured and kind, and takes loving care of Mr. Levy. He dresses him, washes him, brings him snacks, watches over him, tucks him in at night.

During their younger years, although they would see each other in shul at the daily *minyan,* they could never have a meaningful conversation with one another. Mordecai would spend every spare moment engrossed in his studies, while Max would spend every spare moment in some bar. Nevertheless, whenever their paths crossed, Mordecai was always the model of kindness and understanding. When, on occasion, some folks at the *minyan* would laugh at Max's abysmal ignorance, Mordecai was the first to come to his defense. "Listen," he would say patiently, "he never had a chance to study or learn or read. What do you want from him? It's not his fault."

And now, the man Mordecai always defended out of the goodness of his heart is taking excellent care of Mordecai — out of the goodness of his heart.

* * *

General notes on a visit to the Jewish Home: Why are we so delighted and so patient with the antics and the gurgling of an infant who knocks things over and needs help getting dressed and undressed — and so impatient with the antics and sounds of a ninety-year-old who knocks things over and needs help getting dressed and undressed? The same mother who lovingly tends her infant son finds it much more difficult to perform the identical tasks for her aged father.

Of course, the difference is that the mother of the infant is buoyed by the thought of his beckoning future. As for the aged father, the specter of death hovers over his every step. The younger person looking at her aged father sees no future, only the past; not growth, only decay. The younger person is reminded of that which she would like to forget: her own mortality. Some day she might be old and decayed; some day she might need help to get dressed, to eat, to get tucked into bed.

don't leave yet

Five-year-old Jeremy had been having trouble breathing. At first it was diagnosed as asthma, but he did not respond to any treatment. So there were new hospitals, new doctors, new tests, new diagnoses. Finally, a tracheotomy. The hospital chaplain asked me to drop in.

I find the child in the isolation ward, his mother sitting next to his bed. He is in obvious pain, restlessly turning, but because of his condition unable to make a sound. The mother, at least on the surface, is calm. Every few moments she turns her head from me just to stare impassively at the child. I ask her if I can do anything for her.

"Just pray for him to get better."

"I certainly will, but you must pray also. May God grant him a full recovery very quickly."

"Amen," she whispers.

We sit silently, awkwardly. She is not a synagogue member, this is the first time we have met, and she is clearly uncomfortable. I try to put her at ease but am not very successful. I make small talk: where are you and your husband from, what type of work does he do, do you have other children? She squeezes her handkerchief, replies in monosyllables. Finally, I sense that my presence makes her uneasy and that she would rather be alone, so I get up to leave. "No," she says quickly, "please don't go. Stay a while longer."

So I sit down again and read some psalms with her. For a long half-hour we say very little. When I finally leave she thanks me, quite genuinely.

hell hath no fury like a member ignored

The mere presence of a rabbi at times of crisis is important — of this there is no question. And hell hath no fury like a dues-paying, meeting-attending, charity-giving member who feels that his personal time of crisis was ignored by the rabbi.

Just prior to Rosh Hashanah I called a member who had been very sick — someone whom I rarely see in shul — to wish him a good year. His wife answered the phone. Before she put him on, she informed me that she had wanted to tell me something for a long time, ever since her husband took ill. "You paid him one hospital visit, and then forgot about him," she said. "If he were a wealthy member of the shul, you would have made it your business to visit him regularly. I am sorry to have to tell you this, but it has been on my heart for a long time and I just wanted you to know."

I told her that I understood her anger and really had no excuses. What I did not tell her was that after her husband had left the hospital, I did call him on the phone and wanted to visit him at home. But he minimized his illness and told me that a visit was really not necessary. I was foolish to have listened to him, but because I was under heavy pressure at the time, I did not see him again — and after a day or two, he simply slipped out of my mind.

She was right to have pointed out my lapse. I could have told her about my phone call, but in fact it was no excuse. The comment about the wealthy member really stung. I hope it is not true.

Occasionally, however, such things take a different turn. Carl Pariser, for example, is angry at me; unknown to me, he was hospitalized, and I did not call, much less visit. I heard this from three separate people to whom he had confided his pique.

"But Carl," they had each said to him, "did the rabbi know you were sick?"

"It doesn't matter," Carl said, "he just doesn't care about us. Here I was, sick as a dog, and he doesn't visit or even call. I am really upset."

His friends pleaded with him like the friends of Job: "Carl, how can he come visit you if he doesn't know you're sick — what is he, some kind of prophet or something? Listen, your doctor didn't just happen to fall in. He was notified. Why is the rabbi any different?"

"I don't know," Carl mumbled. "All I know is I've been a loyal member for fifteen years, paid my dues, bought raffle tickets, and when I get sick nobody from the shul comes to visit, that's all I know."

So I picked up the phone and called the Pariser residence. Mrs. Pariser answered. She was very sweet and kind. "I understand," she said. "I know you didn't know. Rabbi, don't worry about it. After all, you're not supposed to be God and know everything. We appreciate your call, we really do. It's our fault, we really should have let you know."

She made me feel much better. I hope she has better luck convincing Carl than his friends did.

Pulpit rabbis are held in high and unrealistic esteem and are expected to perform superhuman feats. That is why there is so much resentment against us when we fall short and our feet of clay are publicly exposed. A missed hospital call can do wonders to restore a sense of balance to a layman who until then was convinced his rabbi was a superman.

It is obvious, but so often overlooked: people need attention. They need to be shown that someone cares for them. The rabbi is, in the eyes of many, the deputy of God. If the rabbi shows no concern about people's problems, it is as if God Himself has abandoned them.

Never mind that the rabbi sometimes goes for days without a spare moment. Never mind that he has skipped breakfast and lunch, has snacked on (kosher) junk food all day, has had no time to say hello to his wife and children, or to prepare for the lecture he is giving tonight and the class he is teaching tomorrow morning. Never mind that the rabbi is human and forgets, or that he may not even have known about the illness. A member is in need, and the rabbi did not visit or call. Ergo, the rabbi does not care; ergo, hurt, anger, betrayal, resentment.

to Bella with love

The truth is that people are essentially lonely, even when things are going well. And when things are not going well, they are in particular need of some attention and some kindness.

Bella Goode was the embodiment of loneliness. She would come to talk with me regularly about her problems. She was unhappily married for twenty-five years to an insensitive and rather boorish husband, and had no children. She loved music and theater and reading. He loved nothing. He would come home at night from his grocery store, gulp his supper down without a word to her, ensconce himself before the TV, and sit there until he fell asleep. He followed the same routine every night of the week. Other than a few grunts about food, he rarely spoke to Bella. She went to the theater and concerts alone or with some of her friends.

One day she showed me a book which she had received in the mail on her fiftieth birthday. "Nice, Bella," I said. "Very thoughtful. Who sent it?"

"Open it up to the flyleaf and see for yourself."

I opened it and read the small, neat handwriting: "To Bella — with affection, and much love."

"That's beautiful," I said, "but it's not signed. Who sent it?"

Her eyes brimmed with tears. "I did, Rabbi. I had it sent to myself. I called the bookstore, asked them to inscribe it, and had them send it to me. I just wanted the excitement of receiving a gift — it's been so long since I got one."

the doctor and the mohel

It is the lonely who are most sensitive, and also the poor. I have always tried — but not always successfully — to give special attention to those who are not making it financially, to give them extra time when I see them, to chat with them at synagogue functions, to go the extra mile for them.

Up to a point. Joe and Bonnie Stone, married five years, were barely making ends meet. They lived in a run-down apartment, she rarely wore a new dress, and they drove a battered old Chevy. I tried very hard to be attentive to them, to give them an extra moment or two whenever I met them in the street or at Shabbat *kiddush*.

When a baby boy was born to them, they called me to invite me to the *bris* — but they wanted to use a nonobservant Jewish physician instead of the accepted *mohel*. They felt that the doctor would pose less of a risk to their baby.

I pointed out that Jewish babies have been circumcised by

professional *mohalim* for thousands of years without ill effect, and that the *mohel* was undoubtedly more proficient in circumcision than any doctor, since that is his specialty. I also told them that according to Jewish law the circumciser must be a pious and religiously observant person. But it was all to no avail. They insisted on using a doctor.

I informed them that I cannot attend circumcisions that violate Jewish law, and that, while I very much wanted to attend the *bris*, they would have to understand that I could not be present. They were very upset but told me that their minds were made up: they were going to use the doctor. They regretted that I would not be there, and they hoped that I would change my mind and attend.

I did not attend. A few days later it was reported to me that they were telling their friends that I did not attend because they were poor. If they had been wealthy, they said, I would have somehow found a way to be there.

Poor or wealthy, to appear to ignore people at a time when their loneliness is intensified — at sickness or bereavement or other crisis — is to inflict a profound wound on their very essence. And when that wound, real or imagined, is inflicted by an individual whom they have been conditioned to respect and admire, it cuts deeply. Conversely, when their loneliness is assuaged and their wounds soothed by someone they respect, not only is a great act of *chesed* performed, but it cements the relationship for a long time to come.

Sometimes I wish I hadn't made certain hospital visits at all. Seymour Kreinfeld was sitting in his wife's hospital room, waiting for her to be brought down from the recovery room. They suspected a malignancy and were doing exploratory surgery. He and his family were somber. I tried to lift their spirits, but nothing I could say seemed to help. They remained quite glum. I kept a stiff upper lip and told them not to worry.

On my way out, the daughter whispered to me tearfully, "We got the report half an hour ago. It's a very bad malignancy. They can do nothing for her."

I left feeling rather foolish — me and my phony good cheer.

* * *

There was genuine joy, however, at the synagogue supper where I saw Mrs. Firestone, her husband, and their three-month-old baby. He was an unusually handsome child, very animated, extremely good-natured, enjoying life. Mrs. Firestone seemed especially happy.

One year earlier Mrs. Firestone had panicked when she learned that she was pregnant. She already had four children, and the thought of a fifth made her very apprehensive. She decided to have an abortion. She had already made the arrangements to have it done when she told me about her decision. I was able to persuade her not to do it.

She brought the baby over to me at the supper. I cooed and tickled the child, and then looked the mother in the eye. Neither of us needed to say a word. Both of us were smiling.

words of life and death

Amazing what words can do, the power they have to uplift or destroy, to salve or cause pain. We prattle so much that we don't comprehend the worth of words. We forget that speech is what distinguishes us from the beasts. Onkelos in Genesis 2:7 translates the verse "And Adam became a living spirit" (*nefesh chayah*) as "a speaking spirit" (*ruach memalela*).

It was Mary Lichtman who starkly brought home the value of words to me. Mary is no longer alive, but I remember her well. She had been struggling against spreading cancer for years. Her lungs, her colon, her larynx, everything. She was a remarkable woman; although she suffered much, she was courageous, uncomplaining, always cheerful.

One day her husband called. Her larynx was to be removed the next morning. She would never be able to speak again. She wanted to see me as soon as possible.

As I approached her room, I kept thinking that these were going to be the last words she would ever speak to me. I had to steel myself to walk in. What would I say to her? How should I comfort her? Could I tell her not to worry, that everything would be all right? Should I smile bravely and tell her to have faith? Should I tell her to keep her chin up, it would all turn out fine, the operation would be a success, she had nothing to worry about, we'd all be praying for her, it would all be over before she knew it?

I walked into the room. Her family was gathered around her bed: husband, children, her brothers and sisters and their spouses. They seemed relieved that I had come — as if I had brought with me some magic potion to ward off the impending doom. There were the usual how-are-you's and how's-the-family. Mary put on a good front. "So nice of you to come," she said. The members of the family, as if by some prearranged signal, excused themselves from the room one by one, and I was left alone with her.

As soon as they disappeared, she began to sob. "Rabbi, Rabbi, what am I going to do?"

"Sometimes we have no choices in life. We have to do what we have to do." The words stuck like lead in my throat.

"I'd rather be dead. It would be easier. I don't want to live this way. It's no life, a burden on everybody, and even then I'm not sure I'll ever be all right again." The words, bottled up until now, spurted out in a torrent. She was reaching for some hope, some relief.

My answer was feeble. "But right now this means prolonging your life. What's more important than life? This may give you ten more years, twenty more years, who knows? How can you measure the worth of all those years?" She wanted solace and comfort, but I felt I was feeding pap to her.

"All those years," she repeated. "What good will they be? A vegetable, that's all I'll be."

"Not so, Mary. You'll be able to function very well. You can learn to talk again. They have specially trained people to teach you. And your family — look how much you mean to them."

Futile. She sobbed bitterly and reached out to take my hand. I was silent.

A long minute passed. "Mary," I said, "why don't you say a prayer right now?"

"I don't know Hebrew, and I hardly ever pray."

"You can pray in any language, and God's door is always open. You can tell Him anything you like. He loves you and cares for you very much."

Her face brightened a bit. "Okay, Rabbi, tonight, after everyone leaves, I will say a prayer. And please, you pray for me, too."

"Of course I will. Right now, let's say *Shema Yisroel* together, just you and I. That's the way Jews express faith in God."

She smiled. "Great! That I know in Hebrew. It's the very first thing they taught us in Sunday School."

We said it together, slowly. The first Hebrew words she ever spoke were also the last Hebrew words she ever spoke.

"Rabbi, thanks for bothering to come. (She, a quintessential Southern lady, was thanking me.) I know how busy you are. I'm still frightened, Rabbi, but a lot less than I was before."

We said good night, I went down to my car, sat weeping for a few moments, then drove away.

Chapter 16:
My Most Important
People

Money, giving, sharing: our character, or lack of it, comes to the surface in this dimension of life. What we give and how we give and when we give and to whom we give are among the keys which reveal a person's soul. The Talmud states that a person reveals himself in three ways; "through his cup (i.e., his drinking), his pocketbook, and his anger" (*Eruvin* 65b). The primary key to the character of the giver is not how much he gives, but the manner in which he gives.

Every month I receive a plain envelope which contains two

crisp one-hundred-dollar bills, with a typed note: "Dear Rabbi: Please distribute this to individuals who are in need." The note is unsigned. I have no idea who is sending it to me, but it has been going on for years. Somebody truly believes in giving quietly.

Fortunately, this person is not entirely unique. In the early years, before we had any type of religious high-school education in the community, our best and brightest boys were being lost to us within one year after Bar Mitzvah. Even the finest and most sensitive young man, filled with love and enthusiasm for Torah, hit a spiritual dead-end once he entered a public high school The girls-sports-partying syndrome was hardly conducive to raising a knowledgeable Jew.

We sorely needed a Jewish high school to maintain the commitment of these boys — and girls. But such a high school was not even on the horizon; we were barely managing to keep afloat the newly established elementary day school.

Whenever I noticed a young boy who showed great Jewish promise, I tried to convince him and his parents that he would thrive if he went out of town to a good Jewish high school. By and large I would recommend Baltimore, either the Talmudical Academy or the Ner Israel high-school division. Baltimore was less intimidating to Southern parents than was New York, and both schools ran excellent programs with fine dormitories.

But even if parents were willing to send a thirteen-year-old away, the costs were far beyond the means of most of them. I tried to raise the money myself and negotiated with the schools for discounts and scholarships, but even with all this, the seas were very rough.

the anonymous giver

Then I talked with Morris Levenger. A pious Jew of seventy-five, he arose every morning at four to study Mishnah and *daven*, and then went about his duties, which involved the various properties he owned around the city. He lived a simple, frugal life, but he was a person of means — and he liked to give.

Mr. Levenger was wise and understanding, and I would often share my communal problems with him. I told him about the youngsters and my worries about them.

"Rebbe," he said, "I will sponsor two boys. Just make the best deal you can with the school, try to get the parents to help out, and I will cover the rest of the costs."

That's how it all began. Within a few years the sponsorship of two boys increased to three, then to four, and at one point Morris Levenger was underwriting ten boys and two girls from Atlanta who were studying in advanced Torah schools in Baltimore. He kept this up for years. These youngsters did very well in high school, and most of them went on to advanced yeshivot and seminaries. Today many of them are rabbis, day-school teachers, or fine laymen making excellent contributions to Jewish life.

Morris Levenger played a major role in the religious development of Atlanta, though he never thought of it that way. What distinguished him above all else was that not a soul knew of his largesse — not the students and not their parents. No one but me — and God.

poor Sylvia

Mrs. Sylvia Kraus, extremely wealthy and extremely uncharitable, always nods her head in agreement during my sermons, even when I am talking about people like her. I declare that not only do people rarely tithe their incomes these days, but that by and large people give only tiny percentages of their income to *tzedakah*, and she vigorously concurs. I preach about forgoing the present moment, and about material things being trivial and of little consequence, and she emphatically nods approval. But whenever I approach her for a contribution, she has a reason why the timing right now is not good and why at this particular juncture she cannot support this school, or give to that charity, or help the synagogue with a special new project, or contribute to a fund for homeless children.

There are some wealthy people who give generously, but there are others who are constitutionally unable to open their hands. I often wonder what it is that prevents them from giving. Are they really fearful that some day they might not have enough to support themselves or their children? Do they convince themselves that they have nothing? Or is it simply a bad habit without any basis in rationality — an instinct to clutch and keep? That their luxurious cars, expensive furniture, lavish homes, and extravagant cruises and vacations are not seen as contradictions to ungenerous giving is eloquent testimony to the truth that the mind can rationalize anything.

Sylvia's husband Sam is an amiable sort who would probably give more generously if he had the power, but she is the power and decision-maker in her family. She reached her nadir a few years ago when her aged mother needed some expensive bridgework for her teeth. I had visited the mother at the old-age home, and she asked me to remind her daughter about it.

Sylvia listened to me and then blurted out, "At her age it really doesn't pay to do that."

At first I assumed she was suggesting that her mother's age made this kind of dental work unfeasible. That's not what she had in mind. "I want to help her and all that, but to go to all that expense, I don't know. Let's be realistic — and I hate to sound crude, Rabbi, and forgive me for putting it this way — but at her age it doesn't really pay to do all that."

Crude is hardly the word. Poor Sylvia.

husbands and wives

Husbands and wives do not always synchronize fully with one another, so when it comes to returning to religious practice, it is natural that one spouse is invariably ready to move much more rapidly than the other. This manifests itself very frequently in the giving of *tzedakah*.

When we were raising major funds for the new synagogue building, I went one evening to solicit Abe Katzen. Abe had previously indicated that he would like to dedicate a classroom in memory of his parents and that he was ready to pledge twenty-five thousand dollars over a five-year period. We were working out the details of our understanding in his living room when his wife came home. He had apparently made the mistake of not discussing this with her previously. She joined in the discussion, and after a few minutes she said, "But Abe, how can you give all this money to the shul when you know we have to redo the whole house, and then you promised that we would make this trip to the Far East. I just don't think we can afford to give this money to the shul right now."

That did it. No pledge from Abe — not then, and not later. Abe was humiliated, apologized to me many times in private, but that was that. Once again I found myself feeling sad — not only for Abe, but also for his wife.

On the other hand, every so often Beverly Stein would quietly hand me a thick envelope stuffed with bills, sometimes amounting to hundreds of dollars. "Give it to charity at your discretion," she would say. The first time this happened I sent her a note thanking her for her thoughtfulness. When she saw me next, she told me that she appreciated the note but that it was not necessary, and she asked me not to send her any more thank-you notes. I can't be certain, of course, but the edge in her voice made me feel that, although she earned her own income, perhaps she did not want her husband to know about her personal giving.

the stealthy giver

Simon Berger is an extremely well-to-do investor. Whenever I need something for a special situation — a family in need, a scholarship for a poor boy to go to summer camp, help with a poor child's day-school tuition, anything —

Simon is always ready. I pick up the phone, tell him I need five hundred or a thousand dollars, and the check to our charity fund arrives the next morning.

He is such an easy touch that I try not to ask him too frequently. Once, after a three-month hiatus, he called to complain that he had not heard from me in a while. I told him that I hadn't had any particular needs. "Rabbi, I know you wouldn't lie, but you're depriving me of one of my greatest pleasures." The next day his check for one thousand dollars arrived on my desk, for me to distribute to any needy causes or individuals.

I once sent letters to a small group of wealthy individuals asking them to help me set up a confidential free-loan program. I requested contributions of between five hundred and twenty-five hundred dollars. Simon received my letter and immediately called me. "How much do you hope to collect altogether?" he asked.

"I was thinking of about twenty-five thousand."

"That sounds reasonable. I'm mailing a check to you today. Thanks for letting me know about it."

Two days later his envelope arrived. I had expected about one thousand dollars. The check was for twenty-five thousand dollars. A note was attached: "If you find you need more, let me know."

Simon gives the way some people steal: silently, stealthily, making certain that no one knows what he's doing. He expects no credit, wants no thanks, gives only because he wants to be of help to others. Whatever he earns is immediately tithed and placed in a separate bank account, untouchable except for charity needs. When he makes a deal which nets him, say, twenty-five thousand dollars, he immediately puts twenty-five hundred of it into his charity account.

Here's a man who is truly a spiritual investor. The rate of return he is receiving from the Bank of Heaven is unequalled anywhere on earth, and it's guaranteed by the full faith and trust of God Himself, Who has never defaulted on a payment.

Yes, he is very wealthy. Yes, he can afford it. Yes, he still lives a luxurious life. But the joy he takes in giving and sharing his wealth is itself a joy to behold.

One can give not only with money, but with time and energy as well. An old man who was very poor used to *daven* with us every morning. During the day he used to come into the shul and sweep the floors, dust around the seats, repair torn *siddurim*. On Shabbat he stayed after the *davening* to collect the *siddurim* and *Chumashim*. I offered to pay him for this since he was in such great need. He was horrified. "Oh, no, what I do is nothing. It is an honor to take care of God's house. I look forward to it. If you pay me, you will take away my pleasure." Here was a man who was giving out of the goodness of his heart. But I would have a difficult time convincing synagogues or organizations to give him a testimonial dinner.

saving a Jewish soul

Tzedakah and the hand of God: Larry Romberg, an eighteen-year-old all-star basketball player, had just graduated high school and had been offered a full four-year basketball scholarship at a small college in South Carolina. On the face of it this was a stroke of good fortune, because Larry's parents were barely making it financially and college tuition was far beyond their means. Everyone who knew him was happy for him.

Except me. The college offering the scholarship was a Christian evangelical one, and I was fearful. With Larry's minimal Jewish background and with no Jewish friends or community around him, combined with mandatory daily chapel attendance, required courses in the New Testament, and a totally Christian atmosphere, it would only be a matter of time before he was cajoled into accepting Christianity. He would be no match for the practiced and persuasive missionaries on campus who would be out in force to save the soul of this nice Jewish boy.

I called Larry and his parents in and told them about my

concerns. Larry and his parents scoffed at the very thought that their son would ever abandon Judaism. "Rabbi," said Dad, "we appreciate your worrying about this — but no way is Larry ever going to become a Jesus freak. You don't have to worry."

I asked them if they would switch schools if I were able to obtain a similar scholarship from Yeshiva University, which had a fine basketball team. They all said they would be delighted.

I immediately called the Y.U. coach and told him the story. He said he would be thrilled to have a player like Larry on his team, but that they could not possibly match the full scholarship offer. They would give him a generous scholarship, and in the Judaic program they would place him in a specially tailored academic program for youngsters with weak Jewish backgrounds. The scholarship would partially cover his tuition, meals, and dormitory. But there would still be a five-thousand-dollar gap, and it would be my responsibility to raise it and have it ready before the school year began. It was a very generous offer, and I accepted it. To save a Jewish soul, it was a bargain.

All this took place before Simon Berger came on the scene. Pre-Simon, I had to painstakingly raise the money bit by bit. And since Larry was not the only project I was engaged in, it was not easy.

With exactly one week to go before the school year began and the money due, I was still fifteen hundred dollars short. I had exhausted all my contributors and had no one to turn to.

That afternoon I had an appointment with a wealthy Texas woman who came to see me with her personal problems whenever she was in town. She was highly intelligent but somewhat long-winded, and our appointments invariably took longer than required. But she needed to talk, and I always heard her out. These sporadic meetings had been taking place for several years.

On this particular day she wound down after two hours and rose to leave. "I really appreciate all the time you've been giving me. I'm not even a member, and I have bothered you a great deal. I know you personally won't accept money from me, but I would like to give you some money to distribute to any worthy cause you know about."

"That's very thoughtful," I murmured, thinking of my needs for the Larry scholarship. She reached into her purse, pulled out an envelope and placed it on my desk. When she left, I opened it. In it was a check for exactly fifteen hundred dollars.

The rest of the story: Larry did very well in his studies and on the basketball courts. While there were no further obvious acts of God, I was able to raise the money each of the four years through various sources. Larry graduated with honors, and today he is married to a fine Jewish girl, is an observant Jew, and a successful accountant.

a guilt-edged conscience

Calvin Weiner was not one of those sources. Calvin is extremely well-to-do, but he is distressed at my public and private appeals for various charity needs. For years he has been grumbling to anyone who will listen that I make too many appeals for money. He wants all appeals, even private requests for needy causes, to be approved first by the synagogue's board of directors.

I don't know why Calvin is so upset. He owns a thriving business plus substantial land and investment property, but gives ridiculously little to charity. Worse, he wants to make certain that others give as little as he does. His behavior brought to mind the Mishnah in *Avot* V:16 which discusses the four types of donors to charity. The most admirable is the one who wishes to give and that others should also give; the least admirable is the one who does not wish to give and does not wish others to give.

Calvin mentioned his objections to me a few months ago. "I give what I can. It's not fair to push us all the time," he said. I was noncommittal, but later on I was sorry I had been so tactful. I promised myself that he wouldn't get away so easily next time.

Next time arrived a month later. A tornado had hit Florida,

and the Jewish community buildings and synagogues of a small town were destroyed. There was a nationwide appeal in all synagogues to help them rebuild. After our appeal, one of the Hebrew teachers, whose salary is very limited, pledged one hundred dollars. The next day, Calvin came up to me and handed me a ten-dollar bill. I was very disappointed. His day of reckoning with me had arrived. "Calvin," I said, "I appreciate this, but this is just not enough for a man like you."

"What do you mean, 'a man like you'? How do you know how much I have or don't have?"

"True, I don't know. But one thing I do know. You have much more than Rabbi Ganz, and he just gave one hundred dollars."

"I'm not interested in what he gave. This is what I can give."

I did the unthinkable. I handed him back his ten bucks and said quietly, "I'm sorry, Cal, but I can't accept this."

"You mean you refuse to accept this?"

"I expect a better contribution from you, Cal, plain and simple. I'm very sorry."

Calvin grabbed the bill from my hand, turned on his heels, and walked away without a word.

The incident troubled me all day, but I was not really sorry about it. All his life he had been getting away with inadequate giving. He needed to be called on it once and for all.

Did it change his giving habits? No. Did I create an enemy? No. Calvin is unable to give, but he is not a vindictive person. However, he now offers me exactly zero whenever I appeal for anything. I hope that at least he feels a bit guilty, because a sense of guilt is a wonderful expression of one's conscience. A guilt-edged conscience keeps us on the straight and narrow.

the problem of affluence

Affluent people by and large associate exclusively with other affluent people. As a result, they come to feel that everyone is comfortable and well-to-do, and that no one has to worry where the next dollar will come from. Their chief financial concern is how best to spend or invest their discretionary income. So they grow oblivious to the people around them who worry about paying the rent, who don't have enough for utility bills, who have to scrimp on groceries, who cannot afford new shoes for their children, who can't pay tuition, who can't afford medical insurance, and for whom life is an unending day-to-day struggle.

Among some of the affluent there is a feeling bordering on resentment at being reminded of such things. They forget that their own money is often due to a wealthy father or to a lucky break; were it not for a tiny twist of events they might now themselves be living hand-to-mouth. They forget that not everyone who is a successful businessman is necessarily wise. Money is their due, a result of their own wit, brains, foresight, vision, and hard work. The fact is that there are many people who have worked as hard as they, and are as endowed with fine minds and foresight, yet never made much money. But this does not impress them. This is the genesis of those nasty bumper-stickers I occasionally see: "I Fight Poverty — I Work."

This is why I so value the several people in the community who are well-to-do and give generously. They have not forgotten what it is to be in need. And, incidentally, I value even more the charity of the poor man who, when he gives one hundred dollars for a cause, is sacrificing much more than the rich man who is giving ten thousand.

the machers and the poor folks

The wealthy and the poor: every local rabbi received a letter from the national office of the U.J.A., asking each rabbi to prepare a list of twenty-five of "the most important and influential" members of the synagogue, whom they would invite to a gala city-wide reception to meet the President of Israel on his forthcoming visit to the community.

The supercilious and exclusive concept of "most important" deeply offended me, so I devised a wicked little scheme. I included on my list only a few people of means, those who have been giving unstintingly to everything. The balance of the list consisted of members who, because they were not wealthy and therefore not influential, were invariably overlooked. I chose some good people who were of very modest means; a few outstanding day-school teachers; some elderly people who were barely getting by; some widows, some divorcees, some single men and women. Each of them would be very pleased to receive a special invitation to such a reception and would enjoy mingling with the bigwigs of the community.

It would also be educational and enlightening for the President of Israel to meet some ordinary people for a change. In his travels throughout the United States he is never exposed to a representative cross-section of American Jewry. He sees only the affluent, the big givers, the self-important. In Atlanta he would at least see some of the *amcha,* some of the Jewish masses, and it would do him, and them, some good.

The gala reception took place at the most luxurious hotel in town. All the movers and shakers of the city were present, Jewish and non-Jewish: the governor, the mayor, the editor and publisher of the *Atlanta Constitution,* the consuls-general of the dozens of countries represented in Atlanta, all the rabbis, the archbishop, the wealthiest men in town and their ladies (and several wealthy ladies and their gentlemen), and of course all the big Jewish givers — plus my own select group of people.

It was one of the glitziest parties ever held in Atlanta, and everyone had an extraordinary good time rubbing shoulders with everyone else. What made it particularly delightful for me was the fact that none of the invitees from my congregation knew that I had orchestrated their invitation, since all invitations had come directly from the Special Committee to Welcome the President of Israel. The luminous pleasure and excitement on the faces of my cadre were wondrous to behold.

It didn't take long, however, for the sponsors to sense that something was not right. Many of the prosperous people they expected were not present. When the sponsors inquired as to who was in fact present from my congregation and discovered that I had invited very few affluent people, they were very unhappy. When they asked me about it a few days later, I simply reminded them that they had asked for the most "important" members of my synagogue, not the richest.

anti-establishmentarianism

Somehow I have always taken a delight in not going along with the Jewish establishment's *diktats*. Their leaders are well intentioned and very effective in fund-raising, but they are by and large without any authentic Jewish awareness and knowledge, and overestimate the significance of the role they play in Jewish life. Even though they generously support crucial causes like local day schools and homes for the aged, they are not by training or knowledge equipped to make the decisions about priorities for the Jewish future. But of course they do make such decisions and set such priorities.

I have always had good personal relationships with many of these leaders, and found them sincere and hard-working for Jewish causes, even if, in most cases, they were Jewishly unlettered. (A delicious exchange at one of their board meetings: I had suggested that a certain activity that was being proposed was not in keeping with Torah and Jewish tradition. Piped up a big giver: "Listen, Rabbi, I respect you and what you stand for and all, but let's try to keep the Torah out of this. No one understands it anyway.")

However, I found that an occasional act of rebellion on my part was necessary for my sanity and well-being. As a general rule, community dissension is to be avoided, because the issues are quickly forgotten and character assassination takes center stage. It is debilitating to all concerned and benefits only those who like to gossip. In my almost four decades as rabbi, I was engaged in only two or three major community conflicts. But there were times when the issues were so important that open conflict had to be risked no matter the costs.

One such issue was the decision of the local Jewish Community Center to open its facilities on Shabbat. It was a long and difficult struggle; we even boycotted events at the Center. It split the entire town in half, but the fight had to be waged. In the end, the main building itself did not open on Shabbat, but their outdoor park facilities and swimming pool in an outlying neighborhood did open on Shabbat, over the objections of the traditional community. The one positive result of the conflict was that the community at large learned of the crucial and overriding importance of Shabbat.

Another conflict involved the decision taken by the local community Federation to withhold funds from Israel until the "Who Is a Jew" issue (really "Who Is a Convert") was settled (read: dropped from the agenda) to the satisfaction of the "leadership of our community." This was, in my view, blackmail: you play the game my way or I stop supporting you. Unspoken, of course, was the key fact that so many of the big givers were either married to converts themselves, or had children who were so married. These were all Conservative and Reform conversions which were not recognized in Israel because the conversion procedures did not follow classic *halachic* norms.

The very possibility that Israel might insist on *halachic* conversions was understandably a very emotional issue to such people. On the other hand, I felt that the threat to cut off support for Israel was arrogant and insensitive — in particular when the rabbinic community in the city was not consulted about such a controversial decision. When the Federation publicly issued its challenge to Israel in the name of the community, I publicly denounced the act from the pulpit. This demonstrated, I said, the skin-deep loyalty to Israel of those who have no solid religious moorings; at the first issue that displeases them, they are ready to cast Israel overboard.

I also pointed out the irony of the situation. The Federation prided itself on its unstinting support of Israel; for them, support for Israel was a kind of substitute Judaism. And yet, they were holding back funds because of this one issue. But the Orthodox synagogue, whose rabbi was often accused of not being Zionist enough, had never suggested that Jews should withhold funds from Israel, no matter how egregiously hurtful to religion were some of Israel's past policies.

To their credit, our synagogue's board of directors disassociated itself from the Federation and publicly declared that the Federation did not speak for us. The Federation was, in the words of one of its leaders, "livid" with rage at me and the Orthodox community. They questioned our integrity and accused us of grandstanding. The double standard was illuminating: it was permissible for the Federation to go public with its threats to cut off funding in the name of the community. But it was not permissible for us to declare publicly that they do not speak for us.

the new golden rule

Long before the Israel imbroglio, I suggested from the pulpit that Jews who know very little about Judaism should realize their limitations and concentrate on raising the funds, and that matters of communal priorities and decision-making should be in the hands of more knowledgeable people. This was a quixotic hope at best — a Federation executive kept telling me that their definition of the Golden Rule was that he who has the gold rules. Nevertheless, I occasionally floated such thoughts because firstly, they were true, and because, even if there was little hope of implementing these ideas in practice, it was important that people hear them. The reaction of my congregation was positive, but the establishment was not amused.

I also used our synagogue bulletin to question the universal habit of giving communal honors and awards simply on the basis of wealth. I challenged the community to give recognition to scholars and righteous people who are models of what a Jew should be. The worth of a Jewish community, I suggested, can be gauged by the type of people it honors.

Apparently I struck a raw nerve, for the reaction was swift. On the positive side, one of the local Reform rabbis, for a change agreeing with me, used it as a text for his sermon. But the Federation leadership took it as a personal affront. I received some vitriolic phone calls and letters of protest — all from people not affiliated with our synagogue.

All the old anti-Orthodox stereotypes emerged from the netherworld: Orthodox Jews are not community minded; they think they are superior, they look down on the community, they are holier-than-thou; they are militant, fanatic, inflexible, behind the times; they look down on women and that's why they seat them behind partitions in their synagogues. The usual, tiresome list.

One letter, after the obligatory litany of anti-Orthodox rhetoric, added that "only a sick man would write something like that in the middle of the campaign." (Clear implication: say whatever you want about us, but after the campaign is over.) "The campaign" is that sacred three-month period when all communal activity grinds to a halt while the funds are being raised. The American Jewish fund-raising apparatus has convinced everyone that to criticize it is to criticize God, Torah, the Jewish people, Jewish destiny, and motherhood. Fund-raising has become an ersatz God, and to suggest that their methods need improvement is heresy.

It is a tribute to the power of the written word that the article was still being discussed around town several months after it was written. It is also a tribute to the loyalty of my own membership that throughout this period they did not flinch, but backed me completely.

After the furor blew over — and I was sorry to see it end, because for many people it created a new awareness of the problem — I was sitting at a glittering fund-raising dinner for Israel. The man sitting next to me on the dais was puffing on a huge cigar and was in a very expansive mood.

"Who would have thought ten years ago," he mused aloud, "that today I could afford to be sitting up here on the dais with all these important people."

He meant his statement to be taken at face value, without a trace of irony. Here in microcosm was our problem: who sits on the dais of American Jewish life? He who can "afford" it. And who is important? Also he who can afford it.

pride goeth before humility

The local Israel Bonds organization is less representative of the powerful and the affluent of the community, and therefore much easier to live with. Their task is to encourage investments in Israel, and they have no pretensions about establishing priorities for the Jewish future. While they are a much more benign organization, I had to be watchful even with them.

For example, our congregation, at its annual Israel Bond dinner, never had an honoree and always resisted the accepted vulgarization of these dinners: candle-lighting ceremonies, distribution of award plaques, and the other gimmickry of the Jewish dinner circuit.

On the printed invitation to one particular dinner many years ago, they inserted pictures of the various chairmen and dignitaries of the local Bond organization. They had wanted to include mine as well, but I refused — not out of modesty but out of pride.

Somehow it was beneath my dignity to have my name attached to the tired cliches which adorned every picture: "Exemplary service to Jewish life"; "in the forefront for a secure Israel"; "distinguished business leader . . . many talents . . . strength and inspiration on behalf of many causes . . . dynamic leadership" — all those boilerplate descriptions, used in this town one night and in the next town the next night, that are attached to any warm body that consents to act as a host or chairman. To have such terms used about me was a profound embarrassment, and so I respectfully declined.

Unfortunately, those who noted the absence of my picture assumed I had been neglected by Israel Bonds and wrongly blamed the organization, or thought I did not want my picture included because of my humility and gave me undeserved credit. Sometimes pride goeth before humility.

Chapter 17:
"I'm Not Enjoying
This Mourning"

That unfortunate word "enjoy": how it has been twisted out of shape. I deliver a particularly sad eulogy at the sudden death of a young husband, and his widow tells me amidst her tears that she really enjoyed what I said.

Another example: a young woman whose father has just died comes in to clarify what she may and may not do during the year of mourning. She is not observant but wants to honor her father's memory. During our discussion I explain the purposes of the mourning restrictions: to express tangibly one's sadness at the loss of a loved one's life, so that whenever she refrains from going to a concert or a party she is in fact honoring the memory of her father. To carry on normally as if nothing happened, I suggest to her, is in effect to say that the loss she experienced was not very significant.

A few months later I see her at a meeting. "I want you to know," she says, "that I am not at all enjoying this year of mourning."

Granted, the young woman no doubt meant that to forgo music and partying was not easy, and the widow meant that the eulogy was uplifting — but I wish they would stop using that "E" word.

My other unfavorite word is the "C" word: "comfortable." Every so often a member resigns from our synagogue because he doesn't feel comfortable during services, and joins another congregation where he feels more comfortable. He is not referring to his chair.

These misused words reflect our narcissistic, self-indulgent society. I *daven* because I enjoy it; I do a *mitzvah* because it makes me feel good; I do *chesed* because it gives me a warm feeling inside; I build a *sukkah* because it's fun for the kids; I have a Pesach Seder because it's a great family time. The inevitable measuring rod is one's personal pleasure. The other, or the Other, is immaterial. As soon as the pleasure fades, as soon as I stop feeling good about it, as soon as that warm, comfortable feeling evaporates, then Torah and *mitzvot* and God Himself also evaporate.

This is the criterion by which religion is judged: Does it make me feel good? Does the sermon make me feel comfortable? Do I enjoy praying? That the purposes of God and Torah and commandments and prayer are not merely to help us feel good but to help us become better people, even holy people — this rarely occurs to anyone. They don't occur to anyone because rabbis never talk about it. And when rabbis do talk about it, the people feel uncomfortable and they don't enjoy it and don't feel good about it and resign from the synagogue and find one where they can feel good and be comfortable and have more enjoyment because the rabbi delivers talks on politics or on current books or films.

God of enjoyment and fun

We take our religious pulses too frequently. Am I enjoying the services, is it doing anything for me, is Judaism helping me? Instead, prayer should be focused on reaching out to God and making some kind of spiritual contact with Him. To be solely preoccupied with the question of whether prayer is or is not doing anything for us is really to focus on the self and not on the Other. It is said that the Baal Shem Tov used to say: "If I pray one hundred times without proper *kavannah* and focus and sincerity, and the next time with *kavannah*, that one time lifts up the other hundred times, because that one time creates the breakthrough and pulls the others through the opening with it." One must keep the channels open, and occasionally one will make a spiritual breakthrough. Furthermore, the one hundred inadequate attempts were not wasted at all. Without them, the hundred-first might not have occurred at all.

Enjoyment is not the issue. One is supposed to stand alone before his Maker — a shattering, shuddering moment. How can people talk during serious prayer? How can they chuckle, tell jokes, gossip — gossip! — all before the King of Kings?

Once religion becomes merely comfortable, once it stops pricking the conscience and no longer serves as a goad for selflessness towards other people and towards God, it is no longer religion but a sop. Poor Moses. He tried to teach us how to live lives of discipline, but the people of Moses refuse to budge from their couches. This is today's religious demand: make me comfortable, otherwise I will take my business elsewhere. Without stirring from deep within their lounge chairs, a goodly portion of American

Jews turn their Judaism on and off with their remote control buttons, surfing from one synagogue to another in a relentless search for the one that will deliver full comfort and enjoyment.

The day is approaching when some enterprising prayer committee will change the opening of the *Amidah* to read: "Blessed art Thou, our God and the God of our fathers, God of Abraham, God of Isaac, and God of Jacob, the Author of comfort and enjoyment and fun, Who provides pleasure and gratification to His creatures and will send His Redeemer to us to enhance our good times in this world."

David Morrison is a case in point. Brought up in our shul, married by me, a constant visitor to my study since he was a teenager, he and his wife are resigning to join a Conservative congregation where they "will feel more comfortable."

Having been very supportive of him through his many personal crises, I was quite surprised when he informed me. He must have read my mind. "Rabbi, I want you to know it's not you. You are wonderful, there is no one like you, we love you. (David never quite lost his teen-age effusiveness.) It's just that the shul has become so Orthodox that we don't feel comfortable any more."

"How do you mean that?" I knew exactly what he meant, but wanted him to articulate it.

"Well," he said, "you say things in your sermons that we can't live up to. It makes us feel bad."

"I'm sorry to make you feel bad, but why don't you look at it as a prod to become a better Jew?"

"Well, we think we're pretty good Jews, really. We're not perfect, but we try." They are very fine people, but their observance of Jewish practice does not go beyond Friday-night candles.

I tried to show him that a synagogue is the one place where we should not expect to feel comfortable, that *davening* is not a social event, but an occasion where we meet God and God meets us. Discomfort, I suggested, is a sign that we are growing religiously. But all to no avail.

What puzzled me most was the fact that he had just gone through major surgery. I had visited him several times in the hospital, and our relationship seemed even more solidified than ever.

Again he seemed to read my mind: "I know this will sound selfish, but we've been thinking about doing this for a long time. I wanted to wait until after the operation just in case I needed you."

Well, I hope that at the very least he will have no future need for me. The sad truth is that where he is going, he and his wife and children will have no opportunity for religious growth, since little will be demanded of them and whatever they do will be more than enough. They will remain comfortable and undisturbed.

He brought to mind Walter Greif, highly intelligent and educated, who for years has not moved one iota religiously. The reason: he feels that he is in tune with God, and he constantly receives messages from Him telling him what to do and how to behave. Therefore, he tells me, he doesn't require a Torah or a Judaism, since he has direct access to God and has transcended the religious requirements.

What I found most revealing was that everything God tells him seems to make his life much more self-indulgent. God tells him that he need not observe kashrut, or Shabbat, or any of the *mitzvot*. God supports his decision never to attend synagogue. He makes no demands on Walter. Great God!

I once asked him if God ever tells him what he must and must not do, and if He ever commanded him to do anything that was inconvenient. Walter did not reply.

the rabbi advocates major sinning

We are living not in a time of sinners, but in a time of mediocrities. The story of Elijah's battle with the priests of Baal on Mount Carmel is instructive. Elijah challenges the Jewish people to make a choice: either the God of Israel is the Master, or Baal is the master. Today things are very different. We have no genuine idol-worshipers. Today we have idol-worshipers who are not really committed to their idolatry. Since there are no real idolaters, there are no real Elijahs either. Great sin engenders great saints, and mediocrity engenders mediocrity. And since there are no Elijahs today, there are no obvious miracles, no fires descending from heaven.

Since there are no Elijahs and no open miracles today, it is easier for us to straddle the theological fence, for we are not quite certain if we prefer the Lord God of Israel or the contemporary counterparts of Baal. Therefore, because there are no great sinners and no prophets and no clear signs from on high, and we are not sure where we stand, we have to strain mightily to hear God's thundering voice from Sinai. This means that in the absence of heavenly fire we must create our own fire through serious study of Torah, openness of heart, deeds of lovingkindness, and relentless pursuit of closeness with our Creator.

I tried to explain this idea of religious mediocrity — that even the sinning of our day is mediocre — to one of my adult discussion groups. By the end of the week I heard that people were puzzled why the rabbi was advocating major sinning.

* * *

A mother once called me to complain that the *bris* of her newborn son had to take place on Shabbat. She and her husband would rather have it on Sunday. I told them that Jewish law is clear: a *bris* takes place on the eighth day after birth even if the eighth day is Shabbat, even if it is Yom Kippur.

"But Rabbi, aren't we forbidden to cut on Shabbat?"

I found this hard to take from someone who did not observe Shabbat or much else. "True," I replied, trying to hide my pique at her sudden concern for Jewish law, "but for a *bris* we are not only permitted to cut, we are obligated to cut."

Now the truth emerged. "Well, my husband has a dress shop, and Shabbat is his biggest day. He'll have to close up the store for half a day, Rabbi. That's a tremendous loss on a Saturday."

By this time I had had enough. "You ought to consider this: when God grants you a healthy baby and a happy occasion like a *bris,* perhaps you should be ready to give up a little something for His sake."

"But why is our religion so inflexible?"

"If you have a religion that keeps changing its laws to meet everyone's personal convenience, you end up without any religion at all. Supposing traffic laws changed every few days in order to make things easier for individual drivers. We'd have total chaos."

The *bris* did take place on Shabbat. During the proceedings, as I gave *mazal tov* to the mother, she whispered an apology to me. "I'm sorry I gave you such a hard time the other day, but you know how it is."

I nodded but said nothing. Then she added: "But I still think our religion is inflexible; we should really do something about that."

The comfort syndrome is all-pervasive: religion is to be adjustable and pliable, like a good swivel chair, moving in whatever direction we happen to turn, submissive to our wishes. Even God Himself has to make us comfortable. God help Him if He doesn't.

Rosh Hashanah jogging

Estelle and I were walking home from shul on the second day of Rosh Hashanah. It was a lovely, warm day. Approaching us from the distance was a shirtless jogger in shorts. As he drew closer, I realized that he was a Jew who lives in the neighborhood. He had once been a member of our shul, but a few years earlier he had left us to join the Reform Temple because, yes, our shul made him uncomfortable.

Dilemma: should I wish him a *Shanah Tovah* and possibly

embarrass him, or should I ignore him, say nothing, and be seen as snubbing him?

I wished him a *Shanah Tovah,* and he responded in kind. As he trotted by us he suddenly turned around, smiled, and said: "You gotta admit, there are certain advantages to being Reform. They only have one day Rosh Hashanah."

The implications are fascinating; by withdrawing your annual dues from one synagogue and transferring them to another, you absolve yourself from serving God in a certain way.

For him the "advantages" are that he can jog while I have to go to shul on the second day of Rosh Hashanah. He can have "fun," while I have to pray. He can be Comfortable and Enjoy, while I have do's and don't's to follow in my religious life.

✳ ✳ ✳

The major idea I try to impart with everything I teach my people is this: the religious life in effect boils down to making the choice between bending God to our will, or bending ourselves to His will. The single great foundation that underlies all human behavior is, obviously, self-interest. Torah is the guide that helps us transcend our natural, selfish instincts and turn them into an instinct for service of others and of God.

This authentic religious attitude is not produced by one sermon, or by a dozen. It is the work of a lifetime. That's how long it takes to change a single human trait, much less a fundamental, built-in quality like selfishness.

Enjoyment and pleasure are perfectly acceptable in Judaism; we are not an ascetic religion. But the secret of Judaism is what it lends to physical pleasure. It adds to it a certain permanence by linking it with the timeless and removing its evanescent here-today-gone-tomorrow quality.

The divine irony of it all is this: the less one concerns himself with the enjoyment of religion, the more one can derive profound satisfaction from it.

I don't agree with the Torah

A young Jewish man whom I never met, married to a non-Jewess, called me to arrange a *bris* for their newborn son. Has the wife converted to Judaism? No. In that case, I replied, the child is not Jewish according to Jewish law and may not have a *bris*. Would I be willing, he asked, to convert the baby to Judaism? I replied that this was theoretically possible under certain special circumstances. Would he and his wife, I asked, raise the child as a Jew? He hesitated and finally said that until the child is eighteen they would probably just take him both to synagogue and to church, and then they would let the child choose.

It was the old, thoughtless banality. I asked him if he expected to wait until age eighteen to let his child choose about things like personal hygiene or proper behavior. He didn't see the analogy.

I told him that obviously the way he raised his child was ultimately up to him and his wife, but that not raising his child as a real Jew would make a mockery both of the conversion of the child and of the *bris*.

"I don't see why," he argued. "I feel the baby is Jewish."

I tried to explain that when it comes to living by any system of law, much less God's law, our personal feelings are beside the point.

"I still don't agree with the law," he said. "I feel my kid is a Jew, and I don't see why you should deny the *bris* to him."

"I personally am not denying anything to you. It's really a simple matter. Jewish law has certain requirements for a *bris*. Your situation does not meet these requirements. There is nothing I as a rabbi can do about those basic facts."

Here it all is in a nutshell: subjective religion. Everything depends on what we "feel." Knowledge, learning, standards, personal discipline, Torah, and Jewish law are all beside the point.

Point, counterpoint. A Christian young man called me soon after this *bris* incident. He was married to a Jewish woman, they had just had a baby, and he wondered if the baby should have "the circumcision rite." He had met with a non-Orthodox rabbi who told him that he was attaching too much religious significance to the circumcision, that its major purpose was to identify oneself with the group and nothing more.

But this Christian young man somehow felt that there was more to it than this, and decided to call the Orthodox rabbi. He had heard that the circumcision was a covenant, and thought that maybe it was more of a religious event than the other rabbi had led him to believe.

* * *

Bending ourselves to God's will: my mind drifted back a few years to a Jewish store on New York's Lower East Side. A man — he appeared to be a rabbi but I could not be certain — was trying on a form-fitting *tallis*. It was not really a *tallis* but a narrow silk shawl with tassels and stripes. Most non-Orthodox rabbis wear these instead of the long, traditional woolen *tallis*. Beyond the fact that it does not conform to *halachic* standards, the shawl typifies the be-Jewish-but-not-too-Jewish philosophy: wear a *tallis* but let it resemble a priest's cassock; wear a *tallis* but cut it down to size; wear your tradition but make it form-fitting.

The poor chap was with his wife, and they were having trouble finding just the right item.

"I want something a little more striking. Do you have something with a gold *atarah*?" He went to the mirror and turned carefully from side to side.

"No," said his wife, "it's not quite right. It hangs too long."

The proprietor, ever obliging, scurried to the rear and brought out a dozen new shawls. "These just arrived. Our latest line."

Jewish Miss Manners

The real tragedy of the Conservative and Reform movements is not so much that they legitimize the abandonment of classical Jewish law and tradition. It is that even from their own pragmatic point of view they are unable to retain Jews within their own non-Orthodox fold. Having transformed violations of the most sacred laws into mere breaches of etiquette, these rabbis have turned themselves into Jewish Miss Manners — and with less authority. They have denuded Judaism of any binding force and are unable to offer Jews anything solid to which they can return. Jewish laymen may be Jewishly unlettered, but they are not fools. They can sense genuineness and intellectual honesty, and they can sense the reverse as well. The spiritual facts of life are that you cannot bring people into holiness by compromising that holiness.

I do not like to be so critical of these Conservative and Reform rabbis. I like them personally and have always gotten along well with them. As a rabbi, I know that their lives are far from easy, and I strongly empathize with them. I am also confident that they are sincere in their desire to save Judaism.

The problem is that with some shining exceptions, they seem not to be quite sure just what Judaism is: a form of liberalism, a force for social justice? Their definitions change with the vagaries of the daily headlines and with the latest editorial opinions of *The New York Times.* One gets the impression of a lack of compass and steady vision. This is why their Temples are beset with horrendous rates of intermarriage, which in turn fuels their willingness to perform quickie conversions wholesale and to recognize patrilineal descent. The cold facts are that their track record in returning Jews to Judaism is dismal. They do not develop *mitzvah* observers. They simply have failed to instill serious Jewish commitment or serious Jewish living into most of their people.

Case in point: I attended a certain funeral service although I was not officiating. I heard the son of the deceased ask the officiating Conservative rabbi whether it was necessary to cover the casket with earth after the burial. "If it's not necessary, I would rather not have it done," said the son. The act of covering is, of course, clearly prescribed by *halacha*h.

The rabbi whispered reassuringly, "Well, it's really up to you."

So this is Jewish law: it's up to you; whatever you want; we are here to please. You want to follow Jewish law? We will oblige. You prefer not to? No problem. It's up to you. Deep in his heart, can this mourner have any respect for Judaism?

A teen-ager once told me,"We really have a great religion — it doesn't tell you what to do. It leaves everything up to you." Now I know where he received his Jewish education.

No wonder the non-Orthodox are facing a future of severely declining numbers due, tragically, to intermarriage and assimilation. It doesn't take long to realize that a religion that asks little and demands little is ultimately worth little. Why remain within the fold when, upon inspection, there is no fold?

The Orthodox are far from perfect; we are fragmented and do not quite know how to reach out effectively to the non-Orthodox. But the facts are obvious, and who can gainsay them? The Orthodox change people's lives, have the lowest rates of divorce, intermarriage, and assimilation, send thousands of young men and women to study Torah in Israel and America at advanced levels, and produce committed, learned young people. By contrast, the other movements, despite their tremendous resources and power, have very little of Jewish substance to show for it.

In moments of candor, some of their own leaders admit privately that spiritually and ideologically they are bankrupt. They realize that they are presiding over the spiritual demise of millions of Jews and are unable to stem the tide. This is the great tragedy of contemporary Judaism.

saving Judaism:
the dead-end street

One of the great mistakes rabbis make, including some of the Orthodox, is that instead of fulfilling our mission — which is to teach Torah, uplift people, raise their religious sights, demonstrate the depths and wisdom of our tradition — we try to play God and become obsessed not with teaching Judaism but with saving Judaism. And some rabbis attempt to save Judaism at all costs — even if it means altering and distorting the Torah. We save the patient by killing him.

Our task is not to save Judaism, but to teach it, transmit it, instill a sense of love and sacrifice for God and for Torah — and leave the saving to God. We should do our part and allow God to do His. Otherwise our *ad hoc* attempts to save Judaism for God can lead to all kinds of dead-end streets.

At the turn of the century, Reform tried to save Judaism by expurgating from the prayerbook the Hebrew language, as well as all references to the ultimate return to Zion and Jerusalem. We must be up to date and relevant lest we lose our youth, they said. Yet they lost their youth — and their elders as well — to assimilation and intermarriage. Their modernized prayerbook did nothing to stem the tide. On the contrary, it gave it added force. Many Jews reasoned that if our religion is a virtual carbon copy of the Protestant Church, why not follow this to its logical conclusion and be Protestant in fact? This was a reasonable reaction, but Reform was blind to the facts of life; they were too busy reforming Judaism.

Nowadays, the Conservative movement is repeating the same error, albeit with more caution, because the terrible history of the twentieth century is a restraining force. Nevertheless, the save-Judaism syndrome is tenacious. Their new prayerbook, for example, now refers to the ancient Temple service in the past tense, something that long ago took place in ancient Israel — rather than in the normative future tense, as something for whose restoration we pray.

Their swing to "creative services," their emphasis on "relevance" — these are all integral parts of today's Conservative movement. All are manifestations of the weakening of their belief in Torah, *halachah*, and the processes of Jewish law. Only when the past becomes meaningless is there the drive to resort to more contemporary techniques — all in order to save Judaism, of course.

At a recent national convention of Conservative rabbis, one of America's most famous rabbis stated that it is immoral to follow the attitude of Torah and *halachah* with regard to homosexual behavior. Where *halachah* and morality conflict, he declared, morality must prevail. That human definitions of morality change with the seasons did not seem to disturb him. If it seems immoral to me, claims this rabbi, that is sufficient unto itself. Subjective religion.

This philosophy reared its head some years earlier when this same group debated the issue of counting women to a *minyan*. The issue is not whether women count as people, of course. It is, rather, whether one can count to a quorum those who are not under full legal obligation to pray. Women are exempt from prayer obligations for a variety of reasons.

Arose the chairman of the Law Committee, a prominent Conservative rabbi. "I know that Jewish law does not allow women to be counted as part of the *minyan*. But I think it's immoral not to do so. Hence, I vote that Jewish law be overruled."

If prominent rabbis can base major religious decisions on their personal feelings of the moment, how can I blame a Jewishly deprived young man for saying that even though *halachah* says his child is not Jewish, he feels that it is?

Chapter 18:
For Goodness' Sake

have been noting the Me-ness of our times, the solipsism and the narcissism, the emphasis on enjoyment and personal comfort which drives religious decisions. But let me not be quick to generalize. So many of my people have inspired me with their sensitivity and goodness.

Among them was a ninety-nine-year-old great-grandmother. She had been experiencing frightening dreams of late. Her father appeared to her, crying bitterly; animals tried to attack her; friends appeared and disappeared.

She was a pious lady and wanted to talk to an Orthodox rabbi, but she lived in a small town in Alabama, and the nearest rabbi was two hundred miles away and very much Reform. She had called her granddaughter in Atlanta and told her she wanted to talk with an Orthodox rabbi — even if only on the telephone.

The granddaughter related the entire story to me. Apparently, the grandmother was a very kind lady who, during the thirties, kept the only kosher home in her area of rural Alabama. Jewish peddlers who passed through town selling their wares always knew that they could stop at her house and have a kosher meal. She never asked for money and often gave her own food away to them.

One particular peddler was very obnoxious, had a loud voice, annoyed her with his vulgarity, and also disturbed the non-Jews in the neighborhood with his boisterous behavior. One night during supper she raised her voice and told him to quiet down, and that if he did not, he should never bother to come back to her house. He never returned. That was in 1935.

The incident still troubled her. She was convinced that her dreams were a kind of retribution for being unkind to that man.

I called her. She was of excellent mind, very lucid, though hard of hearing. She wanted me to assure her that I was Orthodox. Ever considerate, she said, "It's not that I have anything against the Reform, but I am used to the old-fashioned kind of rabbi." I assured her that I was quite old-fashioned and told her that God must love her very much to have allowed her to live for so many wonderful years. I asked her what her secret was and how I might get to be her age some day. "Just live the way God wants you to," she said.

She told me about her dreams. I suggested to her that she was justified in being upset with the rowdy guest and that I was certain he had taken no offense, because in his heart he knew that she was right. I also told her that while I couldn't speak for Him, I was pretty confident that the good Lord was not holding this against her. Nevertheless, I suggested to her that she give a small amount of money to *tzedakah* every night before she went to sleep, read some psalms, and ask God to grant her peaceful nights. I also read to her the special prayer for dreams in the *siddur,* the *Hatavat Halom:* "I have dreamed a dream and do not know what it indicates . . . May all my dreams be good ones . . . Protect me and be gracious unto me . . ." She found this very comforting. I assured her that I would pray for her each day, and that I felt optimistic that the frightening dreams would quickly disappear.

She seemed reassured and blessed me profusely with all good things. But her story and her sweet decency have blessed me many times over.

Conscience is the trace of Godliness within us. If we utilize it properly, it is a way to keep us on the narrow track of being human. Do beasts have a conscience? Do they feel guilty after they devour their prey? Only human beings have this brake on their bestiality.

For example, David Berkman, seventy-five years old, came in to see me about a personal problem that was an echo of the Alabama *bobbe.* David had been unable to sleep for two weeks. The reason: last month he had in anger said about someone, "He can go to hell." He had never used words like that about anyone before and was deeply distressed. "Rabbi, I feel miserable, just miserable. I want to apologize to him, but if I tell him what I said it will only make things worse. Is there anything I can do?"

I tried first to relieve his guilt, telling him that he had not committed a dastardly crime and that we are all human and have our limits. His regret, I pointed out, was an indication of the high standards he had always set for himself.

But I could not assuage his pain. "After all these years," he kept muttering to himself, "after all these years to do something like that."

It was deeply ironic: a man who had inadvertently allowed one nasty sentence to slip from his mouth was feeling more remorse than some of the major sinners who over the years have strutted in and out of my study.

My prescription for him was the same as that for the great-grandmother: give some meaningful *tzedakah,* read psalms, and pray for forgiveness if he had violated any of God's laws. He felt a bit better, and I asked him to call me in a few days to tell me how he was doing.

A well-known rabbi's widow arrived in town one day on an unorthodox mission: she was raising money for her late husband's yeshivah in Jerusalem, traveling from town to town throughout the United States in order to save the institution from bankruptcy. Men do this constantly, but the sight of a pious woman going from door to door and from office to office was very disconcerting.

When the woman came to the office of Frank Gardner, a well-to-do member of the non-Orthodox community, he was about to write out a generous check when he stopped. "Tell me," he said, "how much do you hope to collect altogether in Atlanta?"

"About one thousand dollars," she said.

"I am embarrassed," said Frank, "that a fine lady like you should have to do this. I'll make this check out for fifteen hundred dollars on one condition: promise me that you will not go from door to door in Atlanta, Georgia."

She agreed and happily left town the next morning. She told me that throughout her travels in the United States, many people had expressed their chagrin at her plight, but only this man had done something concrete about it.

Some people are blessed with innate sensitivity. I remember Joe Friedenthal's telephone call at six one morning. His voice was very calm. "Rabbi, I'm sorry to call so early, but I wanted you to know that my wife Annie passed away this morning at two A.M."

"Why didn't you call me earlier to let me know?"

"There was no point in waking you and your family up at that hour. She was gone. What more could be done for her?"

I am amazed at the natural kindness of some people. I was

working in my study one late Friday afternoon, about an hour before Shabbat. The phone rang. "Rabbi, this is Lea Sapperstein. I am sorry to bother you on Friday afternoon, I know how busy you are."

"That's okay, Lea. How are you? How's Jake?"

She replied in a calm voice: "Rabbi, Jake just died. Suddenly. He collapsed on the street downtown. They took him by ambulance to the hospital, but it was too late. I'm in the hospital now. Rabbi, what should I do? It's almost Shabbos."

I found out what I could from her and told her to wait right there for my call. Shabbat was now less than one hour away. I quickly talked to the doctors, to the hospital officials, to the mortician, to our *Chevra Kadisha*, to the officials in our shul who handle such things. Gradually, all the arrangements fell into place. One of our good members drove down to the hospital to bring Lea home. I rushed over to her house and found her perfectly in control, calm, composed, magnificent in her strength.

All this was part of the ordinary course of a synagogue day. What was not ordinary was her opening remark when I picked up the phone: "Rabbi, I am sorry to bother you on Friday afternoon, I know how busy you are." A mundane expression, but in the context of her personal shock and tragedy, the mundane words take on amazing new dimensions of generosity of spirit, unselfishness, and consideration for others.

Chapter 19:
God, Would You
Mind Waiting One
More Week

God's very first words to Adam concern food: he might eat of everything in the Garden except from the one tree. Even in Paradise there are restrictions on eating. From the beginning there are limits placed on man's physicality. Animals eat, human beings eat; is there to be no difference between them?

Certain foods are forbidden to us always, and even what we may eat has to be prepared and slaughtered in a prescribed way. Certain foods must be eaten at certain seasons (matzah on Pesach) or in a certain place (the succah). At certain times we may not partake of any food at all (Yom Kippur). Wine and bread are essential ingredients in ushering in holy days. And all food requires a blessing to God before and after we partake of it. Food is an integral part of the framework of the relationship between God and ourselves. The way we view food and utilize it is a litmus test of our humanity, because food, like all physical things, can very easily dominate us. There's much more to food than meets the eye — or the belly.

* * *

Vivian Brown and family, after much agonizing, finally decided to make their home kosher. I was scheduled to come to her house on a certain Wednesday to supervise the complicated turnover process: metalware has to be immersed in boiling water, certain utensils and food items must be discarded, others can be retained. All this requires a rabbi's supervision.

On the night prior to our appointment, she called. Would I mind postponing the appointment for one week? She just discovered a large amount of non-kosher meat in her freezer, and before becoming kosher she thought it more practical that she and her family use it up rather than throw it out.

Again one of those situations for which no amount of study can prepare a rabbi. She was ready to do what it takes to maintain a strictly kosher household, but, dear God, let's be practical. Would You mind waiting one more week before I bow to Your will?

a unique defense of kashrut

Even more absurd was an episode many years ago. Two of my officers, very loyal to the shul and to me, were having a business meeting with two other gentlemen who happened to be leaders in the Reform Temple. The conversation soon turned to that month's hot topic of conversation: my attempts to persuade Jewish organizations that their communal dinners must be kosher. When the organizations balked, claiming that the nonkosher functions were more elegant, I calmly suggested from the pulpit that I saw no reason why our synagogue should support Jewish organizations that publicly flout Jewish tradition and discriminate against observant Jews.

The two Reform laymen felt that I was being too militant and trying to impose my views on the rest of the community.

My two officers defended me very astutely. "We're not personally observant," they said, "but our rabbi isn't telling people what they may or may not do in their private lives. He's only saying that public Jewish functions sponsored by Jewish organizations should respect Jewish tradition. That's not coercion, just plain Jewish self-respect. Is it fair or right that Orthodox Jews should be excluded from the functions of the Jewish community?"

All of which was well said. What was ludicrous — and, in a perverse way, touching — was that they were defending me while partaking of a nonkosher meal in a nonkosher restaurant.

the butcher and the baker . . .

Time was when the only kosher establishments in the city were the butcher and the baker. Today there are butchers and bakers plus a plethora of hotels, restaurants, pizza shops, lunchrooms, supermarkets, caterers, and a host of other establishments under proper kashrut supervision. This has been a blessing for the community, but life for the rabbi was much simpler before we got so organized. Now the rabbi has to deal not only with proprietors of shops, but also with angry catering managers, the threat of lawsuits, defamation of character, Cadillac lusts, private detectives, and the Georgia General Assembly.

It was a few days before a major kosher dinner at one of the elegant local hotels. The lady who was their new catering manager was on the phone: "Rabbi, this man you sent down here to supervise the dinner is insisting on burning out the ovens."

"Correct. Those are his instructions. He's supposed to do that before every function."

"Those kosher requirements are really too strict, Rabbi. The chefs are going crazy. Our kitchen staff can't handle it. We have to do something."

There was a tone of resentment in her voice which disturbed me, particularly since we had been running kosher functions at this hotel for many years without incident.

"Do you boil up pots and pans in your kitchen at home? Do you burn your oven out with a blowtorch every time you eat?" she demanded.

"Of course not. The only time one needs to do such things is when things have become nonkosher. We do this in the hotel because the oven may have been used with nonkosher meat."

"This dinner is for the American Jewish Committee. There will be five hundred guests here. I am willing to bet that not ten of them keep kosher in their homes. Why do we have to be so strict for 490 people who couldn't care less?"

I started to explain that Jewish organizations all try to maintain Jewish traditions in their public functions regardless of the practices of their individual members, when suddenly the obvious struck me. "Are you Jewish? " I asked.

"Yes, of course."

"I knew it."

"How did you know?" she asked.

"Because I cannot imagine a non-Jew speaking to a rabbi about kashrut in such an insulting manner. There are always questions that people have about the kosher regulations. But in the many years I have been dealing with kashrut in this community, no one has ever had the *chutzpah* to question our requirements the way you just did."

She immediately backed off and apologized. I ended the conversation by telling her that we have not had any problems in the past, but that if the hotel wanted to get out of the kosher business it needed only to inform me and I would be happy to advise Jewish organizations and individuals to take their functions to other hotels.

"Oh, we certainly want this business, it's just that what we're required to do seems a bit much."

I was sorely tempted to call her superior and report the incident. But I didn't want her to lose her job, so I did nothing. Since that episode, incidentally, there have been no more outbursts.

we'll let the lawyers decide

One day I noticed an ad in the daily paper: the Jensen Bros. restaurant chain was promoting their "kosher luncheon delicatessen." Jensen is a totally nonkosher establishment which never made any pretense of being kosher. I called the district manager and informed him that the ad was misleading, and that any food, even if it is kosher to start with, that is processed in a nonkosher kitchen is presumed to be nonkosher.

He quickly understood and apologized for the misunderstanding. Like many non-Jews, he thought that kosher simply meant "clean" or "pure." Since he was bringing in delicatessen food from a famous kosher processor in New York, he thought the ad would attract some new customers. He promised to kill the ad that day.

End of story? No. Within a week I received an angry phone call from the sales manager of the kosher purveyor in New York. What right did I have to say that his product was not kosher when it had rabbinical certification?

I explained that the most kosher product in the world becomes immediately nonkosher once it is cooked in the ovens of nonkosher establishments. He would not listen. "If you don't rescind your ban on our product, I'm afraid there will be some problems," he said.

"Sir, I did not ban your product. Jensen can continue to bring as much of it in as it likes. But what Jensen cannot do is prepare it and then advertise it as kosher. Once it enters their kitchens and is processed, it loses its kosher status."

"Rabbi, maybe I'm not making myself clear," he said. "I intend to give this over to our attorneys, because we believe you are guilty of restraint of trade. We don't think you have the right to tell anyone what they can or cannot advertise."

"True, up to a point. But if the advertising is misleading and affects the Jewish community, I think I do have that right."

"Well, we'll let the lawyers decide that. Nice talking to you, Rabbi."

I immediately called one of the best attorneys in town, a good personal friend. He told me that in his judgment the threat was a bluff and that I would never hear from them again. He was right.

the rabbi was the crook

Little did we dream when we granted kosher supervision to Max the Deli Man that one day I would be seeking legal counsel to defend my own good name.

One day our inspector found nonkosher oils on Max's premises. It is tempting to use such oils because they are of inferior grade and therefore much less expensive than kosher oils. Max claimed that the oils had been delivered in error and that he had never used them.

Two months later our inspector found nonkosher oils again. There might have been a delivery error one time, but not two times. We demanded to see his delivery records. "You don't trust me," he whined. "If there is no trust, there can be no relationship between us." He was right on both counts.

"Max, unless we see those records we will have to withdraw our endorsement."

He kept repeating the mantra: "You don't trust me. There has to be trust." But he refused to show us his books.

We publicly announced the withdrawal of our supervision. It is our policy, in order to avoid unnecessary humiliation to the business whose supervision is being revoked, never to divulge the specific reasons for discontinuation of the endorsement. We simply make it known, through pulpit and newspaper announcements, that the endorsement is withdrawn.

In this instance, it turned out, this was misplaced courtesy. Max immediately began a campaign to malign my reputation. He told everyone who would listen that I had demanded from him a five-thousand-dollar contribution to the synagogue, which he had refused because he considered it blackmail, and that this was the real reason the endorsement was withdrawn. In Max's eyes the rabbi was the crook, while he himself was the noble and righteous one who had stood by his principles even though it had cost him his business.

The story was preposterous on the face of it, but he repeated it so frequently that some people began to whisper about it in the community. After all, they reasoned, where there's smoke, there's fire. It must have made great gossip: "You won't believe this, but you want to know the real reason they pulled the supervision from the kosher deli shop? I heard . . ."

But there was not even smoke — only Max's fevered imagination. I finally asked an attorney to send Max a strong letter threatening a suit if he continued this defamation. That finally laid the matter to rest.

I want a Cadillac, not a Chevy

Moe Stein ran a cookie specialty shop under our kosher supervision. He understood that he would have to remain closed on Shabbat, and for the first several years he did. His business was gradually building up, and he made a decent living. But he kept yearning to open on Shabbat; that one day's business, he kept telling me, would equal his profits for the rest of the week. He was clearly champing at the bit, but time and again I was able to persuade him that it would only be a trade-off; his regular kosher customers would leave him if he lost his kosher endorsement by opening on Shabbat.

One day Moe came in to see me. He was an honest fellow and came right to the point. "It's no use, Rabbi. I have to throw in the towel. I have to open up on Shabbat. I know I'll lose the *hechsher*, but I figure that financially I'll do better."

"Maybe financially, Moe. But how about religiously?"

"Look, I feel bad about this, but I just have to do it. There's no way out."

"But Moe, you're making a living, and each year is better than before."

"I know, but it's not enough. I'm not greedy, but I have to have more income, and that's it."

"You're a big boy, Moe. I can't force you into anything. I'm just very sorry and very disappointed."

"You gotta understand. My father drove an old, beat-up Chevy all his life. I want to drive a Cadillac. My father couldn't afford a decent house for us to grow up in. I want my kids to grow up in a big house. All that takes money, Rabbi. If I close on Shabbat, I'll remain with my Chevy and with the same house I'm in now. That's not fair to my kids. What's better, Rabbi, that I never grow financially and remain a nothing like I am now, or that I make some real money and become a somebody? Listen, I don't know a lot about my religion and maybe I should know more, but one thing I do know. God doesn't want me to remain a nobody, does he?"

"Moe, you're a nobody when you ignore your own religion, no matter how much money you make. You're a real somebody when you stick with what you know is right, no matter what it costs you."

"Rabbi, you're not understanding me."

"I'm understanding you, believe me. Tell me, if you had the opportunity to steal a hundred grand, would you?"

"Of course not."

"But look what a hundred grand would do for you. You could buy your Cadillac and make a down payment on a big house. You would be a somebody."

"No sir. I wouldn't dream of it. Not me."

"And violating Shabbat?"

"Rabbi, it's not the same thing."

"It is, Moe. It is. It all comes from the same Torah, from the same God. Why are we forbidden to steal? Not because we think it's bad. We're forbidden to steal because it's against God's law. Why are we forbidden to violate Shabbat? Also because it's against God's law."

"Rabbi, I'm not smart enough to argue with you. But I still don't think it's the same thing. Anyway, my mind is made up. I can't help it. There's no way I can stay closed on Shabbat."

That conversation took place a long time ago. But even now, as I record it, it still aches.

telltale movies

We once gave a kosher endorsement to a new Jewish bakery, with the obvious understanding that no baking would be done on Shabbat. The baking operation itself was at least ten miles from the Jewish neighborhoods, so there was no way we could really check whether the baker was maintaining this aspect of the agreement. However, since he was in shul every Shabbat morning, I felt that all was well.

A few months after he opened, one of our members, himself not a Shabbat observer, called to tell me that at about five A.M. last Shabbat morning he was in his car on the way to the airport when he spotted the bakery truck in front of a supermarket, and that the driver was delivering cartons of fresh bread. I asked him whether he was positive. He said he would swear to it.

The irony of a nonobservant Jew tattling on the non-observance of someone else was not lost on me. But the tattler was essentially an honest person, and it disturbed him that someone was operating under a false front.

I made a personal visit to the bakery. Without tipping my hand, I made a thorough inspection and casually inquired of the baker how his new business was going, whether he was being accepted in the Jewish community, and whether he was picking up business from non-Jewish customers as well. He said that things were moving slowly, but at an acceptable pace.

Everything seemed to be in order, but the Shabbat report still gnawed at me. I decided to ask our janitor to drive by the bakery on Friday night after he left shul to see whether any lights were on inside the premises. John is very intelligent and immediately knew what I was getting at. I urged him not to mention my request to anyone.

On Shabbat morning, John reported to me that he could not be positive, but he thought he saw a dim light and some movement in the back of the bakery. "I would have driven around the back to check," he said, "but it was late at night and I was scared, being a black man and all that, you know."

The next day I called in a private detective agency, told them what I suspected, and asked them to give me a full report on the next Friday night's activity at the bakery.

On the following Monday morning, the detectives came to see me. They had staked out the bakery and found that, while the entire retail business was closed to the public, there was in fact baking activity in the rear. Furthermore, the bakery truck was loaded up at three A.M. and proceeded to make deliveries to a variety of establishments until seven A.M. The detectives, who were in an unmarked van, had filmed the deliveries, as well as some of the activity inside the bakery. Within two days I had in my hands a full written report (plus a whopping bill).

I called the baker and asked him to come to my study. I came right to the point. "Joe, I know for certain that you have been baking on Friday nights."

"What! Rabbi, that's just not so. Somebody's misleading you."

"Joe, I have the proof. Not only are you baking, but your truck is making deliveries early Shabbat morning to several stores."

"There must be some mistake. You know I'm in shul every Shabbat morning myself."

"I know — while your truck is on the street. It might have been better if your truck were in shul instead of you."

"Rabbi, are you calling me a liar?"

"I'm not calling you anything. I am only telling you that I have proof that would even stand up in court. And I am also telling you that this Shabbat in shul I will publicly announce that we are withdrawing kosher supervision from your establishment. We are placing a notice in the newspapers to that effect as well. And, Joe, I am personally very disappointed. Kosher supervision is based on trust, and you broke that trust."

Joe knew he was cornered and put up no fight. He never admitted his violation, continued appearing in shul on Shabbat morning, proclaiming his innocence to anyone who would listen. But within six weeks he went out of the kosher business entirely and opened up an officially nonkosher bake shop.

At least he didn't threaten to take me to court. Too bad. The video would have been interesting.

watching the shochet up close

Some kashrut violations are venal, some less so.

George Jackson was the handyman at Fleishmann's butcher shop in old Atlanta in the forties, many years before I came to town. He was reliable, trustworthy, and never drank. He did all the chores, ran the errands, kept the place clean. He always got along fine with white folks, and he especially liked working for Jewish people. He had been working for Fleishmann for as long as anyone could remember.

Every few days he would bring live chickens from the butcher shop over to the nearby woodshed in the back yard of Rev. Lansky, the *shochet.* There he would wait while Lansky slaughtered the chickens. George always tried to be helpful. Once in a while he would help Lansky chase down a frightened chicken who did not care for the look of the knife in the good reverend's right hand. After the *shechitah,* George would bring the slaughtered chickens back to the shop and help make them ready for sale.

Thursday was the major slaughtering day. One Thursday afternoon George appeared with his chickens but could not find Rev. Lansky. He knocked at his door, called out his name, but Lansky was nowhere to be seen.

George knew that customers were coming in to the shop and that Fleishmann got very upset when the chickens were not ready. George could wait no longer. He knew where Rev. Lansky kept his special knife, the one he used to sharpen so carefully. He opened the drawer of the cabinet, removed the case in which the knife was kept, took out the sheath, and unwrapped the soft cloth from around it. "Ain't no problem for me to do it myself," mumbled George to himself. "I watched him all these years. I'll do it exactly the way he does it. People are waiting." And George slaughtered the chickens exactly the way Rev. Lansky did it. Then he rinsed the knife, placed it back in its sheath in the case, and slid it into the drawer of the cabinet.

George worked for Fleishmann a few more years, and then got too old to work and had to quit. On his last day of work Fleishmann hugged him and thanked him for his steady help over the years. "There's nobody like you," said Fleishmann. "I sure am gonna miss you." And Fleishmann handed him a gift of twenty-five dollars, which in the forties was very generous.

"I'm gonna miss you, too," said George, tears in his eyes. "You're a real good man. One more thing now, before I go — whoever you get to take my place, tell him that if he watches Rev. Lansky close up, it don't take a whole lot of time to learn how to do that there *shekting*. Comes in real handy now and then."

the designated chicken

Down in South Georgia, in a town called Pine Scrub, there lived a single Jewish family, a middle-aged couple named Harry and Maisie Gold. They were the proprietors of Gold's

General Store on the town square. Honest and civic-minded, Harry and Maisie were respected by everyone in town.

They were proud Jews, and although they observed nothing else, they did observe kashrut very strictly. "That's how Momma raised me, and that's how I do it," Maisie would always say.

They went to great lengths to keep their home kosher. Every week Harry would take a couple of chickens out of the coop in the back yard, hop into his 1948 Buick, and drive the thirty miles into Savannah to get them slaughtered by Rev. Schwartz.

One September, on the eve of Rosh Hashanah, South Georgia was struck by a tornado. Pine Scrub itself was spared, but there were no kosher chickens left in the house, and the state police had closed the road to Savannah.

"We'll make do without chicken," said Harry. "We'll have fish and other things. It'll be fine."

"*Yom Tov* isn't *Yom Tov* without chicken, Harry. It just isn't the same."

"We got no choice, Maisie. We'll just have to make do."

"We're talking Thursday, Friday, and Saturday, Harry. Can't eat fish all those meals in a row. Got to have some chicken in there some way."

Maisie went over to her drawer and pulled out a long black knife. "Harry, take this knife and go out there in the shed and *shecht* us a couple of chickens. This is an emergency."

"Maisie, I don't know how to do no *shechting*. I never did it in my life."

"Harry, be a man. You've seen Rev. Schwartz do this enough times for you to know how to do it. You been watching him for twenty years. By now you know what to do."

"Maisie, I'm scared to handle this here knife on a chicken."

"Oh come on, this is an emergency. You got no choice. Go on out there and do it. The knife is real sharp. It won't take but one clean stroke."

Harry shrugged his shoulders, took the knife in hand, and went into the yard to the henhouse. Maisie stayed in the kitchen preparing *kugel*. After a while she looked out toward the shed and, seeing no sign of him, went out into the yard.

There she found her husband lying flat on his back in a dead faint, the long black knife near his outstretched hand. On his chest, strutting back and forth and clucking proudly, was the designated chicken.

the Georgia General Assembly goes kosher

Our attempts to get a kosher food law through the Georgia General Assembly — a law directed against those who falsely advertise their products as kosher — were not without their luminous moments. It was quite a challenge to explain kashrut to the honorable members of the legislative committee.

After my presentation, the questioning got off to a bad start. The legislator from Cordele said, "I get the impression that you people are trying to force your interpretation on the people of this state. You may say 'kosher' means one thing, but what's to stop me from saying it means something else?"

I tried to ignore the 'you people' and explained that "kosher" is a legal and religious term that has only one meaning, and that it should not be used loosely to describe food that is merely spiced delicatessen.

The legislator from Hahira tried to demonstrate how knowledgeable he was: "We got us a deli in our area and once in a while we get a coupla Jewish salesmen to come in there for a corned-beef sandwich."

The chairman of the committee was a bit more refined. "Sir," he inquired, "and I ask this with utmost respect — if y'all can't eat just any food, what do you do for food when you travel, for example?"

"Well, the airlines make kosher food available on request, and in the larger cities there are kosher restaurants. In smaller towns, we just do the best we can. We bring along our own food sometimes, or just eat fruits and vegetables and whatever we can pick up at the local market that is kosher."

"Is that right? That don't make life none too easy, now, does it? I guess you really have to be a believer to maintain that there kosher discipline. Gentlemen, my own opinion is that we here in Georgia have a responsibility to protect our Jewish citizens who practice this, so I'm all for this legislation. You have to respect folks who sacrifice for the things they believe in."

But the representative from Blairsville was unconvinced and bared his red neck. "We all respect a man who believes in his religion, but folks can't come on down here and tell us what is the right way to advertise. We have as much right to say if something is kosher as anybody else."

I was humbled by my ability to articulate the real meaning of kashrut.

To my great surprise, the kosher food bill passed the Georgia legislature by an overwhelming majority. But the endemic anti-Jewishness of some of our honorable representatives was an education of sorts.

the seder that was not kosher

There were other occasions when I was singularly unimpressed with my powers of persuasion.

Just before Passover I met with a group of Jewish students from Emory University who wanted my help in planning a student Seder. These were youngsters with little or no Jewish background, so I knew it would not be an easy meeting. What I didn't expect was that they would want to have the Seder with all the trimmings — the right matzos, the wine, the traditional Seder plate, the bitter herbs, the *charoset,* everything — but that they would want the meal itself to be nonkosher.

When I pointed to the contradiction of having a traditional Seder that violates the tradition, they looked at me as if I were mad. "But we don't keep kosher anyway. Why shouldn't we be honest about it?"

"Yes, but when you have a Seder you are celebrating a major Jewish tradition. Does it make sense to celebrate

Jewish tradition with one hand and to violate Jewish tradition with the other?" I wanted them at least to see the paradox, the inconsistency.

"Well, it's not like we'd be serving ham."

"It's the same thing," I said. "If I were you, I would be fully honest and go ahead and serve ham."

No matter what I said, I was unable to show them that there was at least a moral-religious problem here. Their sterile Jewish homes and sanitized synagogues and temples and Sunday Schools had so desensitized them that they could not see the contradiction in what they were doing.

But when I begin to wonder about the disappearance of the classic Jewish pride in being different, I think of the one student at the university whose gutsy Jewishness is remarkable. Of some two thousand Jewish students from all over the country, he is the only one who is fully observant of Shabbat, kashrut, and *mitzvot* in general. Even more striking, because more visible, is the fact that he never appears on campus without his yarmulke. This takes great inner strength and conviction — to be able to withstand the many social pressures of his peers, particularly at an age when peer approval is so significant. He is an outstanding student and a campus leader. He carries within his soul that classic spirit of Jewish defiance.

treif all year, kosher on Pesach

I have always been struck, incidentally, by the hold which Pesach has over the Jewish people. Almost everyone has a Seder of sorts — and even though it is often a mere family get-together, with more emphasis on the *kneidlach* than on the Haggadah, it should not be denigrated; Jews are still maintaining some form of the ancient tradition. Something about Pesach strikes a deep chord within the souls of all Jews. Even more curious is the fact that there are Jewish families who observe absolutely no kashrut during the year, but keep a strictly kosher home during the week of Pesach: separate dishes, strictly kosher meat — everything. But the moment Pesach ends, they revert back to their year-round habits.

Also odd are the various gradations of kashrut observance one encounters year round. Level I: Kashrut is strictly observed throughout the year, in the home and away from home. Level II: Strict kashrut is observed at home, but one eats in fish and dairy restaurants even if they are not strictly kosher. Level III: Strict kashrut at home, but anything goes away from home. Level IV: Casual kashrut is observed at home — one set of dishes, products are brought in without too much concern for their reliability — and of course anything goes away from home. Level V, as outlined above: Kashrut strictly observed in and out of the home for the week of Pesach only. Level VI: No kashrut either at home or away from home — not even on Pesach — but one never eats shellfish or ham or shrimp or pork. And on the seventh level, thou mayest ingest that which pleaseth thee, be it shellfish, pork, shrimp, be it in thy house or when thou walkest on the way.

Two reactions: a) This is an illustration of the tendency of people to pick and choose from the tradition, to do that which is comfortable for them and to disregard that which causes them discomfort. b) This is an illustration of the tenacity of yet another ancient tradition. Kashrut is not an easy *mitzvah*. The fact that Jews at the end of the twentieth century are still observing even vestiges of it is a sign of the hold which Jewish tradition still has over us. Choose one of the above.

just desserts

In any case, the level of kashrut observance in the community at large is at a much higher level than ever before. How well I remember the days when there was not a single kosher hotel in Atlanta, and not a single place other than the synagogue social halls in which kosher communal dinners could take place. In those days, weddings were held either in one of the posh Jewish country clubs or in one of the downtown hotels. The well-meaning hosts would graciously arrange a lavish fruit and vegetable plate for me. It became an integral part of the menu at weddings and at public Jewish dinners; everyone would eat their nonkosher meals, and the rabbi would have a fancy fruit plate. In those days, I saw so many green peppers, red peppers, oranges and apples and lettuce and tomatoes that it is remarkable that I can still look at fruits and vegetables.

Today there are any number of first-rate hotels that have kosher facilities, and no communal Jewish organizations would dream of serving anything but kosher at their annual dinners. The ubiquitous rabbinical fruit plate has become a thing of the past.

But not entirely. Some years ago, I played a little trick on the late Jacob Rothschild, the local Reform rabbi. A city-wide dinner was being held in our own synagogue social hall. Jacob Rothschild was to be seated next to me on the dais. I instructed our caterer to prepare for him an elegant fruit and vegetable plate. When the time for dinner arrived, everyone was served breast of chicken, but the waiter brought the fruit plate to Rothschild, together with a written note from me: "Jack, since this is a strictly kosher function, we thought you would be more comfortable with a fruit plate."

Good sport and fine wit that he was, he took it all in excellent humor, after which he got his chicken — but not before getting his just desserts.

Chapter 20:
All Rabbis Are Jewish

The major Jewish organizations fret about Jewish-Christian relations. I can teach them a thing or two. A phone conversation between my wife and a lady caller:

"Pardon me for disturbing you," the nice lady said. "I'm a Baptist and I teach Sunday School in Covington. Next week, we're doing a lesson on the times of Jesus, and I wanted to know something about rabbis. Would you mind telling me — what kind of rabbi is your husband?"

"Well, he's Orthodox. There are three major groupings in

Jewish communities today — Reform, Conservative, and Orthodox. The Orthodox are the most traditional."

"No, I don't mean that. What I mean is, is your husband a rabbi like Jesus was a rabbi?"

"I'm not sure exactly what you mean."

"Well, specifically, is he a Christian rabbi?"

"No, he's a Jewish rabbi. There is no other kind of rabbi."

"You mean every rabbi in the world is Jewish?"

"Exactly. All rabbis are Jewish."

the father, the son . . .

Some rabbis, however, speak before they think. When our oldest son became my assistant rabbi in the early 1980's, there was understandable confusion as to how the two Rabbis Feldman should be addressed. A wit suggested that my son be called "Rabbi Feldman" and that I be called "Father Feldman." Most people, however, settled on "Rabbi Emanuel" and "Rabbi Ilan," which helped alleviate the confusion. The father-son team is in itself a subject for a long book. We worked for ten years together, after which he was offered the position when I retired. Having been born in the community, and now working with people who remembered him as a child, it could not have been very easy for him. That during all this time we never had a serious disagreement is one of those minor miracles for which I am grateful.

Late one afternoon I was sitting alone in my synagogue study. The date was December 24. Not a creature was stirring. The phone rang. "Is this Rabbi Feldman?" the lady asked.

"Yes, it is."

"Is this the father or the son?"

Before I knew it I had blurted out, "Neither. This is the holy ghost." It was funny, I suppose, but as I said it I knew I shouldn't have. Perhaps the caller was Christian and would be offended. I held my breath.

I heard a slight gasp at the other end and then, to my great relief, a loud laugh. She was in fact a Christian, but she appreciated the joke. I apologized for my indiscretion. As it turned out, she had simply called to inquire if Christmas has any intrinsic connection to Chanukah. Father Feldman informed her of the distinct difference between the two.

✳ ✳ ✳

A certain distortion of Judaism often surfaces when I address Christian youth groups. I always begin by explaining that we respect all religions and their beliefs, and do not try to convert anyone to Judaism. We believe that the righteous of the world all have a share in the world-to-come, and do not believe that anyone is eternally damned just because he or she does not accept Judaism. That is why we do not have missionaries.

The element of Judaism which many Christians find hardest to understand is that Jews do not accept Jesus as a divinity. "If you don't pray to him, what role does he play in Judaism?"

"The same role that Mohammed plays in Christianity," I reply. "Which means that in terms of religious practice or belief, he plays no role. The point is that we respect all monotheistic faiths, but our approach to God is quite different from that of Christianity or Islam. We do not ascribe any divinity or prophecy to Jesus or Mohammed, and their teachings hold no claim over us. We have only one God, and one Bible and tradition, and that is what we try to live by."

One teenager blurted out: "But if you don't believe in Jesus, that means you don't have Christmas!"

"Correct."

"But what do you do on Christmas day?"

"Nothing special. It's an ordinary day for us. What do you do on Jewish holidays like Passover?"

He chuckled. "Nothing special, I guess."

His friend was shocked. "But the Bible says that Jesus is the son of god."

"That's odd, because my Bible doesn't say that at all. On the contrary, my Bible says that there is only one God, that He is invisible, and that we are not to believe or follow other gods at all." I then proceeded to introduce the group to the concept of the Old Testament and the New Testament. "For the Jewish people, there is only one Bible. You call it the Old Testament, but for us it is *the* Bible, because we do not have any other kind of Bible. For us the New Testament is what the Koran is for Christians: the sacred Scripture of another faith, but a Scripture which is not part of our own faith."

All obvious, simple material, but things which these youngsters had never before heard or understood.

forks, knives, and shivering

Another youngster asked me if Jews use forks and knives when they eat. I was puzzled. "Of course. Did someone tell you otherwise?"

"Yes, sir. My Sunday School teacher told me that Jews don't eat the way other people do."

"Your teacher was referring to our food regulations." I gave her a quick explanation of the rules of kashrut.

The teacher leading the group asked, "This may sound odd, but it has been puzzling me. I heard that when a Jewish person dies, the survivors sit in a cold room for a week."

"I never heard of that myself. We do have the practice of mourning for a week, which we call "sitting *shivah*," but I never heard of sitting in a cold room."

"Oh," she said, "that's it. I heard that Jews sit and shiver for a week."

Probably the most disturbing question I occasionally hear from such groups is this: "Do Jews believe in God?"

I used to be shocked at this question, but its source is rather obvious. Firstly, they assume that Jews are godless because we don't accept Jesus, which in the eyes of some Christians means we are not only damned, unsaved, and unredeemed, but also unbelievers. Secondly, American Jews, sadly, are by and large not religious, and seem quite secular to their religious Christian friends. Thirdly, even religious Jews do not by nature wear their religion on their sleeves.

But it must be faced: from the question "Do Jews believe in God?" there flows naturally the traditional Christian thrust to bring the Jews around to the true belief.

Whenever Christian missionaries knock at my door and ask to talk with me, I suggest that before they try converting the Jews, they ought first to expend their energies on converting Christians to Christianity. Imagine, I say to them, what the world would be like if all Christians actually turned the other cheek, or if they all truly exercised love for everyone in their daily lives.

"Can't we just talk a bit?" they ask, avoiding my suggestion.

"Well, we can certainly talk, as long as it's not about abandoning my faith and accepting yours over mine."

"Oh, no. We respect Judaism greatly. We only want to share some ideas with you." And they begin pulling out their literature.

I try to be friendly but open and frank, and persist in my suggestion about converting Christians to Christianity. This tends to make the discussions very brief.

These people are sincerely concerned about saving me from the fires of hell, and I suppose I should be grateful. They are well trained and well versed — literally — but their knowledge of Scripture is skin deep, limited to the citation of mistranslated verses from the Hebrew Bible. But I worry about their impact on Jews who are without Jewish background and learning.

an open and shut briefcase

An evangelical college asked me to deliver a lecture on the subject "A Jew Looks at Attempts to Convert Him," and I was intrigued by it. I presented a carefully prepared talk on the major differences between Judaism and Christianity, on why Jews do not attempt to convert Christians to Judaism, and on why it might be a good idea for each faith to concentrate on converting its own people to its own faith.

The talk went well, I thought, and the question period was lively. One lady sitting in the first row, obviously a fundamentalist missionary, kept tossing biblical verses at me: "But Isaiah clearly says that the virgin shall give birth and that the child will be savior of humanity. How can you deny that?"

"Ma'am, I would not deny anything Isaiah says, except that he does not say that at all. Remember that Isaiah spoke Hebrew, not the King James English. The original Hebrew of that verse uses the word *almah*. You are translating that as 'virgin,' but the Hebrew word for virgin is *betulah*, not *almah*. *Almah* simply means 'a young woman.'" She asked several such questions, each on the same anxious and somewhat neurasthenic level.

The questions from the rest of the audience were intelligent, respectful, and curious. I felt that it was a worthwhile evening. But when I picked up my briefcase from behind the podium, I found that it had been opened. Nothing had been taken from it, but something had been inserted in it: a whole ream of missionary literature.

Despite the misinformation I frequently encounter among Christians individually and in groups, however, I have rarely sensed any animosity towards Judaism on their part, but rather a deep curiosity and respect — in particular a respect for observing, practicing Jews. Even if many Jews have no idea of halachic Judaism, many thoughtful Christians have a deep respect for it, for in it they perceive the authenticity of the Judaism of old.

Or at least I think so. I received a letter from the wife of a non-Jewish acquaintance: "Dear Rabbi: Douglas and I deeply appreciated your hospital visit. It was good of you to take the time to come visit with us. You truly have a good Christian heart."

the guilt of the victim

Jewish self-distortion is, I think, far more serious than Christian distortions of Judaism.

I was leading a discussion at the Jewish fraternity at Emory University on the subject of anti-Semitism. A student declared pontifically: "Jews bring hatred upon themselves. They like to be martyrs, and psychologically they do things that cause people to persecute them."

"They?" I asked. "Why 'they'? Aren't you a Jew?"

"Well, yeah, but I don't identify with the kind that bring persecution on themselves."

Clearly he had taken an overdose of Psych 101. Probably got an A and never got over it. I asked him if he had ever heard that six million Jews had been slaughtered in Europe.

"Not true," he said. "Besides, six million Gypsies and six million Catholics were also killed."

"Your figures are a bit off, but let me ask you: did the Gypsies and Catholics also bring destruction upon themselves?"

"Yes," he said belligerently.

"What you're saying is that every victim is guilty. Why should the killers who murder us be found guilty of anything? According to you, they really have no other choice."

He was trapped, but he persisted. "That's right. Anyway, you can't argue with rabbis. They know all the answers."

He looked around at his fraternity brothers for some support, but they averted their eyes and stared at the floor.

Another young man spoke up. "It's necessary to look at this in the broader perspective. If the Holocaust becomes just a matter of Jews being killed by Germans and all, it just becomes too simplistic."

"But didn't Jews get killed? In the millions?"

"Yes, but it's got to be understood in context. Things like the militaristic attitude of the government, the willingness of the people to follow orders, the whole business of authority and domination. That way it's more understandable."

"You mean that if we understand the context, then mass

murder is understandable?"

"You're putting words in my mouth. That's not what I mean. It's just that I don't like simplistic categories of thought."

The discussion reached its nadir when the Jewish coed who was moderator asked, "Could not the millions that Israel spends on weapons be put to better use feeding the hungry?"

I ask her, "If Israel will feed hungry people, will the hatred of the Arab masses towards Israel be abated in any way? Surely you know that when Iraqi Scud missiles were flying towards Tel Aviv in the Gulf War, Israeli Arabs actually cheered them on. In an atmosphere like that, don't you agree that Israel should maintain its strength?"

"Well, Israel is just too militaristic."

"Are you seriously suggesting that if Israel unilaterally dismantled its armed forces, peace would miraculously descend over the region? You don't think the Arabs would simply march in and destroy Israel?"

"Well, they should give peace a chance."

the mess of pottage

Rabbi William Bergstein, a Reform rabbi who is an expert on Jewish-Christian relations, was in town for a conference at Emory University. I was invited to meet with Bergstein ,together with a group of Christian professors.

Dr. Fears of the New Testament department engaged us in conversation just before the public session, and discovered that Bergstein is Reform and I Orthodox.

"Aha," said Fears archly, "the Orthodox don't really care too much for the Reform, do they?"

Before I had a chance to reply, Bergstein leaped into the fray. "Well, Orthodox rabbis also have to make religious compromises." He turned to me. "You make compromises just like all of us."

"How do you know?" I asked with a smile. "We were just

introduced."

"Well, don't you?"

"I try not to, really. Not consciously. And certainly not when the principle is vital."

He honed in for the kill. "You're supposed to be Orthodox. Do you have a *mechitzah* in your synagogue?"

"Yes."

"A *bimah* in the middle?"

"Yes."

"Really?"

"Really."

"But I'm sure some of your people ride to shul on Shabbat."

"Some do, but I can't control that. What I am able to control, I do."

He was triumphant. "You see! We all have to compromise."

But Prof. Fears didn't let him off the hook. "It seems to me," he said in his clipped British tones, "that it is only the Orthodox who are today's authentic Jews."

Bergstein was wounded. He had spent a lifetime convincing Christians that Judaism is not very different from Christianity, and along comes a Christian scholar and recognizes Orthodoxy as the true Judaism because of its very difference.

"Well," replied Bergstein feebly, "they may be authentic, but they're not the only ones who are authentic."

Dr. Fears' comment is not unusual, nor is it limited to Christian intellectuals. The Jew who believes that he will gain the respect of the world by assimilating into the majority culture and imitating the non-Jew will be disappointed. In my rabbinate, I have seen just the reverse. If it is the respect of the non-Jew we seek — and, truth to tell, committed Jews have much more significant things to concern themselves with — then living an authentic life of Jewish practice and belief is the way. Adopting the mores of the majority culture only creates contempt for Jews who attempt to pass as non-Jews and who abandon their own rich heritage for a mess of pottage.

friday night joys

Jerry Klein, a successful attorney and a leader in one of the local Temples, would not agree with me. He is trying his best to be recognized as a human being by the non-Jewish world. He has been telling me about the lovely open-air concerts that take place in Chastain Park on Friday nights during the summer months. People bring large picnic baskets, wine, eight-course dinners, and even candelabras. This is the Junior Chamber of Commerce crowd, the upwardly mobile. For them this is the place to be seen on Friday nights. He described the atmosphere to me: the sky overflowing with stars, the moon high, a famous performer on stage. What could be more pleasant?

"How wonderful it is," he said. "My father and mother were killed in Europe by the *goyim*, and here am I sitting with all these different people — Christians, Moslems, and blacks — and enjoying it and no one bothering me."

The joys and benefits of freedom are many, true enough, and I am grateful that no one bothers Jerry because he's a Jew. But I wonder what Jerry's martyred mother and father would think of their son who takes such pleasure in being accepted by non-Jews on the Jewish Shabbat.

I am also not quite sure why people like Jerry unabashedly and casually reveal to a rabbi their insensitivity to Jewish tradition. Does he have to describe to me in glowing terms the Friday-night atmosphere at the concert? Either there is no sense of shame anymore about such things, or he feels he is being straightforward. Or is it none of the above, but simply an indication that he and his friends don't think a rabbi would be offended by such things, since a rabbi is in any case just a professional functionary doing a job?

And the rabbi? How does the rabbi react to such a conversation? Does he say, "But Jerry, you know it's Shabbat. What are you doing there on Shabbat? You really ought to be in shul on Friday night, or with your wife and children at home, not out rubbing shoulders with the nations on God's holy day." The rabbi does not say that. The rabbi listens politely while inside he aches, all the while struggling for the proper response, and finally, not finding one, mumbles something innocuous in order not to offend a Jerry. Instead, years later he records the conversation in his book about the rabbinate, and he changes the real name to "Jerry" — so that the real person will, once again, not be offended.

* * *

To imitate the ways of the majority culture, to blend into the background, not to stand out as a Jew, to be accepted by non-Jewish society: these are overpowering drives. They are not aberrations nor contemporary phenomena. They are natural inclinations, which is why the Torah warns us in Leviticus 18 — the Torah reading of Yom Kippur afternoon — that when we enter Canaan we must not emulate the Canaanites. It is amazing; if Israel is going to find attractive and worthy of imitation the abominations of the hostile Canaanites, with their child-sacrifices and barbarisms and idolatries, how much more so are contemporary Jews tempted to adopt the ways of a civilization which seems friendly, superficially sophisticated, materially successful, and technologically triumphant. The Psalms, written one thousand years before Christianity, say it succinctly: "They mixed among the nations and learned their deeds . . ." (26:35). To remain genuine and faithful to our own authentic modes of behavior and thought is the most difficult of struggles for the contemporary Jew.

the Jewish Baptist

A Bnai Brith lodge somewhere in Texas wants to expel one of its members. The charge: the individual has joined the local Baptist church. He claims that he is still Jewish and has never renounced his Judaism. The tiny Jewish community is in an uproar.

Beyond the madness of claiming that one can pray to Jesus and still be a Jew, another thought crossed my mind: other than identifying themselves with the Jewish people and attending Temple for a few hours on Yom Kippur, no one in this Lodge observes even a shred of Judaism. As far as Jewish knowledge or practice is concerned, they have all but abandoned it.

It is fascinating, however, to see the visceral reaction of Jews to another Jew who makes the break official instead of gradually and unofficially. I suppose there is something to be said for their reaction, but it would be good if they held a mirror up to their own personal practice of the faith which they so zealously defend.

On the other hand, one should not discount the potential of the once-a-year Jew. There is still a vast difference between him and the Jew who never ever appears in shul. The no-show is very far gone; it takes herculean efforts to bring him back. The one who comes to shul just for Yom Kippur is also far removed from Jewish things, but nevertheless displays some connection, tenuous as it is, to Judaism. The spark within him is still alive. And when his friend joins the church, his Jewish soul reacts in pain.

I never met a religious Jew

The living of inauthentic Jewish lives is counterproductive in numerous ways. I met with a twenty-year-old Jewish girl who has become involved with Jews for Jesus. She told me that she had a sincere desire for religion and for God in her life, but was unable to find genuine religious feeling in the Jewish community. Brought up in an assimilated environment, her assessment of what she had experienced was accurate. Only among Christians, she said, had she ever experienced sincere commitment to God and religion. She told me that she had never met a religious Jew.

I was crushed. What an indictment of us! All the Jews she knows, she told me, are secularized. Their only manifestation of Jewishness is their support of Israel — which is expressed only via the checkbook. As for prayer, zero. Awareness of God, zero. Enthusiasm for Judaism, zero. To make matters worse, her rabbi had told the congregation that Jews don't believe in the efficacy of prayer per se, and that God does not listen to prayer. According to him, prayer is only useful as a tool for self-examination. So she began searching in other vineyards because she wanted a God to whom she could pray.

I argued that she had seen only part of the picture and should not make a serious life decision based on partial evidence. I pointed out that there are hundreds of thousands of Jews around the world who are serious and dedicated to their religion, their Torah, and their God; who pray with fervor; and who serve God with a full and sincere heart. I tried to impress upon her that what she had seen in her Jewish community could not by any stretch of the imagination be called Judaism.

She was not convinced, but she agreed to come back and continue our discussion, which means that there is some hope. I will try to get her to our shul on a Shabbat morning, where she can meet some Jews who take their Judaism and their Torah seriously.

This young lady is a natural result of synagogues which have "adjusted" and "adapted" to contemporary life. Their rabbis preach the latest fads and fashions in religion, and in effect are presiding over a self-inflicted national destruction.

As for the real Holocaust, it is clear that a non-Jew, even a well-meaning and sympathetic one, can never fully comprehend its meaning. The very term has become delegitimized, a favorite of demagogues and rabble-rousers. Every act of prejudice or intolerance is, in these days of loose and imprecise language, termed a "holocaust," so that the word itself has been trivialized. I am not condoning prejudice, but the persecuted, tortured, and gassed Jews of Europe would have preferred, had they been given the choice, to have been merely victims of prejudice and discrimination — alive and able to fight it.

When our daughter Chavah was ten years old, she attended a city-wide concert together with her Hebrew Academy classmates. Some of the boys from her school were wearing yarmulkes. A group of boys from a public school taunted them and mocked the yarmulkes. One shouted, "Did you enjoy the concentration camps?"

Just a childish taunt, but in every taunt lies hidden the kernel of a life-view. The sheer cruelty of the remark, the idea that after fifty years the tortured instead of the torturer should be the object of scorn — where do they pick up such sentiments? From their parents? On a downtown street not long ago I heard a soapbox orator declare that Hitler did not finish the job with the Jews. The crowd around him listened quietly; I was the only one who uttered a sound of protest.

Anti-Semitism is not limited to the street. Sometimes it comes wrapped in gracious packages. The Rotarians invited me to speak at one of their luncheons on the relationship of the Holocaust to the State of Israel. During the question period one gentleman asked, "With all due respect, and I don't mean this personally, but really, I find it strange that there are so many Jewish people who seem to control the media and the finances of this country." He was so polite that it was hard to realize that this was the "Protocols of the Elders of Zion" all over again. I suggested that surely he wasn't one of those who was fearful that Jews were out to conquer the world. I pointed out that there were practically no banks, oil companies, or giant industries controlled by Jews, and that if he looked at it carefully, he would discover that the major media outlets were also not Jewishly owned.

At the end of the question period, which was quite friendly, another gentleman arose. "I have always been curious about this, and I hesitate to ask it, but how come so many Communists have been Jews?"

It was the perfect opening for me. "Gentlemen," I said, "I am confused. The first questioner wanted to know why Jews are capitalists, and now this one wants to know why Jews are Communists. Obviously we can't be both. It's clear that some opinions need rethinking. Would you gentlemen care to step outside and settle this between you?"

There were peals of laughter, and I received a round of applause. But I was not very happy.

two bars of soap

During a college lecture I was giving on the Holocaust, I noticed a Christian girl silently weeping. After class I asked her if she was all right and if I could help her. She told me that she had never realized what the term "holocaust" meant until that moment. All her life she had known about the persecution of the Jews, but only now did she begin to understand what it was all about.

She would have understood even more if she had been in shul with me one morning when the meaning of the European destruction was hammered home to me. After Torah reading, a man came up to me with a slip of paper on which was written a long list of names.

"I want to recite a memorial prayer for these names."

"So many names?" I blurted out.

"Yes. They're my whole family and relatives. They were all rounded up and killed together on the same day. Today is the anniversary of their murder."

I apologized and read the prayer:

> *El malei rahamim*...God of compassion, Who dwellest on high, grant perfect rest beneath the sheltering wings of Thy Presence, among the holy and pure souls who shine as the brightness of the firmament, unto the souls of: Leizer ben Yehudah, Chaim ben Yehudah, Elke bas Yehudah, Golde bas Yehudah (*four children*

of one father; my voice began to tremble); Yehudah ben Yosef (*probably the father*); Masha bas Yitzhak (*the mother?*); Alter ben Dovid, Yente bas Dovid, Reizel bas Dovid, Dovid ben Alter, Sarah bas Yaakov, who have gone unto eternity....

Which in turn brought to mind the two bars of soap. The soap manufactured by so-called human beings from other human beings, from Jews. The soap had been in the possession of one of our members ever since she was an inmate in the Stettin concentration camp. For thirty-five years she had carried it with her in her many wanderings, unsure of what to do with it.

Finally, she brought it to me and asked me to dispose of it in some way. Two little bars of soap in a little white cardboard box.

We buried the box the next week in the Jewish cemetery. The mind can hardly fathom it.

About twenty-five people were in attendance, survivors of the death camps. We did not announce it to the public.

We dug a little hole in the earth,
we interred the soap into the earth,
we covered the soap with the red soil of Georgia,
we recited the memorial prayer and the *Kaddish,*
we smoothed the earth back into place,
we installed a small marker,
and we stood there,
numbed.

Chapter 21:
Of Fanatics, Tennis
Shoes, and Burning
in Hell

I **knew I was getting to be an older rabbi when** calls began coming in from younger rabbis inquiring about the formula to persuade Jews to take Judaism seriously. "I wish I knew the formula," I always responded. The younger rabbis were duly impressed with my modesty, but I was only being honest.

Many things have changed in the thirty years since those first calls. But one thing remains unchanged. In looking back at thirty-nine years in the rabbinate I still cannot, even in retrospect, glean any set technique or blueprint for bringing

Torah into the lives of people. (I trust people will still be impressed with my modesty.) The fact is that as soon as community building becomes formulaic, it is doomed.

Probably the worst thing one can do in setting out to build a Torah community is to set out to build a Torah community. It is better to set out to build one individual, then another, then another. The community will ultimately fall into place.

I remember my trepidation when I left Baltimore to take up what would be my first and only pulpit. Raised though I was in a rabbi's home and familiar though I was with life as a rabbi, I was nevertheless filled with a certain anxiety.

My father kept reminding me not to expect to overcome Jewish ignorance and apathy all at once. Be patient, he counseled; stress the study of Torah; work with individuals, and the community will fall into place; don't try to do it all yourself; leave something for God to do, for He, too, has an interest in the outcome.

turn that town upside down

By contrast, one of my friends from the yeshivah (who today is a world-recognized pioneer in bringing Jews back to Torah), an energetic, enthusiastic worker with people, gave me this final charge as I was leaving for Atlanta: "Turn that town upside down. In six months I want you to change their lives." This youthful enthusiasm was much closer to my natural inclinations, and despite my father's more sober advice, I was sure in my heart of hearts that six months was more than sufficient time to revolutionize the community.

In six weeks, I realized that it would take more than six months. In six months, I realized that there would be no revolutions at all, and that if in six years some small fruits of my labors were to become visible, I could consider myself fortunate. It took several years before tentative blossoms began to emerge, and a decade before anyone tasted real fruit.

The first thing I learned was patience. Just as a pregnancy must take a certain amount of time and the process cannot be speeded up, so does it take a certain amount of time for the authentic message of Torah to penetrate the Jewish soul. It was not my task to do everything, just to make some serious efforts. As stated in *Pirkei Avot* 2:16: "It is not incumbent upon you to complete the labor ..." But it is incumbent upon you to make a beginning.

A corollary principle was to try to relax. A rabbi who wears an invisible badge announcing, "I am going to convert you to a better way of life" is doomed to failure. One does not change lives by being eager to show one and all the error of their ways. It is best to allow things to metamorphose in their own time. One should take his work seriously, but not himself.

All this was particularly true in the fifties. Atlanta, for example, was in no mood for serious Torah living. It was an ambitious small town, just beginning to flex the metropolitan muscles which were to transform it into a major cultural and commercial center. Its Jewish community numbered about twenty thousand souls, centered around three Jewish country clubs and three or four synagogues. The clubs and not the synagogues were the dominant force.

you mean well, but you are young

What most characterized this community was the singular gentility of its people, its kindness to a new, young rabbi — and its Jewish apathy. Things were fine as they were. It was not necessary to change. Development, growth, improvement were desirable goals for a businessman; they had nothing to do with one's soul. The mere suggestion that one might also consider one's Jewish balance sheet was met with condescending good manners: you mean well, you are sincere, and you are young.

It was no wonder that Atlanta had not a single Shomer Shabbat who was not a retiree — and a mere handful of those. There were even two or three men who had been Shomrei Shabbat all their lives, but not a single one of their children was observant. This was not entirely their fault. To raise a Jewish child in the thirties and forties was difficult enough in the larger Jewish centers; in smaller towns the most one could hope for was that the child marry a Jew. Children were sent to Sunday School to be taught by well-meaning teachers who managed to stay a few lessons ahead of their students. For some children, there was an afternoon program of some five hours per week. The ability to read a halting Hebrew and to chant a Bar Mitzvah *haftarah* were the hallmarks of a superior Jewish education. Rare was the child who continued even his minimal Jewish exposure after age thirteen. Serious Jewish learning was simply unavailable, and serious Jewish observance was clearly out of the question. This was, after all, America, and one had to be realistic. Thus was an entire generation lost to Judaism.

In all of this, Atlanta was a mirror image of the masses of American Jewry. Having fundamentally surrendered the struggle, their overriding concern was to settle in with a comfortable Judaism that did not have too many distinctively Jewish features. But history has a way of catching up with empty rationalizations, and today it is obvious that this thinking was bereft of substance. Nevertheless, bad communal habits die hard, even when shown to be dangerous to everyone's health — and there remains a heavy residue of apathy even in today's American Jewish life.

One could not attack such a fortress frontally. The only way — and the best way — was to toss some seeds over the walls, with the faith that they would somehow take root here and there. The seeds were small discussion groups, study groups and even private tutoring of adults.

For many years I ran a Hebrew reading class for women, simply teaching them the *aleph-bet*. After they learned to read, we familiarized ourselves with the *siddur,* and learned the meaning of certain basic prayers. Then we moved into a study of the weekly Torah reading, which over the years gradually increased in depth and scope.

deceptively simple Rashi

The intuitive understanding and comprehension of the text by certain women in that group was remarkable. I found myself carefully preparing for this class, and discovered that in many ways they were more perceptive than the men in absorbing the ideas of the most esoteric of biblical commentators.

A little learning is, of course, a dangerous thing. I still remember one woman who, no doubt impressed by the personal progress she was making, told me that she wished I would not stress Rashi so much, because "this group has outgrown Rashi."

"No one ever outgrows Rashi," I replied.

"But Rashi is for children," she insisted. "We need to go into Ramban and others. We're beyond Rashi."

I realized then that though I had taught them many things, I had not taught them humility before the presence of the classic commentators. The great genius of Rashi is that he is able simultaneously to take children and profound scholars by the hand. He is deceptively simple, but so nuanced and so precise that when he uses one word instead of another, it can make a major difference in our understanding of the biblical text. To the uninitiated, Rashi is simple. To the scholar, he is the profoundest and most subtle of teachers.

The same lack of humility confronted me in a Talmud class I was teaching. Here, too, the men were highly intelligent but had had little exposure to Talmudic method. During a particularly intricate discussion, one of the men blurted out, "This makes no sense!"

"Harold," I said, "please add two little words: 'to me.' You cannot say that it makes no sense, period. That sets yourself up as the final arbiter of judgment on the Talmud."

"But it makes no sense."

"To you it makes no sense, Harold, to you. Maybe I didn't explain it clearly enough, so the fault may be mine, but not the Talmud's. Maybe we both need to work at it until it does make sense." I had not succeeded in imparting a basic premise in the study of classic Jewish texts: when they are difficult to comprehend, the fault lies in us and not in the material.

Over the years, however, the various learning groups made remarkable strides, and through their exposure to the original texts they gained a new respect for Judaism — and a new respect for themselves as Jews. Nothing so affects the Jewish soul as exposure to the original source material.

of chewing gum and Isaac's blessing

Inevitably there were frustrations. I was teaching the story of Isaac's blessing, and how Rebecca choreographed events so that Jacob and not Esau would receive the coveted blessing from Isaac. My point was to show that this was a much more profound matter than the simple deception of a blind old man. The very future of the Jewish people was at stake here. I tried to show the layers of meaning that lay hidden within the biblical text.

The class was always over the head of dear old Mamie Susskind. She did not have a head for learning, and she came primarily for social reasons; she enjoyed being with other people, and she liked the give-and-take of the discussion. What we studied was of no concern to her. She would sit there week in and week out tending to her knitting — literally — and chewing gum. She never bothered me, and I never bothered her.

But as I dug deeply into the hidden meanings of this blessing story, I heard her stage whisper to the lady next to her: "I never did care for that Jacob fella anyway." The remark served as an important reminder to me that my fantasies that I was doing an effective job as a teacher were largely delusional.

the taillights

Besides these learning groups, the other essential ingredient in the spiritual growth of the community was the founding of the Hebrew Academy day school in the 1950's. This was done without the support of most of the established Jewish community — with one or two notable exceptions who lent unofficial support and encouragement. Other Jewish schools followed in its wake. Most of the communal leaders, lay and professional, were fearful of charges of ghettoization, of undermining the public school system, and somehow, of being unAmerican.

One of them even suggested to the school's leadership that the name "Hebrew" was too parochial and should be changed to something that sounded less narrow, in order to give the school a broader base. He was ignored. It is a measure of Atlanta's increased Jewish self-confidence that subsequent schools contained in their names even more parochial Jewish terms: "yeshivah," "Torah," and *kollel.*

As in so many matters involving the Jewish future and the setting of priorities, the Jewish establishment was sadly lacking in vision. Only a generation later did the Jewish Federations, in Atlanta and around the country, finally recognize the crucial significance of Jewish day-school education, on elementary and high-school levels, for the Jewish future. One can only speculate what American Jewry might have looked like today if the Jewish establishment had not missed the boat a generation ago. It turns out that the old-world European Roshei Yeshivah who arrived on these shores after the Holocaust, and who had no familiarity with the English language or with American Jewish life, were on target about the Jewish future, while the *au courant,* sophisticated American Jewish leadership had served once again as the taillights and not the head-lights of American Jewry.

* * *

In terms of individual families and the changes they under-take, very much in Jewish life depends on the woman, the wife, the mother. I would estimate that the vast majority of families in this congregation who have moved towards reli-gious observance have done so primarily because of the influence of the woman of the house. If a wife wants to become more observant and the husband claims he is not ready, the family will move forward nevertheless. Conversely, if the husband wants to move towards observance and the wife is not ready, by and large nothing significant happens.

In general, couples who move toward observance inevitably have problems synchronizing their journey. It is not always easy. One partner always moves faster than the other. But it is the wife who invariably leads the way.

the cult leader

Elaine Posner is one of these women. Five years ago she sensed that her family and her marriage were spinning out of control, and she decided that in a life of observance they would all find a sense of purpose. Her husband Ralph didn't care much either way but, good soul that he is, he went along.

She wanted to swallow all of Judaism in one huge gulp. So enthusiastic was she that she wanted to begin observing kashrut, Shabbat, and *taharat hamishpachah* simultaneous-ly. I discouraged her. I recall the odd debate we had in my study, a kind of role reversal, she wanting to move ahead rapidly and I persuading her to slow down. She objected: "I want to be a full Jewess and I am ready for it." Remembering how some of my congregants had gone too far too quickly, and as a result began displaying immediate symptoms of spiritual indigestion, I counseled caution and urged her to take one step at a time. She deferred to my judgment, but very reluctantly.

After six months of kashrut we moved into Shabbat. After several months of Shabbat, we moved to *taharat hamish-pachah*. Their entire lives have turned around. Ralph himself said to me this year, "Why didn't you tell me how pleasant a Shabbat can be? I might have gone all my life without realizing it." Their children are attending Jewish day schools, and they just sent their fifteen-year-old off to a yeshivah in Baltimore for the balance of his high-school years.

For a nonobservant family to make this spiritual odyssey required deep conviction and courage. And it is all due to Elaine. One Elaine affects other Elaines, and gradually a network and a community are developed. She saw things clearly and did what she had to do.

It was not easy for her. When she and her family started observing Shabbat, some of her friends were unsympathetic and laughed at her new mode of life. When she would no longer eat in their nonkosher homes, laughter turned to mockery and ridicule. Although she and her husband are extremely quiet and self-effacing people, the terms of derision were the usual: "hypocrite," "holier-than-thou," and the perennial favorite: "You are looking down on us."

Somehow this is the classic reaction to those who begin to practice more Judaism. The less observant people around them become uncomfortable. Sometimes this discomfort is good; it acts as a challenge and a prod, and it rouses some people out of their lethargy. But sometimes the discomfort results from a perceived threat, and returnees are subject to derision or accused of having hidden motives, of lacking minds of their own, or of simply being misfits.

Misfits — because the general feeling abroad is that the observant life is without joy and without pleasure, and what normal person would knowingly forgo all enjoyment and pleasure in order to become observant? Nonobservant Jews do not realize that just the reverse is true. The returnee finds in the religious life a deeper delight and contentment than anything he has ever before experienced. More than one *baal teshuvah* has said to me, "Why didn't you force me to observe Shabbat years earlier?" The Torah life is not somber. It is serious, yes, but *simchah* and *oneg* are integral parts of Judaism.

Elaine was strong enough to withstand these pressures and not take them seriously. If she weren't mentally tough to begin with, she would not have been seeking a new kind of life. In fact, her example actually led one or two of her friends to begin re-examining their own levels of Jewishness.

Probably her most difficult trial came when she informed her parents that she could no longer eat in their home because it was not kosher. They, old-line members of the Reform Temple, were horrified. They felt that their daughter was rejecting them and rebelling against her upbringing. They were certain that she had fallen into the hands of a cult, with me as the cult leader. But, decent people that they were, they slowly reconciled themselves to her newfound ways. They even had the intelligence to come to talk to me, the cult leader himself, about their problem.

Some cult leader am I. They should see some of my congregants while I indoctrinate them from the pulpit: they sleep, read the *chumash,* stare at their watches, or observe the ceiling.

Sometimes I wonder: if the observant life has such great things to offer; if the difference between us and the non-observant world is so palpable; if we offer meaning and purpose in place of emptiness and drift, how is it that the entire Jewish world is not flocking to us and demanding entry into the world of Torah? There are many reasons, among which are fear of the unknown, ignorance of what we are, coupled with prejudice after generations of anti-Orthodox sentiments in the wider Jewish and secular worlds. But the fact is that we ourselves are not doing a good job. We give off vibrations of arrogance, smugness, moral superiority. We sometimes behave as if we do not care what others think of us because we are so convinced that we are the paragons of ethics and morality and truth. There are tens of thousands of returnees, yes, and every single one of them is significant. But they constitute only a tiny percentage of the Jewish world. So the question gnaws at me: if the Jewish soul yearns for that which is authentic, why are Jewish souls not knocking down our doors?

what a difference a week makes

The pressures on the newly observant are enormous. One week after Ben Gerson first became a Shabbat observer — after a year of wrestling with the idea — he called me on a Friday afternoon with a difficult problem. He was a jewelry salesman and was just about to complete a major deal with Jay Jewelers, a chain of some fifty stores throughout the country. His initial commission on the deal could amount to more than twenty thousand dollars. "Rabbi," said Ben, "they want me to sign on the deal tomorrow morning."

"What are you asking me, Ben?"

"Well, I just became *shomer Shabbat* last week. I'm just wondering — maybe I could just do this one deal and then never again. I mean, supposing I had decided to become observant next week instead of last week?"

"What about your contact at Jay's? He's a Jew, doesn't he understand?"

"Rabbi, when I told him I might not be able to show up because of Shabbat, he hit the ceiling. 'You idiot, do you know what you're gonna lose because of this?' he said to me."

"Listen, Ben, you're a big boy, and I'm not going to tell you what to do. But if you're waiting for me to tell you that it's okay to make the deal on Shabbat, I'm not going to tell you that. Shabbat is Shabbat. But it's your call. I can only pray that you make the right decision." I truly understood the pressure upon him and admired him — he who two weeks ago would not have given this a second thought — for even being troubled. I said a little prayer for him.

Shabbat morning in shul, Ben came over to me and said, "I told the guy I wasn't showing up today. He jumped up and down and called me a crazy Orthodox fanatic. But I'll call him again on Monday, and we'll see. I feel good about it, no matter what happens."

my assistants

Another type of pressure on would-be returnees to Judaism comes from well-meaning friends who are already observant. The fact is that God has too many assistants, too many people too eager to speed others along their way to a more observant life. But the sledgehammer approach is not for me. My own style is to go slowly with people, to nurture them carefully along the path. If anything, my shepherding is too low key.

A young bride-to-be came in to see me. She was very interested in becoming more observant after she married, but had been alienated by all the importunings she had received from some of her friends who were all new returnees.

Perhaps it is because those who are new to Judaism are not yet fully secure in their newfound observance, or because they have had to go to such lengths to reject their own upbringing, that they are so insistent that others follow their path quickly and decisively. Or perhaps it is simply that their enthusiasm is so genuine that they must share it with everyone around them.

This same Ben Gerson, who had hesitated for a long time before moving into Shabbat observance, complained to me years later that I soft-pedal the concept of Divine punishment. "Why don't you tell these people that unless they keep Shabbat they're all going to burn in hell?"

"Ben," I answered, "where would you be today if I had tossed that brick at you from the pulpit?"

I understand the needs and the problems of the newly

observant, but they do not make life easy for their nonobservant friends and acquaintances — nor for their rabbi.

pressure vs. patience

Whenever I begin to feel that they are right and that I should push harder, I try to keep in mind families that changed because of nurturing and not because of pressure.

Carl Sangster, for example, used to drive to shul on Shabbat mornings dressed in his full religious regalia – woolen *tallis* and yarmulke. He was an odd sight as he parked his car, stepped out, and headed for the *davening*. Today Carl and wife and children are full-fledged *shomrei Shabbat,* and Carl himself is one of the best students in our regular Talmud classes.

Laurel Sonnenshein, though she attended shul regularly, was the ice queen. Nothing I said ever seemed to move or affect her. Even during the reading of the awesome admonition sections in Leviticus 26 and Deuteronomy 28 ("If you do not hearken unto Me, I will lay waste your cities and will scatter you among your enemies, and you will be consumed ..."), she would yawn, inspect her fingernails, and whisper to her neighbors. Today she is the proud mother of a young man who is headed for Talmudic greatness. She gets very emotional when she speaks of him. And she listens carefully to all Torah readings.

Sammy Laxe used to go out to his car during the Yom Kippur afternoon break just to relax a bit. He would switch on the radio, listen to the news and to the ball game as he stretched his legs on the back seat. He is now planning a trip to Israel with his wife to visit their son who is one of the top students in a major yeshivah in Jerusalem.

There are three morals to these stories: patience, patience, patience.

Truth to tell, I remain in awe of *baalei teshuvah.* There is much contentment and satisfaction at the end of the road, but along the way life is difficult enough for them. He or she has to withstand the taunts of friends, the raised eyebrows of family, the ridicule of associates, and gnawing self-doubts. Suddenly he does not drive his car or answer the phone on Shabbat; suddenly he does not go out with his old buddies on Friday nights; suddenly he finds himself in shul on Shabbat mornings. And learning Hebrew. And attending classes on Judaism. And studying classic Jewish texts. She makes mistakes, she stumbles, she is sometimes embarrassed, she wonders whether she is doing the right thing, whether she is making some colossal blunder, whether perhaps her friends are right and she has in fact gone mad. It is a tough road back, and it requires a strong character.

A returning Jew once said to me, "I envy you for having grown up in a religious home. You didn't have to struggle the way I'm struggling."

"And I envy you the struggle," I replied.

Returnees are distinguished by certain special character traits: intellectual honesty, fortitude, courage. They have the strength to say to themselves: My past has not been perfect, and I need to make a course correction. No one knows better than a returnee the essential emptiness of the secular life. He knows the depths of despair to which unbridled appetites, lack of discipline, and self-centeredness can lead. He has seen it and experienced it more closely than those born into the religious life. That is why a *baal teshuvah* is concerned with the ultimate questions of living — Why am I here? What is my purpose in this world? — and finds that the Torah offers an answer for him.

Returnees also lack certain character traits: smugness, complacency, self-satisfaction. The road back is rocky and contains many pitfalls. Only special people can navigate it successfully. That's why Jewish tradition holds them in such high esteem. No wonder the Talmud (*Yoma* 86b) states that when true return takes place, not only does God wipe away the past, but past sins are transformed into merits. And elsewhere the Sages declare that in God's eyes a true returnee is more precious than a perfectly righteous person (*Berachos* 34b).

the best shoes I have

Beyond all this, it helps if the returnee has the capacity to laugh at himself. George Bokser, a successful thirty-five-year-old accountant, decided after much soul-searching to move towards Jewish observance. His Jewish background was nonexistent. But there was a yearning within him for spirituality and religion, and he had the requisite backbone. He began to attend an occasional Shabbat service. He was invited to eat Shabbat dinners at various homes and began to meet members of the community, all of which whetted his appetite for more Jewish practice.

Yom Kippur was approaching, and for the first time in his life he wanted to experience a full Yom Kippur day in an Orthodox synagogue. The only Yom Kippur he had ever known was as a child in the Reform Temple which his parents attended once a year.

He wore his best suit and tie, and chose a fine pair of Bally shoes. As he walked into shul, he was immediately struck by the fact that no one was wearing actual shoes. Everyone was wearing cloth slippers or sneakers. He thought it odd but quickly forgot about it in the course of the day's complex *davening*.

Yom Kippur affected him, and he decided to attend shul again on the next holiday, which was Succot. This time, however, he would be prepared. Once again he wore his best suit and tie, and his best tennis shoes, and came to shul. This time he was surprised to find that he was the only one not wearing leather shoes.

* * *

As for American synagogues, this congregation is probably the most unique in America. They are very decent people, and they are curious about their Jewishness. I am blessed to have been their rabbi. Even with all the pain, frustration, and disappointments that I have experienced over the years, I have been blessed. These people have put up with me and allowed me to preach and teach an authentic and basically unpopular Judaism, though many of the early leaders went along more because of personal loyalty to me than because of ideology.

They have not given their rabbi the problems and heartache that so many of my colleagues have experienced, and I readily acknowledge all this. I boast of my congregation wherever I go. They are good people, sincere and considerate. I could not have asked for a finer group with whom to begin my rabbinate four decades ago. Yes, I admit that there are those whose actions make me feel very sorry for them, those who excite my pity because of qualities that make them unhappy and dissatisfied, but I can truthfully say that there is not one person in the congregation whom I personally dislike.

But the uniqueness of this Orthodox congregation lies primarily in the fact that the vast majority of them were not raised in observant homes, and came to Jewish living only in their adult years.

tennis and the road back

Our first true returnee was Nate Cohen. I met Nate on the tennis courts. He considered himself a pretty good player, but, in all due modesty, I must say that I was able to beat him rather consistently. This intrigued him: an Orthodox rabbi who was athletic. Nate had a probing mind, possessed advanced academic degrees from Ivy League schools, and despite the fact that he was a totally nonobservant Jew and was a typical single male with many girlfriends, we became good friends. We were the same age — about twenty-eight — had many common interests, and enjoyed one another's company.

(I must add that the tennis court in particular and athletics in general were the incongruous venues for more than one return to Judaism. They helped break down the barriers that automatically arose whenever the term "Orthodox" was mentioned. The attitude, after they got over their initial disbelief, was: If he plays ball so well, he can't be all that medieval. It kept people off balance; they were not quite able to figure out who precisely this Orthodox rabbi was — which was precisely what I wanted.)

Nate-of-the-tennis-courts married an accomplished artist who was also completely nonobservant. As time went on, the couple's intellectual and spiritual curiosity began to affect them. They appeared in shul from time to time, attended classes and study groups. They asked for reading material on Judaism, and we had many informal one-on-one conversations. They were bright and perceptive, but more important, they were not afraid to buck the accepted life-styles of their oh-so-sophisticated friends.

A few years after we first met, his wife asked me to teach her how to maintain a kosher kitchen. A half year later, Nate asked me to teach him how to don *tefillin*. A few months after that, they asked for instructions on how to observe Friday night. They were not yet ready for a full twenty-four-hour Shabbat, but were responding to an appeal I had made from the pulpit to try at least Friday night as a starter. Not long afterwards they began observing the full Shabbat, then *mikveh,* then daily *davening* — all the time reading and listening and learning. Today, a generation later, not only they, but their children and grandchildren, are observant Jews.

He was the first. Many more followed in his wake. Dr. Frank Fishoff, another wealthy bachelor, used to jog on Shabbat mornings in his posh, yuppie neighborhood. One morning he jogged into our neighborhood, noticed our shul building for the first time, and out of curiosity walked into the lobby. The next week he jogged over and brought some trousers with him so he could sit in the back of the shul. He was intrigued, made an appointment to see me during the week, and he was slowly on his way. The pattern was similar to Nate's.

Several years later, after serious Torah study in classes and with private tutors, by now married and encouraged by his wife, he gave up his lucrative medical practice and moved to Jerusalem. There he intensified his Jewish studies, moved into a pious neighborhood, and they and their six children are today living a rich Jewish life. Beyond all this, he can now make his way alone through a complex page of Talmud. And he still runs.

There are dozens of such stories which I hesitate to record lest they seem self-serving. The fact is that there was a certain magic within our congregation that attracted a diverse number of people back into the Torah orbit. The congregation itself was very accepting of all kinds of Jews, and although the pulpit preached an unadulterated Judaism, people sensed that the congregation was not judgmental and that they could move at their own pace. Many of those who came into the synagogue simply because they liked the people, and who had no intentions of moving forward religiously, somehow found themselves, to their own surprise, in fact moving forward.

the treatment

Perhaps it was that the community was open and welcoming, asking no questions about religious backgrounds or degrees of observance; perhaps it was that we offered something authentic and undiluted that, while it frightened a few Jews away, appealed to many others; perhaps it was the natural friendliness of our people. When strangers walked into the shul, our worshipers did not simply stare at them: they welcomed them, handed them a *siddur,* found them a place to sit, and more often than not would invite them to Shabbat dinner after *davening.* This became known as "The Treatment." It was not an artifice. It emanated from the natural goodness and kindness of our membership — abetted by the genuine hospitality and warmth which is still an integral part of the South, even of a cosmopolitan city like Atlanta. In a city where total strangers say good morning to one another on downtown streets and in shopping malls, it is not surprising that in shul strangers should be made welcome. The synagogue became more than a community; in many respects it resembled a large family.

Chapter 21: Of Fanatics, Tennis Shoes, and Burning in Hell □ 303

Gene and Frances Langer never recovered from The Treatment. Newcomers to town, they were looking for the Reform Temple when they got lost and came into our shul one Shabbat morning. They sat down together, but one of our ushers politely informed them that in our tradition men and women sit in separate sections. They were horrified and rose to leave. Before they got to the door one of our members approached them with a smile, welcomed them, asked Gene to sit next to him, and signaled his wife to take care of Frances. Gene and Frances stayed. They never left. They became, in time, fully observant, and ultimately all their children studied in yeshivot and seminaries.

This is not to suggest that the congregation is monolithic, or to suggest that the returnees are the only good people in the community. Decency and generosity of spirit are found across the board, from the most observant to the least observant. I have always had as much affection for the nonobservant as for the fully observant — and I can get as annoyed with the fully observant as with the nonobservant. A very large number of our congregants still keep very little, which leads me to an odd confession: although it would be good for the Jews if everyone in the congregation were pious and learned, I welcome the challenge of being the rabbi of a community which is not monochromatic.

I once made this confession in public, and added that on the day when the entire membership becomes fully observant I would resign, because my purpose as a rabbi would have been fulfilled. Rebecca Singer, very clever but not yet observant, said to me later: "Now you know why my husband and I don't keep Shabbat. We're doing our part to keep you here."

FFB's and BT's

The resurgence of Jewish practice in the congregation has not been without its inevitable problems. Some people moved forward, but others did not. Those who moved into Jewish practice were occasionally resented by those who did not. The less observant imagined they were being looked down upon by the more observant, and that I favored the more observant. Of course, the newly observant occasionally were a bit zealous in preaching to their nonobservant friends, and when I would privately point this out to them, the reaction was often that I favored the less observant and gave them greater attention.

There was also the disconcerting phenomenon of those who have always been fully observant — known as the Frum From Birth people — who immigrated to Atlanta as we grew. The FFB's, as they were called, were content with their personal religious situation, and some of them were discomfited by the zeal of the returnees. Coming, as many of them did, from metropolitan Orthodox centers, they had never been exposed to large numbers of *baalei teshuvah* who had not been raised to be *shomrei Shabbat,* for example, and for whom every *mitzvah* was a new challenge to be addressed, studied and conquered.

A kind person would describe the Frum From Birth people as being much more relaxed about their Jewishness. They were used to it, comfortable with themselves as Jews, and took it all in stride. An unkind person would say that the FFB's took Judaism very much for granted, that they saw no need to change and to grow religiously, that they were perfectly content to remain exactly where they found themselves spiritually. Which was not entirely fair, because here and there some FFB's were inspired to personal growth by their encounters with the returnees.

To encourage Jewish growth and at the same time to make every type of Jew feel welcome in the congregation — and to make them all want to grow — has been a major rabbinic challenge. Life and change are synonymous, but neither life nor change are easily addressed.

the rabbi as a baal teshuvah

And I? Have I changed for the better? Am I a better Jew now

than I was when I started out? A more effective rabbi? A finer scholar? Who knows? I think I spent more time in personal study in the early years than now. At twenty-four, freshly ordained, I was probably more idealistic. Life was certainly much simpler at that age, when one is blessedly unaware of the complexities, nuances, and gray areas that one encounters later — gray areas that can easily wear away at the sharpness of idealism. That is one of the dangers of the rabbinate.

Another, even more serious danger is that year after year we rabbis cajole and admonish others from our high seats of judgment — and all the time there is no one to admonish us and urge us on to better things. We deliver sermons on repentance, but we ourselves neglect to repent. We exhort the congregants to take up Jewish study, but we ourselves tend to forget the meaning of learning. We willingly take credit for the forward strides in Jewish life, but the blame for its failures we willingly lay at other doorsteps.

Do we really believe that we bear no responsibility at all for the high rate of intermarriage, the suffocating apathy, the lack of Jewish observance, the abysmal Jewish illiteracy which plagues Jewish life today? There is no one to tell us that a lethargic Jewish community is a reflection of an apathetic rabbinate, and that it is not only laymen who need to return to God and essentials.

It would not hurt if, from time to time, someone would remind the rabbi of all these *baalei teshuvah* that he himself, on his own level, should also become a *baal teshuvah*.

* * *

Not long ago it was reported to me that an older member of the synagogue was complaining: "When I joined this shul years ago, it was a nice place. Now a bunch of young fanatics came in and took over, and it's not what it used to be." The complainer was raised in a religious home, still speaks with a Yiddish accent, but is completely nonobservant. The "fanatics" are the young couples who have become very observant.

Somehow, it is the Jew who was raised in an Orthodox home and then rejected it who is the most threatened by any manifestation of intensity in Judaism. *Tzitzis,* daily *minyan* attendance, reciting *berachot* over food, Shabbat observance — such things remind him of his own religious background which he thought he had successfully abandoned in favor of American modernity. But much to his chagrin, he finds that Judaism rears its stubborn head in the most unexpected places.

go out and come in again

In one of his discourses Kierkegaard says that it is easier for someone who is not religious to become religious than it is for someone who is already religious to become more religious. One is always at a disadvantage in regard to his own tradition, because while one is quickened by it, one can also be dulled by it. He goes on to say: "I lack the wakefulness of the stranger. I should conduct myself toward the tradition to which I have fallen heir like an actor who has played a scene poorly. I should go out, and come in again."

From the congregants in our synagogue I have learned to be watchful of this dullness that constantly lurks in the shadows of religious life, especially for those of us to the religion born. When you take a stranger on a tour of your home town, you see things freshly through his eyes. When a rabbi accompanies strangers to Judaism on a tour of this grand tradition, he begins to see with fresh eyes what he has been given. This is one of the reasons these congregants are so precious. Their gift is the gift of a fresh perspective.